THE FIRST FIFTY YEARS
The history of the Evangelical Movement of Wales
1948–1998

The First Fifty Years

The history of the
Evangelical Movement of Wales
1948–1998

Noel Gibbard

BRYNTIRION PRESS

© Noel Gibbard, 2002
First published, 2002

ISBN 1 85049 191 7

Cover design:
Rhiain M. Davies
(Cain)

Cover photograph: Dolgellau
(by kind permission of the Welsh Tourist Board)

Published by Bryntirion Press
Bryntirion, Bridgend CF31 4DX
Printed by Creative Print & Design, Ebbw Vale

Contents

To
Elwyn and Mair
and all the
friends of the Movement

Preface

In 1948, the Welsh-language Evangelical Magazine *Y Cylchgrawn Efengylaidd* first appeared , and its secretary was J. Elwyn Davies, a theological student at Bala-Bangor. He also became the secretary of the Evangelical Movement of Wales. It was a great privilege, therefore, when preparing the Welsh version of this history, to visit Elwyn and his wife Mair in their home in Carmarthen. They were able to share with me the thrilling story of those years of blessing that led to the formation of the Evangelical Movement of Wales. I am greatly indebted to them.

Two other members of that early group were Emily Roberts and Geraint Gruffydd. Emily kept a diary for most of her life. Her diaries are in the keeping of John Emyr, and he graciously allowed me to read them, together with other relevant material belonging to his father Emyr Roberts. Geraint Gruffydd kindly read the Welsh version, *Cofio Hanner Canrif*, and made many helpful suggestions, as well as correcting when that was necessary.

The English translation is the work of Kitty Lloyd Jones, Tregaron. She faced the task willingly and persevered with its completion even while moving house. Many thanks to her for this kindness. There is no doubt that she is an able translator.

Three other persons must be mentioned. Graham Harrison read the English version and made valuable suggestions. Edmund Owen prepared the Index, and Brenda Lewis prepared the work for the press. She worked untiringly and thoroughly on the volume. A huge thanks is due to her.

NOEL GIBBARD

Cardiff
June 2002

Glossary

Noson lawen	a traditional Welsh evening of entertainment
Seiat/seiadau	fellowship ('society') meeting(s)
Urdd	Welsh youth organisation
Urdd Aelwyd	Welsh youth organisation premises

Journals/magazines

Barn	'Opinion': a national monthly periodical
Y Cylchgrawn	'The Magazine': i.e. *Y Cylchgrawn Efengylaidd*, the Welsh Evangelical Magazine
Y Cymro	'The Welshman': a national weekly newspaper
Y Drysorfa	A Welsh Presbyterian (Calvinistic Methodist) monthly periodical
Y Dysgedydd	A Welsh Congregational (Independent) monthly periodical
Y Faner	'The Banner': a national weekly
Y Goleuad	The Welsh Presbyterian weekly
Seren Cymru	The Welsh Baptist weekly
Y Tyst	The Welsh Congregational weekly

Abbreviations

AECW	Associating Evangelical Churches of Wales (initially ACC: Associating Churches Council)
B	Baptist
CM	Calvinistic Methodist (Welsh Presbyterian)
EFCC	Evangelical Fellowship of Congregational Churches
EMW	Evangelical Movement of Wales
I	Independent (Welsh Congregational)
IVF	Inter-Varsity Fellowship (now UCCF: Universities and Colleges Christian Fellowship)
SCM	Student Christian Movement
W	Wesleyan Methodist

1
The New Peace

Throughout the length and breadth of Wales people were celebrating. There were organised street-parties: long tables, laden with every kind of food available at the time, were ranged down the middle of the streets. The singing and rejoicing went on for hours on end. After six years of fighting (1939–1945) the war was over, and peace reigned once more. None the less, some felt unable to make merry. Many a family mourned the loss of a loved one; others were burdened with the agony of waiting, the cryptic words 'missing, believed killed' a constant nightmare. But the war had ended, and people looked forward to a better world.

After the upheaval of the war years, the country's leaders were faced with the task of reorganising and stabilising society. This provided them with an ideal opportunity to fight for social justice. The Labour Government tried to plan carefully. With its stress on public ownership of vital services, it nationalised the coal industry and the health care system.[1] The aim was to secure work for as many as possible, in the hope of creating a contented society in a safe world. When it came to implementing the new state education system, many a wounding battle was fought over the Welsh language, and for those who wished to ensure its future, the establishment of the first Welsh school in Llanelli in 1947 proved a great morale booster. This was a memorable victory, won in the teeth of opposition.

The Welsh-language scene

Both within and without the churches, questions were being asked as to what the war had accomplished. Some regarded it as a just war, while others condemned it outright. The final year of hostilities had seen the publication of a volume introducing the principles of pacifism—*Sylfeini Heddwch* (The Foundations of Peace). Its authors were greatly troubled to find that compulsory national service was to continue in peacetime, and many others shared that view.[2] More often

9

than not their opposition had a religious basis, though for some it was grounded on nationalism. Consequently, as an outcome of the war, the opposition to it, and many a heated debate, pacifism became more acceptable in Wales than it had been hitherto.

Saunders Lewis, an influential poet, dramatist and literary figure, contributed a regular current affairs column ('Cwrs y Byd'—The Way of the World) to the Welsh weekly *Y Faner* (The Banner). Here he argued the rights of Wales as a nation, encouraging readers to 'think European' and inviting them to return to Rome.[3] He also roundly condemned the liberal theology so prevalent in the Welsh pulpits of that period. Another eminent scholar who recognised the failure of liberal theology was J. E. Daniel, but he called Wales to return to the Word of God, the Word that was embodied in Scripture.[4] According to Gwenallt, a prominent Welsh poet, the analysis that *Sylfeini Heddwch* offered of the world's plight and man's need was a superficial one. Scant consideration was given to the doctrine of original sin, and the omission of this made it impossible to reach a satisfactory conclusion.[5] It frightened him to think how easily 'The Fatted Animal' (*Yr Anifail Bras*) had strutted into the fold in Siberia, Belsen, Buchenwald and Hiroshima.[6] The problem was man's sinful nature: the answer, God's invincible power.

And yet the attitude towards liberal theology was tempered. In the early days of peace Bleddyn Jones Roberts said, 'I shall never again believe in the innate goodness of human nature.'[7] Others claimed that Modernism was inadequate to meet the needs of the time, and pointed to secularism and the lowering of the minister's status as signs of the change taking place in the aftermath of war. H. T. Edwards offered the Calvinistic Methodists a practical suggestion: the demolition of three-quarters of the denomination's buildings, to be followed by careful planning.[8] People could not contemplate so rash a proposal at the time; but more recently the denomination has been forced to face just such a prospect, though not necessarily the *demolition* of its chapels.

An attempt to stir up Welsh churches to evangelise was made by 'The New Campaign' (*Yr Ymgyrch Newydd*), an interdenominational movement formed in 1944 but particularly active from 1946 to 1948. It emphasised the need to apply evangelical principles to all aspects of life, venturing into college, factory, coal mine and quarry, as well as the chapel. It operated on much the same pattern as the 'Commando

Campaign' in England,[9] a movement rooted in the Wesleyan denomination that urged the church to go to the people.

The student scene

A certain tension was felt in the colleges too. The Inter-Varsity Fellowship (IVF) emphasised the centrality of conversion and the sacrificial (propitiatory) death of Jesus Christ in both experience and creed; whilst the Student Christian Movement (SCM) placed greater emphasis on the social gospel. In those days, although strong convictions might be lacking, being religious was something taken for granted, and to most students chapel attendance was acceptable.

In University College, Cardiff, the IVF was gaining ground. The work was strengthened during the war years by T. J. Russell Jones and Mair Thomas (later his wife), and by Douglas Glyn Davies (subsequently a teacher in Tonyrefail).[10] These were followed by Gwyn Walters and Glyn Owen, and in 1945 by Wynford Davies, all three of whom were to become Calvinistic Methodist ministers and active in the Evangelical Movement of Wales. Although the IVF was less strong in Aberystwyth and Swansea, there were some in these colleges who were nurtured to be leaders in different spheres and became staunch supporters of the Movement. One such in Aberystwyth was Ieuan Davies, now an elder of many years' standing in Alfred Place English Baptist Church in that town; another was Glyndwr Jenkins, who became a minister and a missionary with the Calvinistic Methodists. In Swansea one of the leading evangelical students was Geraint Morgan of Pontarddulais, who was to become a teacher and, later, minister of the Evangelical Church in Bangor.

Besides bearing witness in the colleges, the IVF ventured to arrange evangelistic campaigns in various places, proclaiming the good news of the gospel and the message 'be ye reconciled to God'. Even during the war years some evangelism had taken place; indeed, there were two remarkable campaigns—one in Carmarthen in 1944, and the other in Llanelli the following year. Seion chapel in Llanelli, which holds more than a thousand people, was full every night for a week, and the meetings were singularly blessed. The local paper voiced some opposition, but that was countered by the Rev. W. M. George, minister of Caersalem (Baptist). Some remarkable open-air meetings were held. During one such meeting, when the speaker, surrounded by a thronging crowd, was challenged by a drunken soldier, a pathway suddenly opened up like the Red Sea of old, enabling him to make his escape.[11]

This campaign bore tangible fruit. This was evident, firstly, in numerical terms. Included among the converts were many who were destined to be involved in the Evangelical Movement of Wales: among these were John Thomas and Eluned Rees, and Hugh D. Morgan and Mari Williams (two couples who were to marry some years later). Another of the converts, Rhoda Bassett, was the first Welshwoman to become an IVF travelling secretary. Secondly, the campaign created a zeal for evangelism, an expression of this being their involvement the following year in several campaigns in nearby villages. Thirdly, meetings for the nurture of the young people were held at Caersalem and in a number of homes. The same thing happened in subsequent campaigns, in Pontarddulais and Ammanford (1946), and in Pontarddulais again in 1947. The thing that caused a sensation in Ammanford was the confession of the Rev. J. D. Williams, minister of Bethany (Calvinistic Methodist), that it was during the campaign there that he had come to assurance of faith in the Lord Jesus Christ.[12]

Meanwhile, in North Wales there were at least two people who were interested in what was happening in the South. J. Elwyn Davies of Caernarfon was a student in Bala-Bangor College. He had come into contact with David Shepherd, the South Wales evangelist, in 1945, and that same year had listened intently to the students preaching in the Llanelli campaign. Herbert Evans of Gellilydan, Merionethshire, was a student in the Normal College, Bangor, and he went down to the Ammanford campaign in 1946 to see for himself what was going on. We must follow the story of these two men in order to understand what was happening in North Wales, and to see how the Evangelical Movement of Wales, which brought North and South together, came into being.

Herbert Evans

At the age of eighteen Herbert Evans went to work in the Civil Service in Llandudno. There he came into contact with evangelical Christians in the workplace, and also in the church at which Horace Jones ministered. (The latter had been raised in the Apostolic Church in Llanelli.) The young man's enthusiasm for the Welsh Nationalist Party and the Urdd (Welsh Youth organisation) kept him busy; but despite this he was restless and looking for contentment in life. Many a time he was challenged by something said by Horace Jones, or by the Pilgrim Preachers at their open-air meetings in Llandudno. By mid-summer 1944 a crisis was approaching: he saw that believing in Jesus Christ meant heaven, and not believing meant hell. He was given grace to respond to the Saviour, and his heart was filled with joy and peace. To consolidate his experience he held firmly to the words in the book of Proverbs that urge a man to seek wisdom: 'Take fast hold of instruction; let her not go; keep her; for she is thy life' (4:13).[13]

Herbert Evans left the Civil Service to enter the Normal College, Bangor. Here he met J. Elwyn Davies, a theological student and SCM member, and I. D. E. Thomas of Rhandirmwyn, Carmarthenshire, a student in the University College who was a member of the IVF. Feeling drawn to I. D. E. Thomas and his companions, the new student joined the IVF. It was only a small group; indeed in October 1946[14] when, on Herbert's advice, Harold Jones joined them, they were just five members; but he too knew that these were his people. Herbert Evans did not enjoy their company for long, however, as his health broke down and he had to go to his sister's home in Bala. There, in the Independent chapel, he met a man who had been converted in India and who told him about a Christian family (the Pantyneuadd family) in the nearby village of Parc.

On the farm at Pantyneuadd lived Mr and Mrs Ellis Davies and their children—Meinir, Mari, Emrys and Bryn (Dafydd Morris and Lina having left home by then). They had moved there from Cynlas, the former home of Tom Ellis, a distinguished Member of Parliament for Merionethshire who was related to the family on the paternal side. Mari had been to Llysfasi Agricultural College for a time, but returned home to work on the farm with Bryn. Meinir had left for London to study music, especially the harp, and had come across the Oxford (or Moral Rearmament) Group started by Frank Buchman. The chief influence on Meinir and others in the family was Peter Howard, an author and the movement's propagandist, who lived on a farm in Suffolk. The moral discipline of the group, with its emphasis on the four absolutes—love, purity, selflessness and honesty—appealed to the family. But while acknowledging the importance of this moral discipline, Herbert Evans was convinced that it was not the heart of the gospel of Jesus Christ, and he spent hours talking and arguing with the Pantyneuadd family, and with John Jones of Brynucha, Llanymawddwy, who was also interested in the movement.[15]

To the family at Pantyneuadd Herbert Evans introduced others who, like himself, had come to faith in the Saviour, and gradually there came into being a close-knit evangelical fellowship. He also arranged for speakers to visit them, among them J. Elwyn Davies, the student from Bala-Bangor. And now we must turn to follow Elwyn Davies's spiritual quest.

J. Elwyn Davies

The story of Elwyn Davies is heavily overshadowed by the war. As a prominent SCM member he was deeply conscious of the need to help those who had suffered through the hostilities, especially in Germany. On their behalf he and his friends went from door to door in Pen-y-groes (Caernarfon), begging for gifts of food and money. On a farm called Parciau-bach they came across Ekkehard Kockrow, a German prisoner of war, and he and Elwyn Davies became close friends.[16] Ekkehard returned to Germany in December 1946; by then, parcels from Pen-y-groes and other places were reaching Germany, and he was truly thankful for such kindness to his people. The enthusiasm for this continued through 1946 and 1947 and spread to other circles. Gwyneth Palmer of Bala told of parcels being sent to the Rev. Robert Belcher, and of how she had received a message from his son, who had worked as a prisoner of war on a farm in Llandrillo, Merionethshire.[17] A local branch of the Urdd in Carmarthenshire was moved to send fifty-seven parcels, all but two of them reaching their destination.[18]

Although busy and conscientious in pursuing this work, Elwyn Davies, like Herbert Evans, was feeling uneasy, and this unease became a restlessness of soul. One day, when cycling towards Pont Seiont near Caernarfon, he knew without doubt that a voice was speaking to him and asking, 'Why are you doing this work?'[19] He felt deeply ashamed, seeing the sin in his heart in a way he had never done before. Here is his own account of this experience:[20]

> Although I preached every Sunday, and was responsible for bringing together over thirty students to the prayer meeting in the outer room of Bala-Bangor by seven every Saturday morning, the

plain truth was that I had never faced the questions, What is the condition of my own heart? What does living a good life really mean? What are God's demands? Although outwardly religious and virtuous, it was self that was on the throne.

Several times before this, his conscience had been pricked by different voices, those of IVF members I. D. E. Thomas and Jim Toothill in particular. And, if at all possible, he used to avoid Herbert Evans, because the reality of his spiritual experience condemned the theological student. Whilst he was earnestly seeking for an answer to his need, two very significant things happened: first, in 1947 he and others arranged an Easter retreat in Plas-y-nant, Betws Garmon; secondly, he was chosen to represent the SCM in a conference in Oslo.

A *turning point*

One of the features of the Easter retreat was the prominent place given to personal and collective meditation; its outcome was that three people experienced conversion, and Elwyn Davies was one of them. His mind had previously been troubled by the verse, 'Awake to righteousness, and sin not; for some have not the knowledge of God: I speak this to your shame' (1 Cor. 15:34), but at Plas-y-nant these words came to him with irresistible force. He knew that God was speaking to him and assuring him of the way of salvation; he was convinced that God had accepted him and forgiven his sins.[21] Although he had known about these truths before, now the Holy Spirit was working effectively on his heart. Referring to the early years of his quest, he says:[22]

> It was a good while later that I came to realise that it was solely by the power of the Holy Spirit that I, and others like me, could know anything of that love and righteousness. Before that could happen I had to be brought to the place where I would be willing to yield my life to God (for the first time, notice) and experience the joy of knowing that He had not only accepted me, but forgiven all my sins. This happened the following Easter [1947] in a retreat for students at Plas-y-nant, Betws Garmon.

When Elwyn Davies returned to Bangor, he and the other leaders agreed to continue the SCM meetings through the final term, although it was the term of their examinations. This gave the young man who had been brought low in Plas-y-nant an opportunity to give his testimony, and a certain Mair Humphreys, who was listening intently, later became his wife.

The spirit of searching spread, and there followed a period of blessing in Bangor when a number of students came to know the way of salvation. During that same period the zealots of the 'New Campaign' were busy in the city, and there was a clash between them and those students who had become evangelicals. The Campaign's approach was to warn the students of the danger of fundamentalism. Elwyn Davies's policy was to avoid public debate and to concentrate on affirming the testimony of those students who had experienced conversion.[23]

Oslo and Berlin

Time came for the theological student from Bala-Bangor to go to Oslo. The small group from Wales included Glyn Owen, who by this time had moved from University College, Cardiff, to Aberystwyth. Their attendance at the conference proved a thrilling experience; it was a privilege to be among thirteen hundred students from all parts of the world and to forge a bond of friendship with some of them, in particular Ingeborg Zieseche, a German who suffered from tuberculosis and was hospitalised during the conference. At the end of one meeting in the church, the hymn 'Thine be the glory, risen conquering Son' was sung joyfully outside the church door, and amid the sound of that rejoicing five of the students went to visit Ingeborg.[24]

> Within half an hour five of us were kneeling by the bed of a young German who had been rushed to hospital that day suffering from TB—she was not to return home like the rest of us, but would have to lie there for two or three years. She was praying, 'Mein Gott und mein Herr' (My God and my Lord), and in that holy place, as among the crowd at the church door, we knew that Jesus Christ was Lord.

Ingeborg showed great interest in Wales and promised to pray regularly for the country.

From Oslo the student from Bala-Bangor crossed to Hamburg, and thence (having obtained permission to enter Germany as a temporary correspondent with the Welsh weekly *Y Faner*) to Berlin. He was taken round the city by his old friend Ekkehard, each glad of the opportunity to meet again, and each saddened by Germany's plight. The temporary correspondent's articles conveyed the complexity of the situation. The title of the first, 'People of Germany fear another war', reflected the prevailing mood.[25] The three dreads that were destroying people's lives were fear, poverty and suffering; to try and forget their misery many resorted to cinema-going and dressing fashionably. Critical observations were also made on Russia and its 'tyranny'. Such comments were generally welcomed in Wales, though Russia found one ardent apologist in a Communist comrade from Goginan.[26]

Germany or Wales?

As he travelled home, a battle was raging in Elwyn Davies's soul. Before him stood an open door to minister to the needy people of Germany; but another door was ajar—to evangelise and serve his native land. When he arrived in London his agony intensified. He met the publisher Victor Gollancz, who advised him to return to Germany to work under the auspices of the Salvation Army's education department. On returning to Bangor he was offered similar advice by a doctor friend, who urged him to go to Germany, saying that he would learn more there in a short space of time than in ten years at a theological college.[27]

The day dawned for the student to inform his Principal of his decision. That same morning he received a letter from Owen Parry, a part-time lecturer in the History department, asking him to call and see him. He had heard about Oslo from someone who had been there, and when Elwyn Davies arrived in his room he saw a map of Europe on the desk and found his eyes immediately drawn to two countries, Germany and Wales. But the lecturer said something that startled him: 'Unless Wales lays hold of true religion in our time, generations will pass without it.' The desire to go to Germany vanished like a dawn mist, and Elwyn Davies went gladly to tell the Principal he had decided to stay in Bangor. This was the second turning point in his life, and it was also a turning point for the evangelical testimony in Wales.[28]

Opportunities for the gospel

Because of the many invitations he received to share his experiences in Oslo, the theological student had little time to settle down. At the meetings that were arranged, usually by local Church Councils, he took the opportunity to present the gospel, and was assisted by others such as Meinir Davies (Pantyneuadd) on the harp and Emily Roberts in song.[29] One such meeting in Blaenau Ffestiniog eventually led to his being called to minister at Jerusalem, the town's Independent chapel.

After consulting with Elwyn Davies and another friend, Herbert Evans wrote to the Bala Council of Churches asking them to arrange a meeting, and they agreed to do so provided that others besides Elwyn Davies took part. That meeting was particularly blessed, and a group of believers there felt convinced that they should meet together for fellowship and to bear witness to the gospel. A suitable venue was found in the home of one of the converts, and Glyn Owen (in Bala Theological College at the time) became a willing leader.[30] The group ventured to ask the town's Council of Churches to arrange an evangelistic campaign, and it agreed to do so.

During the winter of 1947–8 the believers met regularly to meditate and to pray that the evangelical witness might be strengthened, and they decided to arrange a 'retreat' in Dolgellau in early January 1948 in order to prepare prayerfully for the campaign the following Easter. Herbert Evans was the co-ordinator, and he ensured that those who were not college students were given equal opportunity to attend. Among those invited were Emily Roberts and T. Arthur Pritchard: both had been caught in the net of the gospel and were destined to play a key role in the early history of the Evangelical Movement of Wales. It is well worth learning a little about these two lovable characters.

Emily Roberts

When Emily Roberts was born in Derwen, Mynydd Hiraethog, near Corwen, the midwife took one look at the baby and said, 'Poor little thing, she won't live.' She was indeed a sickly baby, her mother too frail to feed her and money too short to buy fuel to warm the bedroom. But the 'poor little thing' did live, and later accompanied her sister Wena to the local Church School, where everything was taught through the medium of English. Welsh was the language of the home, however, and she could read the few books the family possessed. *Teulu Bach Nantoer* (The Little Family of Nantoer) was a particular favourite; and she even thumbed through *Geiriadur Charles* (Thomas Charles' Bible Dictionary) and *Yr Ysgol Farddol* (The Bardic School) —

books belonging to her father, who was something of a country poet. Welsh was also the language of the Calvinistic Methodist chapel she attended, and it was here that she learnt temperance songs and the tonic sol-fa method of reading music.[31]

Having won a scholarship, Emily Roberts went on to Rhuthun School, and then to the Chester Royal Hospital to train as a nurse, working on the very ward where her mother had died. But ill health forced the young trainee nurse to leave, and she was accepted as an uncertified teacher in Carrog school, where W. D. Williams (later of Barmouth) was headmaster. Though uncertain of her future, Emily was convinced that God was leading her; yet she was concerned about the poverty of her religion. Her longing for a personal assurance of God and his purposes for her life was intensified by the testimony of a number of people with a living knowledge of God. Then, some time in 1943, she herself came to that knowledge: she was enabled to cast herself upon the mercy of God and was assured that he had accepted her.[32]

The teacher's uncertain life now had a firm foundation, and she was exceedingly thankful for this when, in 1944, her health deteriorated and she had to spend a period in a Liverpool hospital hovering between life and death. She was spared and, when strong enough, returned to her teaching post, though unsure if this was to be her sphere of service. After her operation in Liverpool she had consecrated herself to serving her God and asking him, 'What wilt thou have me to do?' Maybe he would lead her out of teaching to serve him in some other sphere. When her father died in 1947 (he was buried the day before the great snow came), she thought that perhaps the time had come for her to leave Carrog school. But for many months she had no confirmation of this, and before the door was opened she and her sister Wena received an invitation to the Dolgellau retreat and were asked by the Davies family of Pantyneuadd to stay at their home in Parc, Bala.[33]

T. Arthur Pritchard

Although Elwyn Davies was one of the retreat's leaders, it was felt that they should have another speaker. So Herbert Evans contacted T. Arthur Pritchard, a theological student in Aberystwyth, and he readily agreed to come. Tom Arthur Pritchard, though brought up in North Wales, had been born in the Rhondda, his father, like many of his contemporaries, having gone down south to look for work. Work he did find, but sadly he lost his wife and was left with three young children, Arthur the eldest being only four. The family returned to Blaenau Ffestiniog, and an aunt proved as good as a mother to them. During his teens Arthur worked for a time in the slate quarry, then helped his father to sell milk; but because of his conscientious objection to fighting he had to move to Garndolbenmaen in Caernarvonshire to work on the land. There he attended the Calvinistic Methodist chapel and enjoyed the close-knit fellowship of the village.

But the tranquillity of his life was shattered when the Rev. Owen Thomas, from Llwynypia in the Rhondda, visited the area. He had come to stay for a short while in a cottage owned by the staunch pacifist George M. Ll. Davies. The holidaying minister had decided to attend a week-night meeting at the Baptist chapel; but not knowing the village he happened to stop near Arthur Pritchard's home to ask the way. When, after giving him directions, Arthur said he was on his way to the Calvinistic Methodist *seiat* (society or fellowship meeting), Owen Thomas decided to accompany him there.[34]

The minister from the Rhondda could not be silent about his Saviour, and he gave his personal testimony at the meeting. For the young farmhand this was something totally new and strange, and when asked 'Do you know the Saviour?' he was well and truly cornered. He had no idea how to answer; he did not know such an experience was possible. But when Owen Thomas went to have supper with him, it was this experience that was the topic of conversation.

Owen Thomas went home to Llwynypia, leaving Arthur in spiritual turmoil. But the following year the minister returned, and not only did he answer the questions of the worried enquirer but led him to a personal knowledge of the Lord Jesus Christ. Again Owen Thomas turned his face south, this time leaving the new convert with the problem of finding others with like experience. He heard of two members of the Apostolic Church in Porthmadog and arranged to meet them: one, a baker, was a strongly built man; the other, known locally as 'Ritchie Bananas', was a veritable Zaccheus! The Calvinistic Methodist joined them when they visited the Apostolic Church Convention in Pen-y-groes, Carmarthenshire, and here he met Pastor Dan, that great soul extensively used by his Lord.[35]

T. Arthur Pritchard was exceptionally skilful with his hands and, having set his heart on becoming a woodwork master, pursued a course of training for this in Loughborough. But then, feeling called to preach the gospel, he returned to college, this time as a theological student in Aberystwyth. This is where he was when invited to speak at the retreat at Tyn-y-coed, Dolgellau.

Dolgellau retreat

Twenty-six people arrived on Thursday evening, 1 January, in readiness for the start on Friday. The events of the next four days were recorded by the guest speaker in his diary:[36]

> *Friday, January 2.* The doctrine of justification by faith, based on Romans, chapter 8, was the subject of the morning and afternoon addresses. The evening session was spent discussing some of the perils of the Christian life. A hard day with little freedom, but one of the company came to an experience of the Lord Jesus Christ.
>
> *Saturday, January 3.* A great hardness felt in the morning, someone or something preventing the blessing. The morning spent praying that the hindrance be removed. After dinner one of the company confessing that he had been a hindrance. The Holy Spirit came down in a wonderful way, and the atmosphere changed. Two young girls received the Saviour.
>
> *Sunday, January 4.* Left Dolgellau to preach in Abersoch. Heavy rain on the way.
>
> *Monday, January 5.* Returned to Dolgellau early in the morning. Heard that great things had happened there yesterday. Romans 6 was the subject of the morning address. It is difficult to find words to express what happened at the end of the meeting; the Holy Spirit came down upon the company in a wonderful way. A new and strange experience, an unforgettable day. Many were convicted, and opened their hearts to Jesus Christ. Everyone very reluctant to depart and head for home.

Those are the main facts, but it is possible to fill many of the gaps. T. Arthur Pritchard refers to one person owning up to his sin, but in fact there were two—two of the leaders.[37] The root of the evil, in the case of one of them especially, was pride, and when that was confessed, there was inner cleansing which opened the way for the pouring of blessing upon the whole company. In bed on the Saturday night Herbert Evans had dreamt that he was in a circle of people, the devil amongst them. He approached the evil one and bound him, a sign of the spiritual battle and the blessing that was to follow. On the Sunday night Herbert Evans in Dolgellau and T. Arthur Pritchard in distant Abersoch were awakened at the same time to wrestle with God in prayer. The battle had been won in the secret place before the company came together on Monday morning.[38]

Monday morning's meeting was devoted to prayer, and as he called upon God Elwyn Davies quoted the verse, 'If ye then, being evil, know how to give good gifts unto your children: how much more shall your heavenly Father give the Holy Spirit to them that ask him?' (Luke 11:13). He was just pleading the promise, but before he had finished the Holy Spirit came upon him 'and filled me to such a degree with love for God that I sat down sobbing and laughing at the same time'.[39] The very same thing happened to Herbert Evans.

T. Arthur Pritchard spoke, and when he had finished a circle was formed for prayer and each prayed in turn. Once again the Holy Spirit came down upon the company with the same effects—weeping and laughing, and delighting in the love of God. One of the young people in the circle prayed in a very touching way:[40]

> *Iesu annwyl, gwna fi'n sant,*
> *Cymer fi yn un o'th blant.*
>
> Jesus, make a saint of me,
> Thine own child, O, let me be.

As they continued in prayer, T. Arthur Pritchard had a vision: he felt himself being lifted above the company to look down upon it, and upon Dolgellau, and Bala where the Easter campaign would be held, and then lifted yet again to look down on the whole of Wales. When he told the company of this, his experience was taken as a sure foundation for believing that God was going to shower his blessings on the land. Their hopes were confirmed when a young girl from Bala came to Elwyn Davies and told him trustfully, 'A small stream has started flowing here today; one day it will flow over the whole of Wales.'[41]

In the heat of the Dolgellau experiences Emily Roberts returned to Pantyneuadd to tell her sister Wena what had happened. Before going to bed that night she too experienced the same mighty powers. The Davies family also shared it with each other, as some of them had not been present at the Monday morning meeting. Bryn, who was privileged to be there, summarised it in the words, 'It was nothing less than a revival.'[42] His sister Mari also experienced the mighty working of the Holy Spirit, and it was she who told Dr Martyn Lloyd-Jones about it, knowing how deeply interested he was in Wales, and how ready he would be to support the work and offer sound advice.

Student work at Bangor

The Dolgellau retreat had a marked influence on the development of student work in Bangor. Another retreat, this time for 'freshers' (new students), was arranged in Plas-y-nant at the end of January, but Mari Davies (Pantyneuadd) was also there at the invitation of Elwyn Davies. Late the first night the two of them were sitting in front of the fire, Mari searching the Scriptures for verses about the cross, and Elwyn making notes on a piece of paper. Those notes formed the basis of his addresses, and the meetings were singularly blessed. The Holy Spirit manifested himself in power, and many were overcome, among them most of the SCM leaders in Bangor.[43] According to Geraint Gruffydd, the retreat was 'a spiritual revolution'.[44] Mair Humphreys expands on this: 'We all had to acknowledge our spiritual emptiness and the fruitlessness of our efforts for Christ. We were led by the Christians to see the meaning of the cross in God's plan to save man.'[45]

Back in Bangor Elwyn Davies and others felt an ever-deepening desire for more fellowship with those of like belief and experience. The number of converts was growing, especially through the witness of those who had been to the retreats, and it was vital that they be kept together in fellowship. They needed spiritual food—nutritious food that would satisfy what the Welsh hymn-writer Ann Griffiths termed their 'new stomach'.

Gwilym Humphreys

One of the new converts was Gwilym Humphreys. Geraint Gruffydd had returned from Plas-y-nant at the end of January and shared his experience with Gwilym. That sharing resulted in his conversion and the culmination of a long chapter in his spiritual story.

For a time Gwilym had worked in Llandudno, where he met Herbert Evans and Horace Jones, but because he was a conscientious objector he moved south to the Rhondda to become a 'Bevin boy' in the coal mines. During his stay there his soul was much troubled by the preaching of the Rev. Owen Thomas, Llwynypia, and when Dr Martyn Lloyd-Jones came to preach in the valley the very foundations of his life were shaken. Small wonder, then, that Geraint Gruffydd's experience deepened his desire to be assured of the way of salvation. He was helped by a sermon preached by Bleddyn Jones Roberts on the cross, and by listening to J. Elwyn Davies talk about the German girl, Ingeborg. But it was as he and a fellow student, John Rice Rowlands, were going for a walk together that the truth suddenly dawned— salvation meant putting one's whole trust in Christ alone. Gwilym Humphreys knew instantly that he too had had the same experience as a number of his friends.[46]

Twr-gwyn

Elwyn Davies was one of the SCM leaders, and he had friends in the IVF; but he decided to start a Welsh meeting in Twr-gwyn vestry (the Calvinistic Methodist chapel) for all who had experienced conversion and any others searching for the truth. He led the meetings himself, assisted by Harold Jones of the IVF. Many others whose hearts had been set ablaze by the holy fire visited the fellowship, among them Arthur Pritchard, Emily Roberts and Glyn Jenkins (president of the Aberystwyth IVF). The Spirit was obviously working in the college as a whole: some came to the Twr-gwyn meeting from the Saturday night dance.[47] Meetings were arranged in St Mary's College and the YMCA, and the Bala campaign of Easter 1948 was an outreach by the Twr-gwyn group and a number of friends from North Wales.

Bala campaign

The meetings were advertised in the local paper *Y Seren* (The Star). The editor outlined the background—the 'Oslo meeting' in Bala in October, the prayer meetings held in the town, and the blessing in Dolgellau. 'The campaign to be held in Bala next week is the result of these meetings', declared the editorial,[48] expressing pleasure at the enthusiasm of the town's Council of Churches, and the hope that many would face the challenge of Jesus Christ. The campaign's leader was the Rev. I. D. E. Thomas, a former member of the IVF in Bangor and now a Baptist minister in Glanaman, Carmarthenshire. He was accompanied by Elwyn

Davies from Bangor, and Arthur Pritchard and Griffith Jones from Aberystwyth College.

The previous Sunday Elwyn Davies had been preaching in the Llanegryn area, but for some reason no one could offer him accommodation—'a very unusual thing in those days', he says[49]—so he had to stay in a hotel. He made good use of his time there:[50]

> I had taken two booklets with me: *God's Way of Salvation* and *The Reason Why*. (I still have them today.) And I spent every spare minute making notes of the contents of those two little books! Without a word of exaggeration I learnt more about helping souls to come to Christ during those hours than I learnt throughout my whole theological course in Bangor. It was later that I was introduced to *Drws y Society Profiad* (The Door of the Experience Society) by Pantycelyn, and similar literature.

On the basis of their experiences, Elwyn's two booklets, the leading of the Holy Spirit and the written Word, the company ventured to Bala. Elwyn Davies remembers arriving there with Arthur Pritchard as though it were yesterday. As they passed the Methodist College, Arthur (the car driver!) pulled his hat down over his eyes, so bashful was he to think of the challenge that lay before them.[51]

The meetings followed a set pattern: preaching followed by testimonies, congregational singing, and singing with the harp. The first two nights were rather difficult, with no sign that anything unusual was happening. The third night proved more fruitful, but during the fourth meeting the floodgates opened and the Holy Spirit worked powerfully on the hearts of many. They were convicted of sin, but they now needed to be directed to Christ. A further meeting was arranged for the troubled seekers, when Elwyn Davies explained to all that had stayed behind the way of salvation.[52]

The whole area was electrified by the news. The mighty were brought low and the weak uplifted; prominent men of the town were not ashamed to witness for their Saviour, among them the Calvinistic Methodist minister, the College Principal and the Town Clerk. Rina Macdonald (née Jones) remembers giving her testimony. She was sharing a bed with Sylwen Owen (now Davies), who had come to a saving knowledge of the Lord in Dolgellau, and she was awakened at about six one morning to hear a voice challenging her, 'Will you bear witness to me?' Rina was young in the faith, having believed on the Saviour during her course in St Mary's College, Bangor, but she could not ignore the challenge. On sharing her experience with Elwyn Davies, it was arranged that she should give her testimony in the next meeting. Emily Roberts was also testifying, so one was able to help the other to take part in public,[53] and this created a real bond between them.

The local paper continued to report on the work with obvious sympathy. It recognised the 'fervent zeal' of the young for the Saviour and at the end of the week gave a further account:[54]

> There were excellent services again on Thursday, Friday and Saturday evening, and many testified for Jesus Christ for the first time, reminding those who are middle-aged of the 1904–05 Revival. Many young people from the colleges, and some from Caernarfon and Dyffryn Maelor, had come to give assistance. We hope that this is the firstfruit of a general awakening.

Great things were experienced, but the team continued to expect greater things.

Sad to say, a false step was taken in the final meeting, and the leaders would be the first to admit it. All who had received Christ as Saviour and Lord, and others who wished to do so, were asked to remain behind. Consequently, it was obvious who did not remain and, naturally, many were offended.[55] Yet heaven overruled the proceedings, and the Bala campaign bore lasting fruit—in conversions, in its revitalising effect on Christians, and in the desire to strengthen the witness of the gospel in the future.

In Bala itself, the work of the *seiat* was strengthened. At the suggestion of Mrs Williams, an aunt of the Pantyneuadd children, it was called *Y Gorlan* (The Fold), a suggestion reflecting her desire to see the fold full. The sheep and the lambs were carefully shepherded by the Rev. T. Gwynn Jones (Calvinistic Methodist), Emily Roberts, Elwyn Davies and others.[56] Believers in other places were inspired to do likewise, and the students at Bangor, spurred to greater effort on behalf of the gospel, arranged another retreat in Tyn-y-coed, Dolgellau, in October 1948.[57]

No one took more interest in this evangelical activity than Dr Martyn Lloyd-Jones. He asked I. D. E. Thomas, leader of the Bala campaign, to come to London. Writing from America, the emigrant preacher recalls:

> The following week I received a word from Dr Martyn Lloyd-Jones to go to London to see him. We met in a club near Westminster Chapel. The purpose of the meeting was to give him details of the campaign in Bala. He felt at the time that something new was about to happen in the history of religion in Wales.[58]

But Bala not only gave birth to the children of God. It also gave birth to a new magazine, the direct fruit of the campaign in the town. We must now turn to look in detail at this significant venture.

2
The *'Cylchgrawn'* People

The early days of the *Cylchgrawn* and the *'Cylchgrawn'* Conference

A t the end of the Bala campaign, four people—two students, one teacher and a minister of the gospel—approached the owner of *Gwasg y Seren* (Seren Press) in the town. 'They were bold enough to tell him of their vision—to have an evangelical magazine in the Welsh language—remembering to emphasise at the same time that they had neither movement nor fund nor patrons behind them.'[1] This was a venture of faith. An order was placed for 1,500 copies, and a promise given to pay when ordering the second issue.

The first issue

A small company of people met in Aberystwyth to discuss the magazine's content, decide on a title and choose its cover designer. A whole morning was spent considering different names, one of the favourites being *Llatai* (messenger or love messenger), but the one finally agreed on was *Y Cylchgrawn Efengylaidd* (The Evangelical Magazine).[2] Meirion Roberts was asked to design the cover—a cross, the heart of the gospel, rising out of a Bible, the foundation of true faith. (This is still the Movement's logo.) Conscious that they needed the help of others with more experience, the young group invited the Revs Emrys Davies (Swansea), I. D. E. Thomas (Glanaman) and J. D. Williams (Ammanford) to be joint editors. The first of these was by now a prominent South Wales evangelist and a staunch supporter of the work of the IVF in University College, Cardiff. The second we have already met as one who had seen the Spirit at work in North Wales and played a vital role in the Bala campaign, and he had recently been inducted as minister in Glanaman. The third had succeeded Nantlais Williams in Bethany, Ammanford, following an earlier pastorate in Llangyfelach, Glamorgan. (Here he had been a near neighbour of Emrys Davies, minister at Caersalem Newydd before moving on to Mount Pleasant, Swansea.) J. Elwyn Davies was appointed secretary, and Mrs L. Rees of Glanaman treasurer.

Significantly, the contributors to that first issue of November –December 1948 represented different generations.[3] Owen Thomas (Llwynypia) and Nantlais Williams had been associated with the old *Efengylydd* (Evangelist) magazine; Emrys Davies and Idris Davies (Ammanford) were prominent evangelists; Gwyn Walters and Emily Roberts represented the war period; Geraint Gruffydd (or Griffiths as he was then known) and Gwylfa Davies were the fruit of the spiritual awakening around 1947. The main article was written by Dr Martyn Lloyd-Jones of Westminster Chapel, London (an indication of his interest in the Welsh work and readiness to support it). Herbert Evans and I. D. E. Thomas, two of the four who initially approached the Seren Press, were responsible for the news items.

On looking through that first issue it becomes clear that its aim was twofold: to reach unbelievers and instruct believers. The question posed by Emrys Davies was 'What kind of faith have you?'; the article 'Dewis' (Choice) by Geraint Gruffydd presented a personal challenge. Under the heading 'You are . . .' Idris Davies reminded believers that they were the letters of Christ; in 'Aids to Believing' Gwyn Walters explained the main tenets of the gospel. Owen Thomas in 'Feed My Sheep' reminded readers of the Saviour's command; W. T. Edwards, convinced that he was living in the days of 'departure from the gospel', warned of the heresy of the Jehovah's Witnesses.

Some contributors expressed their belief and experience in poetry. Geraint Gruffydd composed a sonnet 'Ymbil' (An Entreaty); Gwylfa Davies summarised his faith in a poem 'Offrwm' (Sacrifice); Emily Roberts wrote a hymn, 'Iesu Annwyl' (Dear Jesus). Significantly, seven pages of news were devoted to telling the exciting story of the years 1946–1948. Nantlais Williams, with his vast experience of writing for children, contributed 'Sleeping in the Service', a winsome sermonette based on Acts 20:9. Five books were reviewed, among them *The Robe* by Lloyd Douglas and, in stark contrast, *The Victorious Cross* by Rheinallt N. Williams.

The nature of the *Cylchgrawn* was crystallised both in the article by Dr Martyn Lloyd-Jones and in the statement of the magazine's Aims. The 'Doctor' offered three reasons for dealing with 'The Evangelical

Faith': first, the term 'evangelical' needed to be clearly defined; that meant, secondly, creating a consciousness of the past; thirdly, there was a steady growth in the spirit of ecumenism. The stated 'Aims' were threefold:

- To give expression to the evangelical faith which is based on the Word of God.
- To direct others to a saving knowledge of the Lord Jesus Christ.
- To nurture the spiritual growth of believers.

The two key words were 'evangelical' and 'Welsh'. The small group was moved to bear testimony to the gospel in Wales and prayed that the *Cylchgrawn* would be one effective means of doing this.[4]

North–South links

The choice of three editors from South Wales not only gained for the venture the benefit of their experience but also served to forge a closer link between North and South. To a certain extent this had already happened. Some South Wales students had been in North Wales colleges, and vice versa. Some IVF members from North and South had met Gwyn Walters at various conferences—and he, without any doubt, was crucial to the evangelical witness of the early years.[5] Gwyn Walters was exceedingly gifted: every aspect of his work was polished —whether preaching, leading an open-air meeting, conducting a *noson o lawenydd* (literally 'an evening of joy', to distinguish it from the Welsh traditional *Noson Lawen*), playing the organ, or offering a well-reasoned apologia for the evangelical faith. At that time, too, students who were prospective Calvinistic Methodist ministers spent their final year in the Theological College at Bala, and through many of these (Glyn Owen, John Thomas and Hugh Morgan, for example) precious links were forged between North and South. Rheinallt Williams, one of the professors at the college, was the son of Nantlais Williams.

The magazine's committee meetings were also a means of bringing the evangelicals closer together. Despite the convenience of Aberystwyth as a central meeting place, they would sometimes travel to the North or South. When W. H. Davies (Baptist) of Aberduar, Carmarthenshire, was committee chairman, the business meeting would be held in his home, followed by an evangelistic meeting in the chapel that evening.[6] In 1948, Geraint Morgan of Pontarddulais, one of the many teachers who supported the *Cylchgrawn*, was appointed Scripture master in Llanfyllin, Montgomeryshire, and there, through Herbert Evans, he heard of T. Arthur Pritchard, a theological student in his final year. One Sunday the young teacher was invited to preach in Llanrhaeadr-ym-Mochnant, and he mentioned Arthur's name to the elders of the pastorless Presbyterian church. As a result, Arthur Pritchard was invited to preach, and this led to his induction as minister in 1949.[7]

One consequence of T. Arthur Pritchard's coming to Llanrhaeadr was the holding of an evangelistic campaign there, when J. Elwyn Davies, Emyr Roberts and John Vevar (Anglican) joined with him and Geraint Morgan to proclaim the gospel. The one memorable thing about that campaign is the fact that the Bishop of St Asaph prohibited John Vevar from remaining in the area because he had officiated outside his parish without consent.[8]

Emyr Roberts and John Vevar

We have already introduced Elwyn Davies and Arthur Pritchard, but now we must say something about Emyr Roberts and John Vevar. At Easter 1949 a group of young people, led by Elwyn Davies, held an evangelistic campaign in Trefor, Caernarvonshire. The two leaders were staying in the home of the Rev. Emyr Roberts and his wife Grace, Elwyn having come into contact with the minister when he was in Tudweiliog, Lleyn. At the end of the day in Trefor many personal issues were seriously discussed, because Emyr Roberts, though in the Christian ministry, had not yet clearly understood the way of personal salvation. During that week many experienced the light of the gospel shining into their hearts, among them, in Emyr's own words, 'none other than the respectable minister of Gosen'.[9] The said minister referred to his experience a fortnight later:[10]

> I have been given a new book as a present—it's brand new and absolutely brilliant. I have turned its pages in both Hebrew and Greek, English and Welsh—but without the key, although the key is within its own covers: Faith. The Bible has been my food, my drink, my everything for the past fortnight. This may sound selfish. The glorious thing is that Grace is my twin in the Faith. To God be the praise for His unspeakable gift!

It was the testimony of a fifteen-year-old girl that touched Grace Roberts's heart. She had striven to please God, but she now saw that he offered her eternal life through Jesus Christ. 'I remember running home that night [to young Glynneth and Dafydd who were being cared for at home] with the hymn "Mi dafla' maich" (I cast my burden) a wonderful personal experience.'[11]

In its early days the evangelical movement found a wise leader in the gracious person of Emyr Roberts.[12] One of nine children, he was born in Cwm-y-glo, Caernarvonshire. His father was a quarryman, and Emyr followed him to the slate quarry at the age of fourteen. But he felt called to preach, and left to enter Bangor University in 1936, whence he could have moved on to study in Germany. But he chose to stay in Bangor and settle into the Christian ministry. Having served in Tudweiliog for a few years, he moved to Trefor, where he had the experience that changed his life. Throughout his life he remained a fine preacher, and developed into a gifted literary figure.

Whereas Emyr Roberts was a Calvinistic Methodist minister, John Vevar was a curate in the Church in Wales. But he too had been soundly converted. Brought up in Bangor and educated in Llandaff, he commenced his ministry as curate of Llanfechell in Anglesey and was then moved to Newtown. There the preaching and testimony of another curate, Joe Williams, convicted him of his spiritual need, and he came to an experience of God's forgiveness in Christ at a house meeting on 18 January 1945. Soon he was to return to Anglesey, this time to Llanfair-yng-Nghornwy, and it was from there that he went with other evangelicals to hold the campaign in Llanrhaeadr-ym-Mochnant. Later he moved to Botwnnog, where he faithfully served the Church in Wales until his retirement in 1985, a period of nearly 34 years.[13]

Coming together in campaigns and *seiadau* ('societies' or fellow-ships) nurtured a spirit of unity among the evangelicals and gave them the confidence to present the challenge of the gospel to the whole of Wales. A successful campaign was held in Bangor in January 1949, Dr Martyn Lloyd-Jones and Gwyn Walters being the invited preachers. A number of groups received a sympathetic hearing as they testified to the gospel in different North Wales venues. This further convinced them that they ought to think of Wales as their parish—and where better to meet their fellow Welsh-speaking countrymen than in the National Eisteddfod? This was territory they could not afford to ignore.

Dolgellau Eisteddfod, 1949

The venue for the National Eisteddfod in 1949 was Dolgellau, a town that held a very warm place in the hearts of many of the evangelicals that visited the festival that year. Eighteen months previously they had been singularly blessed there, and doubtless the company longed to see God reveal himself once more, albeit in totally different circumstances. Scarcely ever before had anything like this happened in the history of the Eisteddfod—a group of evangelicals, many of them with no experience of speaking in public, venturing into the middle of the bustling throng to bear witness to the gospel of Jesus Christ.

Not satisfied with having a tent as a centre for both the workers and the magazine, Elwyn Davies insisted on having a banner bearing the name *Y Cylchgrawn Efengylaidd* in large letters. But where could such a banner be found? The problem was solved by joining together a number of white flour-sacks and attaching letters made of blue material and secured by tape. Rina Macdonald (née Jones) well remembers being at it until two in the morning getting things ready for that first day of the Eisteddfod![14] One of the company thought the magazine should be distributed free of charge, but others felt a small charge should be made to help defray costs. It was amicably agreed to sell it for a shilling a copy.

In addition to selling the magazine and holding conversations on the field, two meetings were held, one in the open air, and the other a *Noson o Lawenydd* (evening of joy) in one of the town's chapels. Gwyn Walters led the first, accompanying the singing with his piano accordion, and Beth Williams (who later married Gwilym Humphreys) testified to her knowledge of the Saviour, 'her face aglow'.[15] During the evening meeting, led by the Rev. Emyr Roberts, testimonies were given both in word and in song to the accompaniment of the harp. Suitable poems were recited by Gwilym Humphreys and Mair Humphreys, 'Simon, Mab Jona' (Simon, son of Jonah) by the one, and by the other, Gwenallt's 'Beibl William Morgan' (William Morgan's Bible)—the book that to a large extent had moulded Welsh life and was the basis of the *'Cylchgrawn'* people's faith.

Dr Martyn Lloyd-Jones was invited to speak at the evening meeting, but he nearly did not come. The story of how he eventually agreed to come is worth telling.

With Glyn Owen and others, he had preached in Bala earlier in the year to establish the work accomplished there in 1948 and, preaching in Welsh, had experienced unusual freedom. 'The gospel was this time preached with such power and conviction, that those who showed their opposition after last year are dumbfounded.'[16]

The Doctor had obviously liked Bala as a place, and expressed a desire to go there on holiday. He planned to exchange houses with the Rev. T. Gwynn Jones, but the proposed dates turned out to be inconvenient. Mari Davies heard about this and told her mother, who invited the Doctor to stay in Pantyneuadd from 18 July to 10 August. But when asked by the *Cylchgrawn* group to come to the evening meeting at the Eisteddfod, he flatly refused. He had just come out of a Bristol hospital and wished to have a time of complete rest.

One Saturday evening, as he was meditating on the works of Williams, Pantycelyn, the Holy Spirit came upon him in mighty power. He felt his heart being melted by the consuming love of God—the very same experience as he had known in Bristol a few weeks previously, and that which he described as the assurance that he was a child of God (Rom. 8:16). His spirit was revived, and he decided to go to the *Noson o Lawenydd* at Dolgellau on the Thursday. His text was Philippians 4:4, 'Rejoice in the Lord alway: and again I say, Rejoice.'[17]

It is small wonder that the presence of the evangelicals created a stir during that Eisteddfod week. Evangelising on the field was in itself a novel exercise; offering the people a brand new magazine was an additional surprise. The Thursday evening meeting, characterised as it was by the joy of the Lord and the harp in the 'big seat', was so very different from the traditional *Noson Lawen*. For one person who happened to be staying in the same house as a group of team members it proved to be a memorable Eisteddfod. Frances Môn Jones was there to compete in one of the chief solo competitions, but she found herself attracted to the little group and greatly appreciated one prayer meeting in particular. The spirit of that meeting seemed to follow her as she went forward to compete, and while singing on the stage she was possessed by a consciousness of God and given the assurance that Jesus Christ was her Saviour. The adjudicator remarked on the obvious unction in her singing and awarded her first prize.[18]

The evangelical activity drew the attention of the press and radio. The correspondent of the *Cymro* (Welshman), a national weekly, wrote with obvious sympathy. After mentioning the usual things about the Festival, he remarked, 'But a new note has been heard in Dolgellau this year, an evangelical note, both methodist (with a small "m") and Welsh.'[19] He then very skilfully summarised the *Cylchgrawn*'s message: 'Man as he is—both men and women, rich and poor, educated and ignorant—is lost without Jesus Christ', adding, 'Our business, says the evangelical faith, is to respond to the call to repent, and having received mercy by faith, to place ourselves at God's command.'[20] No one on the team could have expressed it better!

J. O. Williams, Bethesda, was responsible for the radio report. After describing the usual Thursday events, he went on to say:[21]

> Indeed, we cannot but notice and feel that there is at present something moving silently through the lives of the youth of Wales. These young people were initially moved by their Welshness as well as their religion, and not by any movement outside Wales. They love Wales passionately, and long to see Wales from the midst of its present-day doubts and materialism experiencing the same joy and confidence as they possess.

The work was firmly rooted in the land of Wales.

The Eisteddfod proved to be an excellent meeting place for the evangelicals. Not only were they able to share the gospel with others, but they also got to know one another. Many a happy marriage stemmed from an Eisteddfod-week courtship, and lasting friendships were forged. Geraint Gruffydd and Gaius Davies met for the first time at the Caerphilly National Eisteddfod, and their friendship greatly benefited the *Cylchgrawn*, both of them in later years contributing in turn to a column under the pseudonym 'Meirchion'.

Aber-rhiwlech

One member of the Dolgellau team, Emily Roberts, was on fire for her Saviour and for distributing the *Cylchgrawn*. By January 1949 she had joined the seven good men and true on the *Cylchgrawn* committee and met with them at Aberystwyth. She felt an inner yearning to serve her Lord full-time, but she was still a teacher and could not leave her post without clear guidance. Was her involvement with the *Cylchgrawn* a call to leave teaching? And what about the proposed and much-talked-of 'home' for the *Cylchgrawn*? Was such a 'home' available? Emily was anxiously waiting for answers.

The dream for a 'home' was indeed realised, a place being found in Aber-rhiwlech, Llanymawddwy, through the kindness of John Jones, Brynucha, and his uncle, William Jones. The committee believed that Emily Roberts was the right person to go there, and she was very happy to agree. She and her sister Wena were to move there in the spring, and on 23 January 1950 she was able to say, 'I have been given wonderful assurance that we are in the path of his will.'[22] A letter received two days later doubly assured her:[23]

> I have had a letter from Herbert with the verse Josh. 1:9. What joy! That was the word that enabled me to face the challenge of leaving the school, and again today on the crossroads of Awelfan– Aber-rhiwlech the same word has returned. 'Have not I commanded you?'—Yes, and I am now at peace concerning the venture.

Emily and Wena were on their way to Aber-rhiwlech. A great deal of cleaning and tidying had to be done, and Gwilym Humphreys, Mair Humphreys and others scrubbed and polished to get the house ready for the two sisters. Mair Humphreys will never forget the move from Dyffryn Clwyd to their new home:

> Suddenly, coming down Bwlch-y-groes (a dramatically beautiful, but very dangerous, mountain pass), my leg slipped against the gear lever where the road was steepest—and it was only the swiftness of the driver pushing it back that saved the van, the furniture and us from going headlong down the steep drop parallel to the road.'[24]

On 30 March Emily Roberts was able to write with great satisfaction in her diary, 'Last night, the first night in Aber-rhiwlech, "I laid me down and slept; I awaked; for the LORD sustained me." This is the beginning of a new chapter.'[25]

A few days later, on 3 April, the first visitors arrived: Elwyn Davies, Emyr Roberts, Gwilym Humphreys and Mair Humphreys, to be joined the following day by Arthur Pritchard. They shared sweet fellowship for three days—fellowship that further assured Emily Roberts that she had taken the right step.

The sisters' home was not only a place of fellowship; it was also the place where the magazines were packed after the stock had been moved there from Blaenau Ffestiniog. Emily Roberts would take a bundle with her to whatever chapel invited her to preach on a Sunday, and to weekday meetings or campaigns. But the remoteness of Llanymawddwy made the task of distributing the magazine difficult, and it soon became apparent that a car would be invaluable. Between them the friends of the *Cylchgrawn* succeeded in raising the sum necessary to buy an Austin Seven. Its arrival was described by Emily in her diary:[26]

> *15 January 1951.* About 8.30 in the evening the little Austin FF 4361 arrived in the 'garage', John Brynucha behind the steering wheel. Scarcely has any car been so prayed over in the whole of Wales. May the Lord give me the grace to express my thanks by fuller and deeper dedication to his service.

In no time at all, FF 4361 became very familiar to the patrons of the *Cylchgrawn*.

'Missionary' travels

For some months Emily was exceedingly busy, and on 20 July 1951 she was officially appointed to travel the length and breadth of Wales promoting the *Cylchgrawn*'s circulation. Her 'missionary journey', as she called it, began in Bala on 23 October 1951, when she visited representatives of each chapel in the town and succeeded in recruiting magazine distributors.[27] The following day (General Election day), she arrived in Caernarfon and contacted seven churches in the town. By the end of the year she had been to numerous places in Caernarvonshire and moved on to Dolgellau, as well as visiting Aberystwyth and attending the Bala *seiat*. She knew full well that this work was a venture of faith and was exceedingly thankful to receive in December a gift of ten pounds, the exact sum needed to pay for her car licence.

It was Emily Roberts who did the travelling, but she was ably supported by countless others, including the editors, the committee and many volunteers. Among the latter was Luned Gruffydd (wife of Geraint Gruffydd), who helped to prepare the magazine for the press in those early years. The situation was such that every article had to be presented handwritten, and it was Luned who painstakingly copied each one in turn.[28] Such kindnesses were a feature of the early years that greatly enhanced the witness of the *Cylchgrawn*.

Emily Roberts had visited South Wales before being officially appointed by the committee, but she went there again before the end of 1951, visiting believers in Llangeler, Llanpumsaint, Llanybydder and Cross Hands in Carmarthenshire. She met Trefor Dakin, a member of the Elim church, Tumble—a quiet man full of zeal for his Lord, who, with Gwynfor Jones, a teacher from Cross Hands, arranged evangelistic meetings in various parts of the county, inviting students and other evangelicals to accompany him. He identified himself with the work of the *Cylchgrawn* and was closely associated with the evangelicals of the Ammanford–Llanelli area. This was an area Emily Roberts was particularly fond of visiting. She was warmly welcomed in many a home, one being that of Mr and Mrs Thomas and their daughters Morwen and Enid in Bynea, Llanelli. Emily and Morwen (later to become the wife of the Rev. Vernon Higham) became close and lasting friends.

Another visit to the area was undertaken in 1952. As well as meeting friends in homes and at meetings, Emily met the evangelical leaders of the area: ministers such as J. D. Williams in Ammanford, W. M. George in Llanelli and H. H. Williams in Cross Hands, where great blessing had been experienced between 1948 and 1952. At Easter 1952 a notable campaign was held in Foelgastell, near Cross Hands, led by a group of young people; among them were Eifion Evans, Gareth Davies and Leslie Jones, three who entered the Christian ministry during H. H. Williams's pastorate. To announce the coming meetings—and at the same time share the good news—they procured an amplifier, connected it to a car battery, attached it to a sledge and dragged it from place to place. The week's meetings were particularly blessed; God's presence was so real that people found it difficult to leave at the end of the service. Even after leaving the chapel, many could be seen sitting on the gravestones enquiring about the way of salvation. One of these was Sulwyn Jones of Penrhiw-goch, Maes-y-bont, subsequently minister of Hebron Evangelical Church, Dowlais. With night closing around them, many received the light of the gospel and, in the abode of the dead, experienced the power of the resurrection.[29]

Emily Roberts and her fellow workers continued the Eisteddfod tradition. Many a time they had to flee for shelter from the rain: Aberystwyth in 1952 and Ystradgynlais in 1954 were particularly wet, though sunny Rhyl in 1953 lived up to its name! Eight hundred copies of the magazine were sold in Rhyl, and in Ystradgynlais they had all gone by the Wednesday. (That year saw the introduction of a new rule forbidding selling on the field. But the heavy rain drove the crowds into the tent, resulting in a sell-out!)

Remarks made by visitors to the tent are worth noting. One commented that the Magazine tent had more young people working in it than any other on the field, and that they seemed to be enjoying their work. Another, asked to buy a *Cylchgrawn*, said that she received it regularly—'O yes, *bach*, I send away to the North for it. It's good— very good.'[30] Within a few years the circulation had reached the three thousand mark.

The first camp

It was in the *Cylchgrawn* tent in Rhyl in 1953 that another significant development was first considered. Elwyn Davies, Herbert Evans and Arthur Pritchard met Morwen Thomas, who had just returned from the camp run by the South Africa General Mission, and all four felt a burden to arrange something similar for children and young people here in Wales. Morwen was persuaded to consider arranging it in co-operation with Emily Roberts. They both agreed, and so a Welsh camp for girls was arranged in Bangor, 17-27 August 1954.[31]

Thirty-four girls each paid the sum of three pounds to spend ten days in Bangor. Many of them were led to a personal knowledge of the Lord Jesus Christ, among them Iola Williams, who later became the wife of the Rev. Geoffrey Thomas of Alfred Place, Aberystwyth. Iola was one of the group that had come from Blaenau Ffestiniog, and she returned home to tell her sister Rhiain, who already believed.

The camp was significant for four reasons: it was the first to be held; many came to a knowledge of the Saviour; the fact that Morwen Thomas was unwell and unable to enjoy most of the camp led to the organising of a second girls' camp in 1955; and in 1956 it was decided to arrange a mixed camp for boys and girls. Annual camps have continued to be held from that year to the present day.

The *Cylchgrawn* conference

From 1948 to 1952 the friends of the *Cylchgrawn* had been meeting at
the Eisteddfod and in campaigns and *seiadau*, and the students among
them had also met in IVF conferences. But the need was now felt for
an annual gathering, at which supporters of the magazine from all parts
of Wales could come together. The first '*Cylchgrawn*' conference was
held in Bala, 11-14 August 1952; the meetings were in the Theological
College, and the conference members stayed in various homes in the
town.[32]

One of those who attended that first conference was Ceinwen
Swann (née Matthews). She was to stay with the Davies family in
Pantyneuadd. On the first night, Mari advised the visitor to cast her
burdens on the Lord and not take them to bed under the blankets with
her. She is unlikely to forget that bed, a huge four-poster that had come
from the home of Tom Ellis, the Merionethshire MP whose statue
stands in Bala. The following morning the family breakfasted together
at a round table, with the servants at a long table nearby. She went to
the conference thirsting for the Word, and was satisfied beyond her
expectation.[33]

Arthur Pritchard was the main speaker, and his subject was 'The
Lordship of Jesus Christ', based on Luke 9:23. In his first address he
stressed the importance of 'following Christ', who specifically calls
his disciples to deny self and deal harshly with their sinful tendencies.[34]
To enable himself to do this continually, the believer must feed on the
Word of God, and the speaker's exhortation was, 'Let us consecrate the
mind to serve God.' The second address, 'Taking up the Cross',
emphasised two things: following meant moving onwards; and the
cross to be taken up was that which already existed, not a cross
fashioned by the believer for himself. In his final address the speaker
explained the difference between 'willing' and 'desiring': willing is
desiring put into action. The constant aim must be to glorify Christ.
The proof of sanctification is that the image of Jesus becomes more
apparent in the Christian's life; sanctification is not for its own sake,
but for his sake. Quoting from a Welsh hymn by Williams Pantycelyn,
he urged his congregation to consecrate themselves fully to the Saviour:

Cymer, Iesu, fi fel 'rydwyf,
Fyth ni allaf fod yn well;

> *D'allu Di a'm gwna yn agos,*
> *F'ewyllys I yw mynd ymhell;*
> *Yn Dy glwyfau*
> *Byddai'n unig fyth yn iach.*

Literally translated, it runs:

> Take me as I am, Lord Jesus,
> I can never better be;
> 'Tis Thy will to draw me closer,
> Mine to wander far from Thee;
> In Thy suff'rings
> Only shall I be made whole.

Addressing the first meeting, J. Elwyn Davies expressed his joy at being in an evangelical conference, and that conference conducted in the Welsh language. He knew, he said, that all present had the interest of Wales at heart. Then, referring to an article in the current issue of the *Cylchgrawn* on the Revival in the Hebrides, he said that revival was the only truly satisfactory answer to the country's problem. But revival must begin with personal renewal. This he stressed again when leading Tuesday's prayer meeting, exhorting those present to pray without ceasing for revival, to desire holiness and to have a burden for lost souls.

Emyr Roberts, in the Tuesday evening meeting, pursued the same theme, 'The need for revival in Wales'. He too stressed the importance of holiness, and the great need for believers to be salt and light in society. 'The Lord has no interest at all in creating saints and then keeping them in a glass case.'[35] He compared the situation in Wales to that in the time of Eli, when family and society had become degenerate and the word of God scarce. Many of the people were religious enough, but they were serving God before the high priest in the temple without a personal knowledge of him. He suggested that there would be no pilgrimages to 'Our Lady of Fatima' in Bala if the spirit of Thomas Charles were once more to occupy the land. Internationally, he believed, God's wrath was against self-righteous nations, and one of the features of Welsh life was religious self-righteousness.

A talk by William Nagemba, a visiting Ugandan, on 'The Person of Jesus' riveted the listeners' attention. His message profoundly impressed Emily Roberts:[36]

We would see Jesus. You come to Jesus; stay there—that is the Christian life. No, don't go forward, you stay with Jesus—grow, no, you stay. The Holy Spirit will always point to Jesus. We want Revival—yes, very well—we want Jesus. That's all, but He's everything.

The same spirit of expectancy and the same pointing to Jesus characterised the afternoon open-air meeting and the young people's meeting on the Thursday evening.

Because of the blessing experienced in Bala, another conference was arranged for 1953, this time in Caernarfon. The invited speaker was Dr Martyn Lloyd-Jones, and many of those present remember his masterly addresses on John chapter 17, and his sermon on the woman of Samaria—a sermon preached with the unction of the Spirit. The following year, the fiftieth anniversary of the 1904 Revival, the venue was Llanelli and the speaker J. Elwyn Davies. Naturally, revival of religion was given prominence, and as an aid to keep alive the spirit of expectation there was a visit to Loughor, where the mighty work of God began. In 1955 the conference was in Denbigh, and the 'Doctor' was once more invited to speak. His addresses were on the work of the Holy Spirit and included a discussion on Ephesians 1:13.[37]

Patagonia

The *Cylchgrawn* continued to be distributed throughout Wales by Emily Roberts, church representatives and the Eisteddfod team. It also went over the border to England, and across the sea to many distant countries. Geraint Morgan of Llanfyllin diligently sent it to no fewer than sixty missionaries, and received many an appreciative letter.[38] He was especially pleased to add Patagonia in Argentina to his mailing list, and mentioned this to Mair Davies (Pentre-cwrt, Llandysul), who was teaching in Welshpool at the time and seriously thinking of going to work in the Welsh colony there. All the letters he received from Patagonia were passed on to Mair, so that when she eventually arrived she knew that the *Cylchgrawn* had gone before her. It was obviously warmly appreciated: a letter from the Rev. Tudur Evans on receiving a bundle of magazines tells us, 'I have nearly distributed them all and I asked everyone, when they had read the magazine, to pass it on to Luned's Library or the J. C. Evans hospital.'[39]

Young people

Many school pupils were zealous for the work of the gospel both in campaigns and at the Eisteddfod. Interest in spiritual matters was reported in the schools of Llanelli, Gwendraeth and Tonyrefail in the South, and Llangollen, Dyffryn Nantlle, Bangor and Blaenau Ffestiniog in the North. During 1952, many pupils in Llangollen came to know the Saviour, and as a result they arranged meetings, initially during the dinner hour, but later after school every other Thursday evening. They were given permission to show the Fact & Faith film *Dust or Destiny?*[40]

In Dyffryn Nantlle Grammar School, a Missionary Circle was formed to discuss the work of missionaries in foreign lands. The members held a Missionary Concert, giving most of the proceeds to the Ludhiana Mission and sharing the remaining eight pounds between other missions. Many from outside joined with the pupils to support the work, one woman giving the sum of twenty-five pounds that she had put aside for her husband's gravestone. The money was fittingly used by Ludhiana Hospital to buy a bed to commemorate him.[41] The Circle received the willing assistance of a new teacher from Porth in the Rhondda. Although not Welsh-speaking (though he did acquire some knowledge of the language), Brynmor Pierce Jones zealously shared the gospel in a predominantly Welsh area.

In Blaenau Ffestiniog Elwyn Davies, then minister of Jerusalem Independent Church, regularly met with candidates for church membership. Besides teaching them, he questioned them personally, clearly showing that they must believe in Jesus Christ and accept him as Saviour and Lord before becoming church members. The Holy Spirit spoke to a good number of them, and they came to the Manse to seek help.[42] Because there were so many it was decided to hold a Scripture Union meeting (*Undeb yr Ysgrythur*) in Jerusalem vestry. Some of the believers were very young, but they had the root of the matter in them and were carefully pastored by Elwyn Davies and Herbert Evans.

When Elwyn Davies left Blaenau Ffestiniog, the responsibility of leadership fell on the shoulders of Herbert Evans. Most of the meetings he took himself, but he also invited visiting speakers such as John Vevar, Mari Davies (Bala), and Emyr Roberts (Trefor). Author Patricia St. John and Sudan missionary Lavinia Hawkins made a particular impression on their young audience. Having himself a lively interest in the missionfield, Herbert Evans procured missionary books, and the young people enjoyed reading the story of John and Betty Stam and of Isobel Kuhn. Indeed it was the reading of such books that led Nerys Roberts to work in India for a period.[43]

The young people assisted their elders in many ways, holding open-air meetings, giving out tracts, distributing the paper *Challenge* in Llandudno, and taking hospital services. Nor was humanitarian work forgotten; for some time, clothing parcels were sent to various European countries. But an occasional Saturday afternoon saw them relaxing and enjoying each other's company on a hike or picnic.

While many in the district admired them greatly, there was also opposition. One schoolteacher was far from happy that so many pupils were 'obsessed' with religion. When one of them wrote an essay on 'Conversion', some of its content annoyed him intensely. He turned on the class and, doubtless thinking of the Scripture Union meetings in Jerusalem chapel, asked, 'How many of you believe such rubbish?' He was shocked to find that most of the class attended those meetings![44]

Herbert Evans was chief co-ordinator not only for the Blaenau Ffestiniog district but for North Wales generally. Realising the value of bringing young people from different areas together, he rallied groups from Blaenau, Pwllheli, Porthmadog and Caernarfon to united meetings. To make arrangements for these 'rallies', which became an important feature of the work at this period, he corresponded regularly with area representatives. According to local people, the Blaenau Ffestiniog postmaster regarded Herbert Evans and Dafydd Orwig of Plaid Cymru (the Welsh Nationalist Party) as his two most faithful customers![45]

The determination of some young people to attend these meetings was astounding. Not having the money to pay her bus fare, one girl gladly agreed to clean her grandmother's house every Saturday morning. The two shillings she received for doing this, plus a further two shillings from an uncle (a total of twenty pence in today's money), sufficed to get her to and from her destination.

The rallies continued for many years. The young people enjoyed one another's company, but they were also grounded in the Truth and helped to live their lives as witnesses to Jesus before going out into the world to follow their different callings.

3
'The Evangelical Movement of Wales'

Organisation and development: a bird's-eye view

The evangelicals were drawn together by the magnet of the Holy Spirit. The fellowship in the *seiadau* and conferences, and in campaigning together in various places, was very sweet. By this time, too, there were growing links with evangelicals in the non-Welsh-speaking community, particularly in South Wales. With a view to keeping the evangelicals together and promoting the work, it was felt that further organisation was needed.

In 1955 some significant steps were taken in that direction. Here are the main events and decisions of that year:[1]

March: The first issue of the English magazine, *The Evangelical Magazine of Wales*, appeared.

The nature and membership of the *seiadau* were defined.

J. Elwyn Davies was invited to work for the IVF as Welsh travelling secretary, on the understanding that he should combine with this the work of the *Cylchgrawn*.

May: Elwyn Davies was appointed General Secretary, and Bryn Davies Treasurer.

July: A 'Credo' or Doctrinal Basis was drawn up for committee members.

Subcommittees were appointed to be responsible for camps, evangelism, rallies and literature.

Three men were chosen to represent the English side of the work.

August: The *Cylchgrawn* Conference was held in Denbigh.

By now the work had developed into an 'evangelical movement'—indeed, that is the way that others described it. An official title had been considered in 1954, when a small group (Elwyn Davies, Emyr

Roberts, John Vevar, Herbert Evans, Bryn Davies and Emily Roberts) had met together in the home of Mrs Smith (at Llys Gwyrfai, Pwllheli). Once more we are indebted to Emily's diary:

> We discussed whether it would be appropriate to form an Evangelical Movement, realising that we had everything pertaining to a Movement but the name, and that had already been given us by others.[2]

It was agreed to put the matter before the 1955 Conference in Denbigh. There the title was officially accepted, with the enthusiastic backing of Dr Martyn Lloyd-Jones, in whose opinion this name was particularly appropriate, as there was an Ecumenical Movement already in existence.[3] The title 'Mudiad Efengylaidd Cymru' (Evangelical Movement of Wales) was, in a positive sense, a recognition of seven years of evangelical witness and, in a negative sense, a protest against the Ecumenical Movement.

The newly fledged Movement was to be led by a General Committee. Other matters of importance, such as the organising of sub-committees, were agreed on at that Denbigh Conference:[4]

Appointments made by the General Committee held during the Denbigh Conference, August 1955

The constitution of Sub-committees

The Conference accepted the following pattern:

1. The General Committee members to be members of all the Sub-committees.
2. The General Committee to elect Sub-committee officials, namely the Chairman and Treasurer.
3. The annual Conference to elect two members on each of the committees.
4. The elected Sub-committee members to remain in office for one year only, unless elected by the General Committee for a further period.
5. Every member of the Sub-committees to be asked to sign the Doctrinal Basis of the Movement.

Appointments for the year August 1955–August 1956

Camps Committee. Chairman: the Rev. I. D. E. Thomas, Caernarfon. Secretary: Miss Morwen Thomas, Llanelli. Members:

Miss Beth Williams, Cardiff; Miss Rhoda Bassett, Llanelli.
Literature Committee. Chairman: the Rev. Emyr Roberts, Trefor.
Secretary: Miss Ceinwen Matthews, University College, Aberystwyth, and the Rev. Gwilym Humphreys, Bethesda.
Evangelism Committee. Chairman: the Rev. J. D. Williams,
Ammanford. Secretary: the Rev. J. Elwyn Davies, Blaenau
Ffestiniog. Members: Mr Gareth Davies, Cross Hands, and the Rev.
Jim Walters, Llanfyllin.
Rallies Committee. Chairman: the Rev. Glyn Owen, Wrexham.
Secretary: Mr Herbert Evans, Bala. Members: the Rev. Gwyddno
Rowlands, Holywell, and the Rev. John Vevar, Botwnnog.

Immediately after 1955, some ministers felt that the General Committee had too much authority. They thought it wrong that appointments to office should be made solely by the General Committee, with no voice given to the Movement's supporters. Subsequently, therefore, though authority remained firmly with the General Committee, greater powers were given to the subcommittees, and opportunity provided to discuss the work of the Movement in annual meetings held during the English and Welsh Conferences.

Staffing and centres

When J. Elwyn Davies was asked to work for the IVF in 1955, he and his family moved to Bala, and in March 1956 Mair Jones from Llangennech, Carmarthenshire, joined them there as secretary. By 1958 Eryl Aran had been procured, and this became the North Wales centre until Bryn-y-groes (the house next door) was purchased in 1960. The need was felt for a South Wales office, and one was found in Port Talbot. Thanks once more to Emily Roberts for the details:

> *24 May 1962*. Gwilym Humphreys and family. The surprising news that Elwyn is moving to Port Talbot to the home of Mr and Mrs Cooke, given them rent free for seven years on payment of rates and repairs. The Movement taking a shop in Wrexham and also a shop in Swansea Market. What a surprise! they have offered the job of looking after it [the Wrexham shop] to me! Well, well.[5]

Emily did not go to Wrexham, but Elwyn Davies and his family moved to Cwmafan, Port Talbot, and thence to the manse when he became minister of the Independent chapel there. And 55 Station Road, Port Talbot, became the Movement office in South Wales.

The appointment in 1964 of Brenda Lewis to assist the General Secretary ensured more efficient organisation. One effective method of promoting the work was the formation of regional committees, operating through the medium of English or Welsh as appropriate. Because of the faster growth of the English work, the proceedings of the General Committee soon had to to be conducted in English. In 1966, in order to safeguard the Welsh side of the work, an Executive Committee was formed (eventually becoming the permanent Welsh Executive Committee).

By the end of 1970 the Movement had acquired new premises for a South Wales centre at Bryntirion, near Bridgend. In March 1972 the Movement office, with Brenda Lewis and Mair Jones, was transferred to this spacious building from Port Talbot, and in 1973 J. Elwyn Davies and family followed them to live in Bridgend town.

The expansion of the work required the creation of new posts. In 1974 Edmund T. Owen was appointed to assist in the Office and develop the literature work, but before long it became clear that another worker was needed. The appointee, E. Wyn James, proved to be a choice acquisition. Responsibility for the Movement's publishing work, especially that in the Welsh language, fell on his shoulders. A native of Troed-y-rhiw, Merthyr Tydfil (an Anglicised area), he had graduated in Welsh at Aberystwyth. In time he proved himself able not only to look after what developed into the Evangelical Press of Wales (Gwasg Efengylaidd Cymru) but also to produce books of his own, a number of fine volumes appearing in print.[6] He is currently Senior Lecturer in the Welsh Department at Cardiff University. Wyn James also took responsibility for the Evangelical Library at Bryntirion, a project begun by Alan Gray in Cathays Terrace, Cardiff.

When J. Elwyn Davies retired in 1990, further changes occurred. His had been a wise leadership, and many tributes were paid to his patient dealings with people, his wisdom in committees and, above all, his burden for the evangelical witness in Wales.[7] The Movement's debt to him is immeasurable, nor will it ever fully appreciate the role played by his wife Mair. It was a joyous experience to attend the service held in Carmarthen on Friday evening, 17 July 1998, for the launch of his book *O! Ryfedd Ras* (O! Wondrous Grace). Appropriately enough, it was his old friend Geraint Gruffydd of Aberystwyth who addressed the meeting—one who, like Elwyn Davies himself, had been present in that remarkable meeting at Plas-y-nant in 1948.

Gerallt Wyn Davies of Cardiff, a native of Caerwedros in Cardiganshire, was appointed to succeed Elwyn Davies.[8] Brought up in a home where the Truth was cherished, and taught by faithful Sunday School teachers, he had heard the gospel clearly proclaimed by preachers such as the Rev. M. P. Morgan, Blaenannerch, a man whose soul never lost the fire of the 1904–05 Revival. After national service in the Navy (during which he was baptised in St Paul's Bay, Malta), he studied at Aberystwyth, his first contact with Elwyn Davies (and hence with the Movement) being through the Christian Union there. On leaving university he entered the Civil Service, and then, after a period as a lecturer, became Dean of the Newport College of Higher Education. He began his work as Chief Executive in 1993, his task being to promote the Movement's vision in co-operation with the Management Committee.

A bilingual work

From 1955 until today the Movement has sought to promote the work through the medium of both Welsh and English. Owing to the fact that the English work has grown so much faster than the Welsh, it has not always been easy to give equal prominence to both. But there remains a sincere desire to protect the emphasis on the Movement's Welshness.

Some of the ministers involved in the work were not fluent in Welsh, and many had been called to minister in English churches. Two such were John Thomas (Aberafan), and Hugh D. Morgan (Gelli, Rhondda); while others like Wynford Davies (Tonypandy) and Derek Swann (Pontnewydd) spoke no Welsh at all. It was imperative, therefore, to cater for them and others like them, and for their people.

The English Magazine

The first step was to produce an English Magazine. *The Evangelical Magazine of Wales* appeared in 1955, edited by J. Elwyn Davies (Blaenau Ffestiniog) and J. Glyn Owen (Wrexham).[9] The first issue emphasised three things: there was need for a magazine to proclaim the whole counsel of God; it would not focus on any particular aspect; and it was published by the committee of *Y Cylchgrawn Efengylaidd*.

49

The unity of the witness through the medium of both languages had to be safeguarded.

Many of the articles were written by regular contributors to the Welsh magazine, such as Gwyn Walters, John Vevar and I. D. E. Thomas, but new contributors were welcomed to the early issues—men like Paul Tucker (Barry), Arnold Aldis and T. R. Loveridge (both of Cardiff), Omri Jenkins (London) and Hugh D. Morgan. 'Auntie Ruth' (Ruth Evans) was responsible for the children's corner and, later, 'Auntie Brenda' (Brenda Lewis). In the first issue I. D. E. Thomas dealt with revival in 'The Ploughman Overtaketh'—the first of four articles highly praised by Dr Tecwyn Evans of Rhyl, a leading Wesleyan Methodist minister. In 1956, this series was published under the title *God's Harvest*, a second edition appearing in 1997.

From the pen of Gwyn Walters came a comprehensive article entitled 'Good News for Today'. This begins by dealing with the difficulties facing the evangelical witness. Many will say that we need to *live* the gospel rather than discuss its content; others will argue that sincerity is of greater importance than wasting time explaining doctrinal minutiae; prejudice will raise its ugly head; whilst some will say we should forget our differences and come together as Christians. The all-important factor for the witness to bear in mind, however, is that he is witnessing to a *Person*—the one who came into this world to die for sinners, and who finished the work once and for all. He was buried, but rose on the third day. And he is the one who changes people's lives and makes them members of his own body. He is Lord of every aspect of one's life. What people need to hear is this scriptural message, not philosophical and psychological ideas.

The first English Conference

Like the Welsh-speaking evangelicals, the non-Welsh speakers and the English felt they needed a conference as well as a magazine. The first Conference, in 1957, was warmly welcomed to Sandfields, Aberafan, where John Thomas ministered.[10] The Conference Secretary, the Rev. T. J. Russell Jones, Risca, preached on the first evening and was followed during the week by Wynford Davies, I. D. E. Thomas and Derek Swann. The main speaker was Dr Martyn Lloyd-Jones, whose addresses, based on Ephesians 3:14-19, were emphatically God-centred.

One of those present was Eluned Harrison (née Cornish, then in Cardiff), urged to attend by her boyfriend, Graham Harrison, who was doing holiday work in the steelworks. Being a student in London, she was accustomed to hearing the Doctor preach, but in Sandfields 'the passion and power of his addresses went beyond what I had known of him before.'[11] He showed clearly that the 'doctrinal' is the foundation for the 'experiential', and that the knowledge of God is something into which one penetrates. One should never be content with superficial experiences. The more the inner man is strengthened, the more will the Christian experience God's presence, a presence manifested in times of revival in the Church's history.

According to Eluned Harrison, the stage was set for Elwyn Davies's address on Friday morning. Dr Lloyd-Jones, knowing that he had to leave early, had arranged for the former to take the meeting, his parting instruction being, 'Tell them about what happened in Dolgellau.'[12] Elwyn Davies obeyed, and not only were many blessed by what they heard, but it reminded them of the Movement's Welsh beginnings in the late forties, marked by notable movements of the Spirit. Derek Swann well remembers on that Friday morning feeling disappointed that the Doctor would not be addressing the meeting, but his disappointment soon vanished into thin air. So conscious was the congregation of the presence of God that they were reluctant to leave. Derek Swann went back to his room in John and Eluned Thomas's home and spent the afternoon alone in the presence of God.[13] He was to preach that evening and knew that this was the best possible preparation.

Another who was at that first English conference was Elizabeth Braund, daughter of an English judge. For a long period she had no interest in the gospel, but as a BBC employee she had been asked to prepare a documentary programme on Mildred Cable and her friends who crossed the Gobi desert. Her interest in Christianity was kindled, she began reading the New Testament and eventually came to faith in Jesus Christ under the ministry of Dr Lloyd-Jones at Westminster Chapel, London.[14] While at Sandfields, Elizabeth Braund suggested launching in England a magazine similar to that of the Movement. She, Elwyn Davies and Martyn Lloyd-Jones discussed the matter, and even considered such a magazine for Scotland and Ireland. In April 1958 the Doctor met with some of the evangelical leaders at Bala,[15] but though promising his full support, he could not give of his time to the venture.

A fruitful partnership

The possibility of a magazine for Scotland and Ireland was not realised, but one was established in England. It was the fruit of further discussions between Elizabeth Braund, Elwyn Davies and J. I. Packer, the three becoming joint editors, and all three in close connection with Dr Lloyd-Jones. Two-thirds of the content was common to both *The Evangelical Magazine* and *The Evangelical Magazine of Wales*, and in this way many of the best authors of the English evangelical world became known to the people of Wales. Alan Stibbs wrote on 'Parenthood';[16] J. A. Motyer on the first chapters of Isaiah;[17] and J. I. Packer contributed two series on the doctrine of God. (These were later to become the foundation of his influential book *Knowing God*.)[18]

In one of his articles Dr Packer expressed surprise that many evangelicals, whilst mastering other disciplines, were so undisciplined when it came to doctrine. One unavoidable consequence was a clash between doctrine and devotion, often leading to the separation of one from the other. Devotion must be founded on doctrine, because it sets out what the Bible says about God, and it enables the believer to get to know him better. Without doctrine the Christian will be self-centred, a condition which makes it very difficult for him to love God with all his mind (Matthew 22:37). In another article he dealt with God's holiness on the one hand and his fatherhood on the other, ending with a masterly practical application:[19] the secret of praying, contentment and perseverance in the Christian life is realising who the holy Father is. So little has been clearly written on the fatherhood of God, and it was good to have a contribution of that calibre.

Nor were the magazines' contributors confined to England and Wales. A most interesting article by Arnold Dallimore, a minister in Canada, reflects his experience on reading George Whitefield's diaries in preparation for writing a biography of that great divine. And the succinct but comprehensive article on the atonement contributed by the Scotsman, Professor R. A. Finlayson of the Free Church College, Edinburgh, is a veritable gem.[20]

Christian Bookshops

One effective way of promoting the witness of the Movement was to open bookshops for the sale of Christian literature in both English and Welsh. Beginning on a very small scale in Bala, the work developed to some extent when the office moved to Port Talbot in 1962, and in that same year shops were opened in Swansea and Wrexham. Further bookshops were later opened in Cardiff, Bangor and Llandrindod, and for some time one that opened in Llanelli was under the Movement's care. By 1998 the number had increased to eight. During the early years Betty Cooke of Port Talbot diligently looked after the work of the shops as well as the sale of cards and calendars, but later on local committees were formed to support this work. Nonetheless it is the shop managers themselves who bear the main responsibility.

Ministers Conference and Fellowships

Early in the fifties a group of Presbyterian ministers felt the need to come together to study, pray and campaign. They believed that through meeting together they could minister to each other, receive help to minister in their churches, and have opportunity to consider how best to face the world outside the church. They shared the dual conviction that the people around them needed the gospel, and that the country in general needed a spiritual revival. Many of them already met to arrange campaigns, and in 1954 they voiced a desire for more effective organisation.

At a meeting held on 19 November 1954, the forthcoming rallies were arranged as usual (the next two to be in Nant-y-moel and Gelli), but another important matter was raised: 'A proposal by the Rev. R. Emlyn Jones and seconded by Wynford Davies that a fellowship of evangelical ministers be formed, was adopted'; and, 'Instead of the April [1955] meeting a conference to last three days was to be held.'[21] I. B. Davies (Neath) was appointed Chairman, and John Thomas (Aberafan) Secretary. Dr Martyn Lloyd-Jones was invited to speak at this conference, and he consented, on condition that it was not confined to the Presbyterians but open to evangelical ministers from other denominations. It was agreed that others should be present by invitation, and the conference was held in Barry.

In the meantime, a list of a hundred ministers had been drawn up with a view to inviting them to a conference at Cilgwyn, Newcastle Emlyn, in 1956. The invitations were duly sent, but during the intervening months several of these 'others' had opportunity to attend occasional meetings of the Presbyterian Ministers Fellowship in Glamorgan, though that Fellowship was 'still . . . constitutionally

Presbyterian'.[22] By the end of 1956 the number attending from other denominations had increased: it included members of the Monmouthshire Prayer Group, and individuals such as Vernon Higham, then at Pontarddulais (Calvinistic Methodist), and Malcolm Evans at Llantwit Major (Congregational).

A third conference was held in Cilgwyn in 1957, again under the auspices of the Presbyterians, but during that week a significant change occurred. In one special meeting the chairman, Dr Lloyd-Jones, steered the discussion between the Presbyterian representatives and representatives of the Movement's General Committee. Among the decisions taken were the following: 'That a Sub-Committee of the Evangelical Movement of Wales be formed to care for the Ministers Conference and Fellowship'; and that 'Ministerial Fellowships for Evangelicals were to be formed in various parts of the country'.[23] Thus it was that the activities of evangelical ministers came under the wing of the Movement.

In that first conference in 1955, I. B. Davies declared that their main emphasis must be the preaching of the crucified Christ. As in the Denbigh Welsh Conference of the same year, the Doctor spoke on the work of the Holy Spirit, based on Ephesians 1:13-14 and 3:14. He claimed that it was possible for every believer to have a deeper, out-of-the-ordinary experience of the Holy Spirit. It was not a second blessing, nor was it a special step in the process of sanctification, but the love of God being poured into the heart, giving assurance of salvation and new power to live the Christian life.[24] Nonetheless it was an experience that affected the sanctification of the believer. In local ministers' meetings, as in the conference, priority was given to exposition of the Word: Emlyn Jones of Neath, for instance, chose to open the Epistle to the Philippians, and T. J. Russell Jones of Risca the book of Malachi.

Until 1961, the annual Ministers Conference was held in Cilgwyn, but the following year it moved to Bryn-y-groes, Bala, and this has been the venue ever since. Reflecting the steadfastness of the surrounding mountains, its pattern has remained the same: a strong emphasis on teaching and expounding the Word, discussion meetings, historical papers, and an overall view of mission work. But the prayer meetings and Dr Lloyd-Jones' address in the closing meeting deserve special mention. The Holy Spirit often gave great freedom in prayer, and there was fervent supplication, frequently interspersed by the 'Amens' of George Griffiths (Cwmtwrch) and Luther Rees (Llansamlet). And the Doctor's comments were not only relevant to ministers in their local situations, but also helped them to understand what was happening in the wider evangelical world.

Besides his earlier visits to Cilgwyn, the Doctor attended all the Ministers Conferences between 1962 and 1979, unless prevented by illness or absence from the country. One central theme in his sermons and discussions with ministers was 'Life'. His greatest joy was to know that God was actively blessing his church: his greatest concern, lack of life in individuals and churches. In the 1971 conference he chose to deal with some of the causes for this lack of life—religiosity, professional religion, ineffective evangelism—and then went on to explain how depending on apologetics to introduce and defend the faith, emphasising the application of the gospel rather than the gospel itself, and scholasticism, which could lead to Deism, were detrimental to the life-giving work of the Spirit. He reminded his congregation, from Acts 13:24-42, that God is the living God, the God who is at work, and he traced his mighty works through Scripture. He also reminded them what their forefathers did in times of spiritual drought: they cast themselves down before God in repentance and sought him anew.[25]

Although the mountain fastnesses remain unchanged, each generation gives birth to new shepherds. The same is true of the Church. Delightful as it was 'to shake hands with old faces', in the words of one chairman, quoting the Welsh-language writer D. J. Williams, it was a joy to see new faces among the old. The number of ministers increased to a regular attendance of about a hundred, many coming from across the border, and some from distant Scotland. Speakers also came from further afield—for example, Iain Murray, G. N. M. Collins, Douglas Macmillan and Maurice Roberts from Scotland. As a result, the occasional Welsh meeting that had been a feature of the early conferences was discontinued. This ultimately led to the formation of a separate Welsh Ministers Conference, one that the small company gathering together annually finds both uplifting and challenging.

Over the years the means of travelling to conferences has changed dramatically. Although Omri Jenkins and Dr Lloyd-Jones arrived for one of the earlier gatherings in a brand new car, and Elwyn Davies and Gwilym Humphreys once cadged a lift in a Tate & Lyle lorry,[26] public transport was the order of the day until Dr Beeching wielded his axe and the number of private cars escalated. As the years progressed, so did costs increase: the £2-5s-0d for accommodation in 1956 became £24.50 in 1985 and £50 in 1997.

The agreement made at the Cilgwyn conference to form ministers' fellowships was immediately implemented, and within two years there were groups in Wrexham, Bala, North Cardiganshire, Port Talbot, Monmouthshire, Caernarfon and Ammanford. A syllabus of study was prepared for them, covering a variety of topics. Here are some classified examples from the early period:[27]

Biblical: The Epistle to the Ephesians, the Pastoral Epistles, Titus, Proverbs

Doctrinal: Regeneration, the Work of the Holy Spirit, Providence, the Fruit of the Spirit

Biblical: Acts 20, using Richard Baxter's *Reformed Pastor* and Charles Bridges' *Christian Ministry*

Historical: William Williams, *The Experience Meeting/Drws y Society Profiad*

Pastoral: Jonathan Edwards, *The Religious Affections*

Missionary: Paul's Journeys

Apologetics: 'Earnestly contending for the faith'

The Religious Affections by Jonathan Edwards was a study that the ministers found particularly challenging. Compelled to question themselves about their own spiritual condition and the nature of their personal life, they were sobered, and driven to commit themselves more thoroughly to the ministry of the Word.

Courses

The English side of the ministers' work developed apace, and the same could be said of other aspects of the Movement's work, though Welsh needs were not forgotten. A *Theological Training Course* was begun in 1972 under the directorship of the Rev. Graham Harrison, to prepare men for the ministry of the Word.[28] By 1980 seventy-four had been prepared for different kinds of work, and twenty-seven of them were by then in full-time ministerial positions. By now the figure has risen to about two hundred and fifty. The course appeals especially to older men who have family commitments that would hinder them from attending a full-time course, and also to those who feel strongly that they want to prepare for the ministry while remaining in the context of their local church. In addition, a number of men already in the ministry but wishing to compensate for what they feel has been an inadequate or non-existent college course have joined the Theological Training Course.[29] From the beginning, the Course included a number of Welsh-speaking students. The year 1976 saw the introduction of a Welsh Theological Course, which was structured to help people to be leaders in their churches.

A *Christian Study Course* was provided in 1974, followed by a parallel Welsh course. This was a guided reading course in Christian doctrine, biblical studies and church history with a view to equipping church members, Sunday school teachers, etc., for Christian living and church involvement. From 1968, too, for a short period, a *Christian Training School* was held in Cardiff (1968) and Swansea (1969). At these day-courses for believers the lectures concentrated on church history, Christian doctrine, biblical studies and the Christian life.

Annual English Conference

After the first English conference at Aberafan in August 1957, the venue shifted to Aberystwyth, where it has remained ever since. One happy feature of the early years was that a number of Welsh-speaking Christians were also present, particularly those with young families, taking the opportunity to combine conference attendance with a week by the seaside. In view of this, and in order to serve Welsh-speaking people in the locality, on two evenings of the week the conference held both Welsh and English preaching services. But when, in August 1966, the Welsh conference was itself transferred to Aberystwyth, this practice naturally ceased.

Attendance grew steadily, often requiring a move to a larger hall of residence or chapel. Then, as numbers began to increase dramatically and include many from other parts of the UK, there was timely provision in the growth of the university campus, with its increased residential accommodation and its Great Hall for main meetings.

The conference programme has remained basically the same: prayer meetings each morning followed by the main conference addresses (with separate provision for children); some afternoon open-air meetings on the promenade, and preaching services each evening. In earlier years there was a historical lecture recalling our Christian heritage in Wales. More recent features have included a seminar on a relevant topic and, since 1991, the Missionary Exhibition that is by now an integral part of 'Aber' week.

It is encouraging to see the large proportion of young people present. This is to some extent a by-product of the camps work—it is not unusual to overhear 'See you at Aber!' as the parting shot of youngsters leaving camp. In the last few years the introduction of 'Extra Time', the late evening programme for young people, has been a valuable added ingredient.

The conference has been indebted down the years to a succession of hard-working and efficient secretaries, and to others working faithfully behind the scenes. In days of spiritual declension, the opportunities that this week affords for seeking God together, hearing his Word expounded, and enjoying fellowship and friendship, have been highly prized.

Camps

The Welsh camps that began in Bangor in 1954 moved to Glynllifon, near Caernarfon, in 1956. The first English camp was held at Eryl Aran, Bala, in 1959, moving next door to Bryn-y-groes the following year.[30] In 1961, a bilingual camp was attempted, but the experiment proved unsatisfactory and was not repeated. Considering that only twenty-six attended the initial Welsh camp, the growth over the years has been phenomenal, and other venues besides Bryn-y-groes and Bryntirion have had to be found to meet the demand. (See also pp. 107-9.)

But the camps would not have been so successful were it not for the constant care of the wardens and their wives and the diligent work of secretaries. Down the years there have been countless leaders and chaplains, some regularly sacrificing their holiday time for this work. Who can forget the priceless contribution of 'Auntie Bessie' (Mrs Elizabeth Jones)? Over and above her role as caterer and cook for the camps season, she contributed significantly to camp life, caring for some of the younger campers and taking part in the *noson lawen* with her kitchen helpers. She became friend, mother and counsellor to dozens of young people, and three of her kitchen colleagues became overseas missionaries. Her gift for alerting campers to practical needs and inspiring a response led to Bryn-y-groes receiving packets of needles, a rubbish bin and even a carpet for the stairs!

The appeal to the denominations

Through the Movement, evangelicals could enjoy fellowship across denominational barriers. Most supporters felt no tension between working within the Movement and being faithful to their denominations. They belonged largely to the historical denominations and genuinely desired the revival of their churches. The appeal that was sent out to the Welsh denominations in 1961 reflects that desire: its burden was a call to repent, to seek God anew, and to pray for an outpouring of the Holy Spirit. That, they believed, was the path of blessing.

This appeal was the outcome of careful consideration by the members of the General Committee. J. Elwyn Davies addressed them initially, speaking of the responsibility of the Movement to Wales and applying the four aspects of Jesus Christ's ministry to the Welsh situation. Just as he ministered to those who attended the synagogue, to the crowd outside, to the church leaders, and to his own disciples, so the Movement should think about the people within the chapels, those outside, the religious leaders, and the members of the *seiadau* (evangelical fellowships). He stressed that the call was primarily to the churches. Although they were in decline, the Bible was still open, and it should be borne in mind not only that God is merciful, but that tares have always co-existed with wheat in the Church down the centuries. After lengthy deliberation following this address, a promise was made to 'encourage one another to walk the path of submission and repentance, asking God to give us progressive grace until we meet in Bryn-y-groes, November 15-16, for prayer and discussion.'[31]

Those responsible for the appeal believed that they were acting in accordance with what is frequently found in the Old Testament, when God called his people to return from their wanderings, and also in accordance with what the nonconformist fathers had done in the past. To kindle a spirit of prayer, the Ministers Fellowships were advised of their intention. Some ministers expressed willingness to visit churches to preach the Word—the Word that would promote the call to repentance. When the appeal was announced, it was kindly received by the Presbyterians and the Wesleyans, but no obvious action was taken. On the whole, the response was disappointing, some challenging the Movement's right to make such a call.

This disappointing response gave rise to mixed feelings among evangelicals. While some were resolved to work harder within their denominations, the hopes of others were shaken, and some were even convinced that they should consider leaving their denominations. Dr Martyn Lloyd-Jones was clearly very sensitive to the reactions. The denominational situation in Wales was a matter on which he had been deeply exercised for some years; he had discussed it with Elwyn Davies as early as 1953.[32] Even then he foresaw the day when the evangelicals would leave. But they would have to be certain that the time was right; unless there was just cause for leaving, ministers should stay within their denominations.

Uniting the denominations

On top of the disappointing response to the 1961 appeal, there was a movement afoot to unite the Welsh denominations. After protracted consultation in 1962, a Committee of the Four Denominations (Pwyllgor y Pedwar Enwad) was formed, comprising Presbyterians, Independents and Wesleyan Methodists as full members, and Baptists as observers. The principles of union were published in a series of leaflets, such as *Tuag At Uno* (Towards Union, 1963), *Cynllun Uno* (The Union Plan, 1965), and *Cyfamodi yng Nghymru* (Covenanting in Wales, 1968). This was another challenge that the Movement had to face.

In an attempt to respond to the ecumenical emphasis and the plan to unite the denominations, four positive steps were taken. First, a meeting was arranged between the denominational leaders and the Movement.[33] Here they voiced their differing standpoints in a friendly manner, but the evangelical representatives made it perfectly clear that doctrinal agreement had to be reached before they could move on to talk about union. Secondly, the General Committee asked individual members to keep a close watch on developments and on press reports.[34] Thus, when *Tuag At Uno* appeared, these members and others had ample opportunity to comment. Thirdly, the Movement published pamphlets by way of response, the first being *Eglwys Unedig Cymru* (The United Church of Wales) by J. Elwyn Davies.[35] Fourthly, after much discussion in various Movement committees, it was decided to publish booklets on the Church.

The Christian Church

In the period between 1962 and 1966 careful preparation was made. Some of the preparatory work was done by Graham Harrison, Noel Gibbard and Hugh D. Morgan; this was then enlarged by Graham Harrison and submitted to the Ministers Subcommittee. A copy was sent to Dr Lloyd-Jones, who responded, 'I think that this is excellent.'[36] A group of ministers met at Llandrindod on Friday 14 January 1966 to deliberate for the last time, and the plan was presented to the General Committee the following day. At that meeting Graham Harrison was thanked for his painstaking work, and it was arranged that on 15 March 1966 a meeting be held in the Heath Church, Cardiff, at which he would present his work and the Doctor would preside.[37]

On that day the Declaration was accepted by a substantial gathering of ministers. They had received a copy of it beforehand, together with a letter from the Rev. J. B. E. Thomas explaining the background and intention. The final version of *The Christian Church* was written by Graham Harrison, and Emyr Roberts was responsible for the equivalent Welsh version, *Yr Eglwys Gristnogol*. Initial work on a second document was undertaken by Gilbert Evans, Graham Harrison and Gordon Macdonald, and the final version—*The Ministry and Life of the Christian Church: A Basis for Discussion*—was published in 1968.[38]

Ecumenical union was high on the agenda in England too, and Dr Martyn Lloyd-Jones was in the forefront of the battle there, as in Wales. But we must not overlook the fact that for over six years, between 1955 and 1961, he regularly attended discussion meetings with those who opposed his stance.[39] It was in the Evangelical Alliance conference held in London in 1966 that he declared that evangelicals should seriously consider their position within the denominations and be ready, on the grounds of their evangelical convictions, to leave them. For those ministers to remain within the denominations, he maintained, would be to be guilty of schism. He urged evangelicals of all denominations to stand together on the basis of the gospel on which they all agreed. In that historical meeting he was opposed by the Rev. John Stott of All Souls Church, London, who argued that Scripture and history were against the Doctor's position. In 1967, the Doctor reiterated his appeal to his fellow evangelicals in another London meeting arranged by the British Evangelical Council.[40] These developments had a marked influence on many ministers in Wales, but it must be remembered that the meeting at the Heath Church, Cardiff, predated both the London meetings.

By 1966 the church situation in Wales was even more complex than in 1961. The evangelicals in the Church in Wales stood firmly behind John Stott; the position of some ministers within the denominations became even more entrenched; some ministers decided to leave, but only when the time was opportune; others felt they could no longer stay and were ready to leave immediately. Furthermore, there were a few who thought that the presence of an evangelical within a mixed denomination condemned him, even if he strongly opposed the Ecumenical Movement. This attitude disappointed many of the Movement's friends. At the same time, many of those who left could not understand how ministers could stay within a mixed denomination. The situation was really complicated.

Affiliation of churches
The Movement's leaders made every effort to keep its supporters, especially the ministers, together. One of the steps taken, in 1967, was to make it possible for churches to become formally affiliated to the Movement. Elwyn Davies introduced a paper as a basis for discussion, and he, John Thomas (Aberafan) and Luther Rees (Llansamlet) were appointed to consider the constitutional changes required for this. Their suggestions, submitted to the General Committee on 1 May 1967, were accepted on the understanding that they were not forming another denomination (though it should be noted that two members withheld their vote).[41]

A number of churches immediately took advantage of this provision: Cephas, Heolgerrig, Merthyr, was followed by King Street, Wrexham; Heath Evangelical Church, Cardiff; West Cross, Swansea; Calvary, Rhymney, and Carmel, Plas Bennion, near Wrexham. The Fellowship at Caerphilly was also affiliated. During the seventies and eighties the number grew steadily.

Affiliated churches were required to agree with the Movement's doctrinal basis. The supporters of this move were convinced that lack of discipline was the prime reason for the churches' decline. For example, those who were accepted into church membership were seldom asked for a testimony to show that their profession was both scriptural and genuine.[42] It was accepted that individual evangelical churches held different views on matters such as baptism and church government, and they were given freedom in these matters, so long as such differences did not prevent fellowship between the various congregations.[43]

These ecclesiastical considerations were not confined to Wales, for in 1967 arrangements were made for the Movement to affiliate with the British Evangelical Council. Until then, the BEC had not numbered a 'movement' among its members, but the fact that individual churches were connected with the Evangelical Movement of Wales made affiliation possible. This bond gave the Movement, through its representatives, a better understanding of what was happening in Britain as a whole and, evangelically, worldwide. It also afforded opportunities to contribute to discussions.[44] The relationship was strengthened when J. Elwyn Davies, the Movement's General Secretary, was appointed Chairman of the Council that same year.

Some ministers were able to contribute directly to the administrative work of the Movement. For a time after Elwyn Davies's retirement, Peter Milsom took additional responsibility as General Committee Chairman with executive powers. From 1982 to 1992 the Rev. Gwynn Williams of Sandfields, Aberafan (now Cardiff), contributed on the administrative side, and the Rev. Hywel Davies, Llangefni (a son of Elwyn Davies), was appointed Secretary of the Welsh work in North Wales, a position he still holds.

4

The Trumpet and the Fold

Preaching the gospel and shepherding the flock

The hearts of the converts of 1947 and 1948 were consumed with a zeal for evangelism, and under the direction of the Holy Spirit they held campaigns and meetings throughout the length and breadth of Wales. The desire to proclaim the good news was a predominant feature of these early years.

Preaching the gospel

We do not have a full account of every meeting and evangelistic campaign held during 1949, but the extensive list of places visited is in itself quite astounding. In South Wales are listed Llanelli, Llwyn-hendy, Burry Port, Kidwelly, Llandybïe and Pen-y-groes: in North Wales, Glasgoed, Port Dinorwic, Nant Peris, Cwm-y-glo, Tudweiliog, Llansannan, Llanfairfechan, Carrog, Coed-poeth, Llanymawddwy, Mold and Trefor.[1] At these meetings students joined with those not in college to bear witness to the gospel, the younger ones taking the introductory parts of the service and the older ones (usually ministers) invited to preach. As with the 'Oslo meetings', the Free Churches were responsible for arranging many of these evangelistic campaigns.

One of the campaigners at Pen-y-groes (Carmarthenshire) was speaking for his fellow workers when he said,

> What we have found after a week of meetings preaching the gospel of Jesus Christ is that the gospel itself continues to attract people. The Pen-y-groes campaign has proved that there is nothing to compare with the gospel of Jesus Christ, and hundreds came to the meetings to hear it.[2]

The length of these campaigns varied—from one or two days to a whole week or even longer. In the case of Trefor (Caernarvonshire), meetings continued over three weeks, and the services held in the slate quarry left a lasting impression: 'In these meetings, as in the evening services, the quiet seriousness of the listeners and the polite welcome given to the missionaries and their message testified to the fact that the Holy Spirit was convicting many of their need for a living Saviour.'[3]

Caernarfon had been the meeting place for those who bore witness to the gospel prior to 1950, and it was here that they returned in that year. As the headline in the local paper testified ('The Young Call for a Religious Campaign'), it was the young people of the town who had asked the Caernarfon Council of Churches to arrange a campaign for April. This was subsequently reported in the press, and we also have Emily Roberts's personal memories of the week:[4]

> It was good once more to be an eyewitness to the miracles of grace—in a home, in powerful meetings on the *maes* (square), in after-meetings, in the Majestic [cinema] and wherever. I shall long remember two after-meetings with Gwyn [Walters], and his Saturday evening sermon on the Good Shepherd (what an unction of the Holy Spirit!); Wednesday evening's open-air, Elwyn and his white tract in the fading light and the Saviour calling; the one and a half thousand children in Moreia on Thursday afternoon; the saved rising boldly and firmly to their feet in Monday evening's service; Lilian's thrilling singing; the promise I had from Idris Davies before Tuesday evening's meeting, namely II Chron 20.12; sharing the work with Morwen; the solemnly serious discussion with Arthur, Elwyn and Mair concerning the work in the North; the prayer with the 'woman of Samaria' in the Majestic; the tears of a girl from Llanrug; and the worrying strain in Edward St. But thank God for each and every one of them.

Mair Davies (née Humphreys) well remembers the enthusiasm in Caernarfon, and the frequent references to the Good Shepherd. It was the topic chosen by David Shepherd in addressing the children: clutching one of his fingers, he emphasised '*my*' shepherd. Gwilym Humphreys sang of the shepherd, and hearing this prompted Gwyn Walters to preach on Jesus Christ the Shepherd. And he had great freedom in his delivery.[5]

A rally could kill two birds with one stone: it could build up the young in the faith and offer the gospel to unbelievers. More people than usual came to the rally in Pwllheli on 23 January 1953. Seeing such a crowd, one young minister present was overwhelmed with tears of joy, and an older and more experienced minister—the Rev. Enoch Rogers, Tudweiliog—expressed his gratitude through the composition of a Welsh hymn.[6] Similar meetings were arranged in Cricieth, Bethesda, Llandudno and many other places.

Nor were the evangelicals in South Wales idle; indeed, many of them were zealous evangelists. A group of Presbyterian ministers arranged English rallies with the same dual purpose as those in North Wales. Four hundred and fifty gathered in Sandfields chapel to hear Gwyn Walters preach on 'Running the Race'. At the evening service, which was more evangelistic, Wynford Davies, Tonypandy, preached the gospel.[7] These ministers did sterling work, and this aspect of their witness came under the wing of the Movement.

Many of the leaders of the rallies in the fifties were men who were the fruit of the student campaigns of the forties—men such as John Thomas (Aberafan) and Hugh D. Morgan (Gelli, Rhondda). Outside the colleges, Emily Roberts was the most prominent person: she was present, for instance, at the IVF campaign in Ystalyfera in 1954, where 'God caused his face to shine upon us and we saw fathers and mothers, young people and children come to the Saviour.'[8] People flocked to the meetings, and the local paper reported that more were going to the chapel than to the pubs. On the last Sunday evening Gwilym Roberts, IVF travelling secretary in Wales, preached in a local cinema full to overflowing.

Evangelism is primarily a matter of attitude and desire, and that is certainly what characterised the group of ministers that ventured into Cardiganshire in November 1959, among them J. Elwyn Davies, Arthur Pritchard and Vernon Higham.[9] The first meeting was held in Llanilar on 17 November, and the final meeting on 27 November at Llanddewibrefi, where Vernon Higham was minister.

The formation of Regional Committees in 1961 made it possible to concentrate on a specific district within an area. The West Glamorgan committee was especially diligent, and many a series of meetings (those in Ogmore Vale, for example) experienced tangible blessing,[10] the presence of God being so real that people were loath to leave at the end of the final meeting. The Cardiff evangelicals felt compelled to go to the Valleys: they visited Rhymney, Bryn-mawr and Tongwynlais.[11] Occasionally there were experiments with new methods such as informal meetings, games, and a coffee bar. This deeply concerned a number of Christians, who expressed their worries in the English Magazine.[12]

The seasons of agricultural shows and fairs provided excellent opportunities for selling books and bearing personal witness. Brynmor P. Jones, assisted by Roy John with his technical skill, undertook this work for a period of three years, the two of them sleeping in the wagon behind the Bedford van. Selwyn Morgan and Peter Thorneycroft also excelled in this kind of work, visiting as many as possible of the fifty agricultural shows held annually in Wales and the Border counties.[13] At first, visitors were none too anxious to buy or to open their hearts, but patience reaps its just reward. Because of the stall's welcoming atmosphere, an individual would occasionally stop to talk and engage in serious discussion: one teacher, for instance, enquired persistently about intellectual problems, and returned the following morning to buy five pounds' worth of booklets.[14]

Evangelists

As well as arranging individual meetings and campaigns, the Movement had a strong desire to see evangelists being set apart to work in Wales. The challenge of this work was continually being put before the Movement's supporters, and a few felt led to respond to it.

During his term as warden of Bryn-y-groes, Ifan Mason Davies felt convinced that he should bear witness to the gospel in Merionethshire. The Movement offered its full support and agreed to appoint him to the work officially in 1967.[15] Within two years he was finding it difficult to fulfil the dual role of looking after the centre and evangelising regularly. The Movement's General Committee agreed to release him from Bryn-y-groes, on condition that his help be available, should need arise. He arranged his programme: itinerant evangelistic work with the van, selling books, showing films, and holding meetings whenever and wherever possible.[16] Within a short time, his work was approved by the General and Welsh Executive Committees, and he was authorised to buy an amplifier for his use. In 1980 (by now living near Aberystwyth), instead of working with the van he concentrated on door-to-door work in the villages with a view to establishing *seiadau*. A joint understanding between the Movement and the Welsh Evangelical Church in Aberystwyth facilitated the settlement of financial terms for this work.[17]

When, in 1973, Irvon Parry left the Anglican ministry in Wales, he came to share the work in Merioneth with Ifan.[18] He had been in charge of Ystradmeurig 'College' in Cardiganshire, but felt a strong desire to be free to share the gospel. The Movement agreed to accept him, and appointed a small committee to advise him and be responsible for his financial support.[19] Irvon settled in Blaenau Ffestiniog, and was prepared to travel from there to different places in North Wales. It was emphasised that this was a venture of faith, and appeals were made to individuals and churches to invite the evangelist to hold meetings, and to contribute towards his maintenance.[20] Although both men witnessed mainly in the North, the South was not totally unfamiliar to them, and they held a series of meetings at Cwm-twrch in Glamorgan and Bryn Moriah in Carmarthenshire.

After urgent attention to necessary van repairs, the two evangelists ventured to Conway Fair. In one memorable open-air meeting there, a gang of young people stopped to listen intently to the gospel, and some of them responded positively to the message. Their efforts were concentrated on Merionethshire, especially the areas around Llandderfel, Cynwyd and Llandrillo. A circular letter was sent to homes, and suitable tracts distributed. Perseverance was the order of the day: 'Our plan was to call twice, if possible, in each home. But we found that some places desired a third visit, and we were requested to call again.'[21]

Those are the bare bones of the work, but it is possible to put some flesh on them. Ifan Mason Davies found the work in Bryn-y-groes, and especially the support of the believers there, of great spiritual benefit to his ministry. He testifies that he went out in fear and trembling, conscious not only of his own weakness but also of the prejudice in many places against the Movement. Selling Bibles, hymn books and children's books helped to break down the barrier between preacher and congregation. Finding a suitable parking spot for the van was a constant problem. For one Dolgellau fair he had conveniently parked it outside the Pigley Wigley café the night before, only to find, on returning the next morning, that it had been shifted way down the road!

Sometimes the opposition was more personal. Driving along in the van one day, he saw a farmer at the roadside. Thinking this could be an opportunity to explain the nature of his work, he opened the window.

But he had scarcely opened his mouth before the farmer tersely stated his doctrine: 'When I die, I will be six feet under.' The evangelist began to explain why he disagreed with this statement, and the next moment a hand grabbed his nose through the open window. Realising this was no time to argue, Ifan sped away like Jehu of old!

Sometimes there was opportunity to talk to someone who opposed the evangelical faith. In the Bala area Ifan Mason Davies came across a woman who was extremely cross because evangelicals were deserting the chapels. He did his best to explain the current situation, but left her unconvinced. Shortly afterwards, when visiting the Maelor Hospital, Wrexham, he saw on the patients' list the name of a woman from the Bala district and so went to the ward to see her. Who should be sitting by her bedside but the woman to whom he had been speaking, having come to visit her sister! Despite the initial awkwardness, Ifan was able to steer the talk to more profitable things, and as he left he offered the visitor a lift back to Bala. She gladly accepted, and on leaving the car pressed a note into his hand with the words, 'Five pounds for the cause.'[22]

There were others who diligently proclaimed the gospel in different areas: Kevin Adams in Llanelli and district, and John Puckett in mid-Wales. In 1982 Ioan Davies began a lengthy period of tireless evangelising. His experience as minister of Caersalem, Caernarfon, over a number of years stood him in good stead as he travelled the hinterland seeking to lengthen the cords. These extracts from his diary are taken from an article he wrote for the *Cylchgrawn*, sharing some of his experiences:[23]

> *Tuesday*. Called to see B., the Vicar thought I could help her. Her mother also there. A cup of tea and a long chat with B., who was very bitter towards S., another young girl who had made life unbearable. Came back to her need, urging her to read once again the Gospels' account of the life of Jesus.
>
> Called with a man who had lost his wife over a year ago, and had started coming fairly regularly to the meetings. His wife had come to believe during her months of illness. This fact a great consolation to the family and a help to me as I try to minister to them.
>
> *Tuesday*. Another fine morning. Visiting in Bethesda. In the first house succeeded in getting a man out of his bed! Apologised profusely, and left leaving *Ffydd i'n Dydd* (Faith for our Day) in

his hand. In the next house, told bluntly by a young girl that she had absolutely no interest at all, but allowed to explain briefly who Jesus Christ was, what he had done and why we should consider his claim on our life. 'Cast your bread upon the waters, for you will find it after many days.'

Tuesday. [Bethesda again] One woman I wanted to see going out, one man in hospital, and no answer in another house! Turned to go home, but called to see a man to enquire about his wife who had been in hospital in Liverpool the previous week. Was told that she had gone down to town! That was good news. More rain after dinner. Went with Glenys to hold a service in the home of the church's oldest member who is 93. Then called with her neighbour who has appreciated regular visits since losing her husband two years ago. Took both friends to the centre for the aged, and because it was still raining heavily met Esther from school and went to Plas Hedd before tea.

Wednesday. Visiting with Andre in Bangor. Had many brief chats today, one or two prepared to listen, some very short and one downright rude—'I want nothing to do with you.' No opportunity even to ask the reason why. The two of us showing a video about the life and work of Corrie ten Boom in the Glan Adda Club for the Disabled in the afternoon, and had an opportunity to discuss matters of consequence afterwards. Requested to show Joni next month.

The work of these evangelists was not only praiseworthy in itself, but it was also a challenge to their fellow evangelicals, reminding them that they belonged to an evangelical movement, and that spreading the good news was its *raison d'être*. The response was not always as good as it might have been, but it must be remembered that many of the independent evangelical churches that were supporting the Movement were themselves wrestling with the problem of how to present the gospel to those outside the Church.

Missionary concern
Another aspect of the evangelical witness was interest in the work of the gospel in foreign lands. It was realised from the outset that horizons needed to be widened lest the Movement become too insular. Elwyn Davies had visited Oslo, and two of the early workers,

A. L. Hughes and his wife Bronwen, had been in India for some years. Others, such as Glyndwr Jenkins and Gwyddno Rowlands who went to India, had left Wales for the mission field during that period, and a man from Africa was present in the first annual conference in 1952 (see p. 41).

The two magazines played a part in fostering missionary interest. Herbert Evans contributed to the *Cylchgrawn* a series of articles on various missionaries and missionary movements, and in the English Magazine there was regular updating of news about missionaries, especially those from Wales. In 1970, *Into All the World / I'r Holl Fyd* was published,[24] a bilingual booklet giving information about missionaries who were from Wales or had close connections with it. In that and the revised 1973 edition there were a hundred or so names, representing more than thirty missionary societies, most of them inter-denominational.

Amongst evangelicals at this period there occurred a definite shift from supporting denominational missionary societies to supporting those whose witness was more clearly evangelical. A number of Welshmen became prominent in different societies: Omri Jenkins (Llandybïe) and Glyn Owen (see chapters 1 and 2) in the European Missionary Fellowship; J. Roderick Davies (Brynaman) in the Brazilian Bible Mission; David James-Morse (Tonyrefail) in the Regions Beyond Missionary Union; Glyndwr Davies in the Dorothea Mission; Leslie Pick (Resolven), founder of the Christian International Refugee Mission; Ernest Williams (Porth) in the Apostolic Church Missionary Movement; and Colin Nicholas (Ammanford) in the Worldwide Evangelisation Crusade. Of the eighty or more Welsh missionaries included in *Into All the World*, some twenty were Welsh-speaking.

Besides seeking to foster missionary interest amongst readers in this country, the English Magazine, like the Welsh (see p. 42), has down the years been sent abroad to missionaries with Welsh connections to help maintain their links with home. Numerous non-Welsh-speaking missionaries have been added to its mailing list, and from time to time requests for the Magazine have come from national pastors. The packet often takes a while to reach its destination, but it is a service that is appreciated. One missionary spoke of 'devouring' it when it arrived!

Patagonia

The 'Welsh Colony' of Patagonia attracted particular attention. The *Cylchgrawn Efengylaidd* had already prepared the ground for Mair Davies of Bercoed, Llandysul, who arrived there in 1963 (and still remains there, her energy unsapped and her vision clear). She began her work under the auspices of the American Episcopal Methodist Church, but from the very beginning evangelical friends in Wales supported her both financially and in prayer. Her regular prayer letter and the news bulletins in both magazines constantly reminded her supporters of the need in Patagonia. In 1974 the Colwyn Bay Welsh Evangelical Church agreed to channel gifts donated for her support. The possibility was discussed of Mair Davies being employed directly by the Movement, and from 1979 it became responsible for paying her salary.[25]

Mair Davies, who is able to minister through the medium of both Spanish and Welsh, has done a great deal of Sunday school and youth work, and she preaches regularly in the Welsh chapels. Her personal care for her people is phenomenal. But much of her work has been centred round the bookshop in Trelew, which not only sells Christian literature but welcomes visitors. Its recent move to more convenient premises should further enhance its witness and boost sales. These words from Mair in the 1991 Welsh Conference express her missionary spirit and willingness to do God's will: 'As I look back over the years—you may not believe me, but it is the honest truth—if I had the choice of living my life over again, I would not have wished for another path. I have thanked Him many times for the path He prepared for me in love.'[26]

Not only did Welsh people respond by prayer and financial support, but some felt called to short-term service in Patagonia. Among them were the Revs Goronwy Prys Owen (while at Carmarthen), J. Elwyn Davies, Ifan Mason Davies and Ioan Davies, together with their wives; also, Dr Phil Ellis and family, and Mrs Hazel Charles Evans. Robert Owen Jones went with his family to do research work and had opportunities to minister. Gwilym Humphreys also visited and, like the others, returned with treasured memories. On arrival he found he was expected to preach three times on a Sunday, and also to visit the sick in hospitals and in homes. On his very first Sunday he was thrown in at the deep end, when a Sunday School class was placed in his care!

And so, on the first Sunday morning, I found myself teaching an adult class of more than twenty scholars. The other classes were being conducted in Spanish. Everything was done so well, the singing and the word to all present at the end of class time so heart-warming. The Tabernacle vestry has been extended during the past years to make it suitable for children and young people. The same pattern is followed in the Gaiman, the teacher of the adult class being Moelona Roberts de Drake, the great-niece of Eluned Morgan.[27]

Gwilym also mentions his first journey from the Chubut Valley to Comodoro Rivadavia, a city some four hours' journey south by car:

For fifteen years, Mair has travelled annually to Comodoro taking Christian books to be sold there. This year a life's dream has been realised—a new Christian bookshop has been opened in this big city. It was a privilege to witness the venture and to see the shop opened in January. There is a small flat behind the shop, a convenient place for Graciela, Alicia's sister, to live. The two sisters, of Indian extraction, are of inestimable value to Mair— Alicia runs the shop in Saint David's Hall, Trelew. She has been to Wales to learn Welsh and she continues to speak it.

Third World Literature Fund

In 1988 another means of contact with the wider world was adopted, through the establishment, by two friends of the work, of the Third World Literature Fund[28]—a channel by which many Evangelical Press of Wales publications were sent to churches, colleges and workers in the Third World. During the venture's first year, 916 copies of 27 titles were sent to Nigeria, Sri Lanka and Sierra Leone, and the following year 600 copies of various titles to Nigeria, Malawi, the Philippines and India. Realising the serious lack of books among theological students, suitable literature was sent to Central and South Africa: many copies of Peter Jeffery's *Christian Handbook*, for example, were sent to Uganda.

A number of the recipients responded expressing their gratitude. A Methodist minister in Sierra Leone testified that reading the books he had received from Wales had enabled him to persevere despite fierce opposition from his Muslim parents. One correspondent expressed appreciation of Douglas Macmillan's *The Lord Our Shepherd*; another of Dr Martyn Lloyd-Jones' *Why Does God Allow War*? Indeed, all the gifts of books were warmly received, and especially so in India and the African countries, where poverty is such a dreadful problem.

Cefnogi

The missionary aspect of the Movement's witness receives the support of an American husband and wife, Don and Joan Phelps of New York State, who have set up 'Cefnogi' (Support) to channel financial contributions to the work with a view particularly to promoting good Christian literature in the Welsh language. They also maintain a link with the Maerdy Evangelical Church in the Rhondda Fach.

And so, in different ways, the Movement seeks to serve Wales without forgetting the big outside world.

Shepherding the flock

Jesus Christ is the Good Shepherd who has great concern for his sheep, but he has also seen fit to raise pastors to care for them in his name. The Movement's leaders were quick to realise that this pastoring aspect was all-important to the success of the evangelical witness. They knew full well that the small flock was precious in the eyes of the Great Shepherd, and they also had before them the example of the eighteenth-century Welsh Methodists who established *seiadau* (societies) country-wide. This is what one minister wrote in a letter to a fellow minister:[29]

> I sincerely hope you have fellowship with your little ones in Trefor. More likely than not, you do. My heart is full of joy when I think of the *seiadau* that are being established one by one. The Christian must have a *seiad* (Mal. 3:16), says the 'genius' of the Methodist Revival, quite rightly in this instance, but for that matter he only followed the Protestant and Apostolic tradition— the church in the house of . . .

There are many significant things in this letter: the information that *seiadau* are being formed, that fellowship between Christians is precious, that leaders have a sense of history, and that the *seiat* is a small church for evangelicals, although they are at the same time faithful members of the historical denominations.

T. Arthur Pritchard was writing to Emyr Roberts. But the addressee was equally convinced of the value of *seiadau*:[30]

> I am perfectly sure that in these *seiadau* I have had a clearer vision of the meaning of the Church of the Lord Jesus Christ than I have come within a hundred miles of seeing in BD textbooks. The secret of new life for our nation is that which we, debtors and sinners, have received, plus that great promise of sustenance and inspiration on the pilgrimage to the Other Side.

The writer of the letter considered belonging to the people of God to be one of life's greatest privileges—belonging to them, whatever their background and condition. In the world's opinion they are 'odd'; the wise think of them as 'cranks', the secular society as 'beneath notice'. But they are God's children who have experienced mercy, and experiencing mercy is what counts, not thinking about it 'as a peroration theme for speech-makers who are like weathervanes on a church roof'.[31]

Experience was the great thing in the *seiat*. It was the place where people had opportunity to bare their souls and get timely help to face life's difficulties. It was also where personal testimonies of conversion were shared. Emyr Roberts, Presbyterian minister of Trefor, gave his testimony in the first united *seiat* held in the village, and invited another to do the same. 'I will give my testimony—for the first time ever in public. If you, or anyone else, wish to do the same, you may do so—but I shall not ask you, I will leave it to the leading of the Holy Spirit in your own heart.'[32]

Other *seiadau* came into being: in Tudweiliog, Pwllheli, Caernarfon, Porthmadog, Bala and Chester in the North. A small group had come together in Caernarfon early in 1948, but the end of that year and 1949 saw a revival of the work. New faces joined the old in different venues—in private homes, such as that of Mr and Mrs Gwilym Owen, and in a chapel vestry, as had been the case in Caersalem when the Rev. I. D. E. Thomas was ministering there. After giving an account of her conversion Joan Hughes recalls those times in Caernarfon:[33]

> After this I joined in fellowship with others who had come to a knowledge of the Lord Jesus Christ as Saviour at about the same time—from Bryn'refail, Penisa'rwaun, Beddgelert, Llanberis and Deiniolen. The *seiadau* were held regularly in Caernarfon—in

Caersalem when the Rev. Isaac Thomas was minister there, after that in Ebeneser vestry on Saturday evenings. Every month, or every other month, we would visit other *seiadau*, in Pwllheli, Porthmadog and Blaenau Ffestiniog. I continue to feel very thankful for the ministry of the Revs Emyr Roberts, Arthur Pritchard, Elwyn Davies, Dr Gwyn Walters and Emily Roberts. Another very dear person who used to come to the *seiat* was Horace Jones, Llandudno. He used to say that he was 'dotty on choruses'. One of his favourites, and one that struck a chord in his heart, was 'He walks with me, And He talks with me, And He tells me I am his own'.

The responsibility of leading the Caernarfon *seiat* was shouldered by a succession of ministers—I. D. E. Thomas, Dennis Jenkins (Deiniolen) and Gordon Macdonald (Aberystwyth)—and much valued encouragement was given by the Rev. W. M. Jones (Calvinistic Methodist) and Henriw Mason (Wesleyan). In 1964 the *seiat* found a home in Noddfa, where Emily Roberts, now a Sister of the Forward Movement, ministered.

The year 1949 also saw the formation of the Pwllheli *seiat*. There was a stirring of the Spirit in the area—in Trefor and Tudweiliog—and a desire to hear God's Word. Dr Martyn Lloyd-Jones visited the town, and his ministry bore visible fruit. Amongst those who believed was Catherine Hughes, and she had further help from Alwena Roberts the harpist, who was present at the meeting. Catherine and others gathered together to form a *seiat*, beginning a work that continued for over thirty years. As in Caernarfon, these believers had a lively interest in those who had newly come to a saving knowledge of the gospel, Captain Humphrey Jones, Singapore (known as 'Bible Jones') being one of them. Another who frequently attended these Saturday meetings during College vacations was Harold Jones.[34] This *seiat* too was blessed with safe leaders: the Revs Emyr Roberts (Trefor), T. Arthur Pritchard (while in Nefyn) and Irvon Parry (while at Blaenau Ffestiniog), and also Keith Lewis, when a schoolteacher in the town— to name but a few.

As its leader in the early years, T. Arthur Pritchard also played a key role in the history of the Chester *seiat*. Geraint Morgan, Llanfyllin, would stay in Arthur and Eirwen's home in Llanrhaeadr-ym-Mochnant over the weekend and go with them to the Chester *seiat*. Many of the members had moved to the surrounding area to find work, but as the years went by a number moved on to 'pastures new'. Despite every attempt to meet in Oswestry, and from time to time in Welshpool, this *seiat* came to an end after six or seven years.[35]

Experiences and subjects

One of the prominent themes of the *seiadau* was how to live the 'more abundant life'. It was the issue discussed in Trefor on 25 September 1951, and in Chester on 17 November that year; and it was also the subject of one of the *seiadau* in Llanymawddwy:[36]

> We thank God for tonight's *seiat* led by Elwyn Davies and dealing with three questions:
> 1. What is Christ to me today?
> 2. What would Christ wish to be to us?
> 3. How to come into this experience and gain possession of the abundant life.
>
> *Present*: Greta, Joanna, Mrs. Griffiths and Pearl (Gorseinon), Sylwen, Carys, John, Gwilym, Mair, Elwyn and the two of us [Emily and her sister Wena] (12).

The members of *Y Gorlan* in Bala were concerned that they were losing their zeal, and when Elwyn Davies visited them it is no surprise that they discussed[37]

> How to rekindle the old daring Evangelical zeal which once possessed us in Bala. Professor Williams was inclined to suggest that we have lost our first love—in the first flush of love the young man would pick up his girlfriend's handkerchief, but later he would become less attentive, but that did not mean that he loved her any the less. Whether that is true or not, it could be that we have lost sight of the urgency of the Gospel.

This is a common experience for Christians. Zeal so quickly grows cold, but although the flames die down it is good to know that God keeps the fire alive.

The hill-farmer's seasonal work was the background of many of the themes developed by Emily Roberts in the Llanymawddwy *seiadau*— tasks like the marking of the sheep she skilfully applied to the Christian life.[38] The Rev. Bryn Roberts, Carmel, would occasionally develop an old saying, such as 'Look after that which is hidden and that which is visible will look after itself.'[39] Idleness in the hidden place is a dangerous thing which prevents fellowship with God, and therefore it is impossible to function properly in public. There must be constant renewal before greater things can be expected from God.

The development of the *seiadau* gave no pleasure to the flesh, the world or the devil. To the world outside they had no meaning and, within, the flesh could be stubborn and the devil cunning. Some in Caernarfon, influenced by the Jeffreys brothers from Maesteg in Glamorgan, considered it a virtue to bear witness to their personal salvation whenever opportunity arose, whatever the feelings and condition of the believer. Some stressed rules and laws, while others cherished the beliefs of the Holiness Movement. The group was severely tossed by many a wave, but managed to ride out the storm. Emily Roberts confides in her diary:

> Went to the *seiat*—the *seiat* that they speak of closing—but that God will not allow—He saw to sending 14 of us there, and gave his own fellowship and blessing on our coming together. We thank him for it. Doubtless the crises were for the good.[40]

Emily Roberts did a phenomenal amount of personal work.[41] On 9 September 1959 she went to a *seiat* in Eryl Aran, Bala, to listen to 'Remembering 1859'—a tape of the address delivered by Dr Lloyd-Jones during the Caernarfon National Eisteddfod[42] on a subject dear to his heart and the hearts of the gathered company. And she made her visit to the *seiat* an occasion of calling on various people. A visit to the Pwllheli *seiat* gave like opportunity to drop in on Mrs Smith, Mrs Evans, Alwena and Catherine.

After the frenetic excitement of the early years there came an opportunity to concentrate more on teaching. More time was given to studying the Bible and discussing topics, but the experiential emphasis did not disappear. It was possible to arrive at a happy combination of the objective and the subjective, as in Trefor:[43]

> The 'flu has played havoc with our *seiat* since the beginning of the year. We meet every Tuesday evening to meditate on the Sermon on the Mount—guided by Wesley's sermons. Afterwards, I now think we shall go through *Theomemphus*. There is still the sound of coming in about the *seiat*, thank the Lord.

The staunch Calvinist valued the help of the Arminian to study the Word. And one cannot think of a better combination of doctrine and experience than the work of Pantycelyn.

The Aberystwyth Evangelical Church also realised the importance of sharing experiences and studying the Word. The work started in the *seiat* led by Bobi Jones continued; and the Rev. Gordon Macdonald visited Caernarfon for a period, leading a series of studies in the letter to the Galatians. Later, the Aberystwyth church was responsible for the formation of *seiadau* in Penrhyn-coch and Llanrhystud, those in Tregaron and Cemaes having existed for some years.

South Wales Fellowships

South Wales too had its *seiadau* or fellowships scattered from east to west. The earliest examples, of course, in Llanelli, Ammanford and Pontarddulais, sprang from the campaigns of the forties, and Rhymney and Caerphilly likewise began after student campaigns of later years. Some of them (Brynmawr and Blaenavon, for example), besides meeting regularly for Bible study and fellowship, sponsored monthly evangelistic rallies.

The *seiat* at Pontarddulais was led initially by Geraint Morgan (on his home soil). One of its later members was Mrs Gwenfyl Williams, who in 1962 became responsible for the Movement's newly acquired bookshop in Swansea market—an eminently suitable appointment, for prior to this she had been faithfully visiting the homes in her area with Christian literature. In the sixties, under the leadership of Malcolm Denning, the *seiat* studied the booklets on the Church published by the Movement, and this led some of them eventually to join together to form Noddfa Evangelical Church.[44]

The Maesteg Fellowship began in the mid-60s in a chapel vestry, and besides meeting together for fellowship and teaching they arranged monthly preaching rallies in the area. During the Rev. Eryl Davies's ministry in the town they obtained the use of one of the oldest inns in Maesteg ('The Three Horseshoes'), renamed it 'The Way' and made it into a coffee bar and youth centre. The large hall at the back was also used for missionary meetings and Sunday night evangelistic meetings. As with Pontarddulais, this Fellowship naturally ceased to function upon the emergence of Peniel Evangelical Church.[45]

The Caerphilly Fellowship (known as ECU—Evangelical Christian Union) first met on the night after the Welsh IVF campaign finished there in 1955. The Rev. Elwyn Davies (then IVF travelling secretary) led that meeting in the Twyn Chapel (now the Community Centre), and people of all ages gathered together from a wide area.[46]

They met on Saturday nights for fellowship and teaching, but the group also sought to reach out—through open-air and hospital meetings, through after-church 'Teddy boy' meetings, and even for a few years running a part-time bookstall at the local market. Dilys John, a founder member, recalls two notable incidents in connection with these after-church meetings. A lad who was in the park, overhearing the words 'I'm a Teddy boy pastor', went along to the Teddy boy meeting. He was subsequently converted while in a remand home and bore a clear testimony throughout his life. One Sunday night Dilys John was approached by a policeman, who expressed his bewilderment: in the Teddy boy meeting that night there had been two rival gangs, and the police had been monitoring the building expecting trouble—yet no fight had occurred. The secret, she said, was prayer: they met to pray together before church on Sunday mornings, following afternoon Sunday school, and also during the week.

This Fellowship continued for over twenty years, led initially by Charles Rex and then by Bryant Seymour. In the sixties, it took advantage of the provision for affiliation with the Movement. Several of its members (Arthur David of OMF, for example) went into full-time Christian service.

5
Church and Movement

Forming new evangelical churches

Within the Movement different views developed on the relationship between evangelicals and the traditional denominations. In this chapter we shall deal with the various attitudes.

By 1966 a process of leaving the denominations had started, and this deeply concerned some ministers. In that year a group of people left the Baptist Church in Heolgerrig, Merthyr Tydfil, and in the following year a Welsh Wesleyan minister felt he too would have to leave his denomination. These are the first two instances that demand our attention.

Cephas Church, Heolgerrig
An elderly pensioner sent a postal order for ten shillings (50p), payable to 'The Cowshed'.[1] That was the very first gift received by the small group that came out of the Baptist Church in Heolgerrig. Having done so, they rejoiced in the fact that they had found a home, even though it was only an old cowshed. It was now possible to plan for the future.

The leader was Mel Jervis, a National Coal Board employee and a Baptist preacher. He and his wife had settled in Heolgerrig in 1959 and joined the Baptist chapel there, contributing greatly to the life of the church, especially the Sunday school and the prayer meeting. Within a few years, however, a disagreement arose between Mel Jervis and a few others on the one hand, and some of the traditional Baptists on the other. The church suffered, and by the beginning of 1966 the only people attending the prayer meeting were Mel Jervis and his wife. Both were convinced that the only possible path for them was to leave the church and start a cause on scriptural foundations; it seemed to them a fruitless task to be contending ceaselessly for essentials of the faith, such as regeneration and the authority of the Word of God. They decided to leave in April 1966.[2]

The Cephas church building was opened on 4 September 1966, and six weeks later Mel Jervis was set apart as pastor. Before long a new home was found for the church, and the preachers in the opening services in 1972 were J. Elwyn Davies and Hugh D. Morgan.[3]

Gordon Macdonald

Leaving a denomination is no easy task. Indeed, it caused Gordon Macdonald great anguish over many years. Having entered Handsworth Theological College in 1954, he came across Robert Haldane's work on Romans and A. W. Pink's *The Sovereignty of God* and was led to accept Calvinistic doctrine. In 1958 he began his pastorate in the Aberdaron circuit, but by this time he was harbouring doubts about children's baptism. In view of the fact that he was now a Calvinist, and that he did not think Scripture warranted the baptism of children, what was his responsibility to his denomination?[4] He tried to face the question honestly.

In 1960 Gordon and Rina Macdonald were moved to Ystumtuen, near Aberystwyth, to a manse that at that time had neither running water nor electricity. During 1961 his denominational unease deepened, particularly on account of the Wesleyan stance on the uniting of the denominations. The troubled minister read chapter 52 of Isaiah's prophecy, and was convicted by the words in verses 11 and 12 that those who bear the vessels of the Lord must be clean. When the family moved to Comins Coch, Montgomeryshire, in 1965, the vexed question arose of accepting young people into church membership. The minister met with a small group, instructing them from the Scriptures and the Wesleyan Service Book. But the young people showed very little interest; some of them attended preparation classes but not Sunday services. To accept such young people into membership, Gordon Macdonald believed, would be an irresponsible step. Many in his congregation did not share that view, however, and the minister was criticised for refusing to accept new members. He felt he was in a situation that made his ministry impossible.[5]

Once again he turned to Isaiah chapter 52, and knew deep down in his heart that he would have to leave the denomination. Glyn Davies, a schoolteacher in Tonyrefail, happened to pay the family a visit, and as they talked together he suggested that the minister should indeed leave. The following morning, after sitting in the study in silence for a whole hour, he and Rina turned to each other and in the same breath said, 'There is nothing for it but to leave.'[6]

That same year Gwilym Humphreys ended his term as warden of Bryn-y-groes. The Movement's General Committee suggested that Gordon Macdonald might be the one to succeed him. He readily agreed to consider the work, but stated his intention of starting a new evangelical cause should he move to Bala. The committee did not feel that this would be right, and the minister grew more and more perplexed. A few days after receiving the committee's suggestion he was in a day-conference in Bala, and during his address the main speaker said words to this effect: 'I believe that the scriptural answer to theological and moral error is separation.' With these words a beam of light pierced the searcher's heart, giving him peace of mind. The battle no longer raged, and all was calm and peaceful.

The *seiat* in Aberystwyth heard of his decision and invited him to become its leader. He accepted the invitation, and received another at about the same time—to work for the Movement in North Wales as an assistant to J. Elwyn Davies. Accepting that offer too, Gordon Macdonald had opportunity to combine two aspects of evangelical witness in the land: shepherding the flock in Aberystwyth, and seeking to spread the good news in North Wales.[7]

Cephas Church is an English cause, but Gordon Macdonald, being Welsh-speaking, was concerned to serve those who worshipped in the Welsh language. The opportunity had now come for him not only to promote the general evangelical work in the north, but also to establish a Welsh cause. It is possible to follow the history of this and the other Welsh causes; but as the English causes are more numerous, it will be necessary to select from among them and concentrate solely on the early period of departure from the denominations.

New Welsh-language Churches

Aberystwyth

For evangelicals in Aberystwyth, 1967 was an eventful year. Not only was it a turning point in Gordon Macdonald's life, but it was also the year when seven students left the town's Theological College. One who had a great interest in these events was Bobi Jones: it was at his room in the university that the Welsh students' Bible class was held, and he and his wife Beti had opened their home for the *seiat* to meet there regularly. Some members of that *seiat*, under the leadership of Gordon Macdonald, felt led by God to establish an evangelical church. The sixties had already seen the undermining of the old conservative social system: now in Aberystwyth they were witnessing the fragile shell of the old religious system being shattered.

Three other local men, quite unconnected with Gordon Macdonald, felt convinced that they should leave their denominations, two of them Calvinistic Methodists and the third an Independent. They came together to pray and discuss matters, and decided to meet weekly for prayer over the summer of 1967. They were preparing, and being prepared, for the next step,[8] which was to hold the first public meeting in the YWCA on the first Sunday of October 1967. The group settled down to worshipping together and bearing witness to the gospel.

A close connection with the students, and with Alfred Place where Geoffrey Thomas was (and still is) pastor, was of inestimable help to the fledgling church. On Christmas Day 1968, the two congregations agreed to hold a united bilingual service—an arrangement that continues to this day. The new Welsh church began to spread its wings by establishing Bible classes in villages within reach of Aberystwyth. By 1974 the the congregation had outgrown the YWCA and moved to the Urdd Aelwyd).[9]

When Gordon Macdonald retired after forty years of faithful service in the ministry, Ifan Mason Davies followed him as pastor. He was a local man who had helped the church from 1977 until 1984. From the very outset John Ifor Jones was an elder and one of the mainstays of the church, but a few years ago he and his wife were released to assist the Welsh side of the work in the Lampeter Evangelical Church. The present elders of the Aberystwyth church are the Rev. Ifan Mason Davies, Gwyn Davies, Ieuan Jones and Keith Lewis.

Bangor

The church that was established in Bangor in 1969, when a number of students and a few other individuals came together to worship because they were uneasy about the condition of the denominations, was a bilingual cause. They were seeking a suitable meeting place, and when it became known that Ebeneser (Independent) was for sale, they purchased it. The group received remarkable financial help from all over Wales, and from as far afield as Swaziland and Australia.[10]

The friends met together for the first time in October 1970, and agreed on the bilingual pattern to be adopted: a 10 a.m. Welsh service, to be followed by an English service at 11.15 and a united English service at 6 p.m. The chapel was decorated and a thanksgiving service arranged for the first Sunday in August 1971, at which J. Elwyn Davies was invited to preach. Many students subsequently found work in the area, and this helped to put the church on a firm footing. It was agreed that when increased numbers justified such a step, the congregation be divided into separate Welsh and English causes.

This agreement was implemented under the leadership of Eryl Davies, but they faced the problem of finding a suitable building. The Ebeneser building had deteriorated by this time, and finding an alternative was proving difficult. But the sale of Ebeneser made the acquisition of new premises possible. The English members, with Eryl Davies as pastor, secured St Paul's, and the Welsh group moved to Hirael.[11]

Dafydd Job was invited to be minister of the Welsh church and commenced his ministry on 10 October 1985. The church later found a new home in the Garth Community Hall.[12] It was from this fellowship that Derrick Adams went to Llangefni, and then to Penrhyndeudraeth. Ioan Davies, an elder in the church, left to minister in Bala. The loss of whole families naturally led to a decline in membership, but nonetheless the church extended its horizons, establishing contact with Christians in the Czech Republic, sending provisions to help them after the revolution of 1989, and financially assisting a Prague student who was preparing for the ministry.[13]

Colwyn Bay

The evangelical cause in Colwyn Bay began as a small group meeting in the home of Geraint and Idwen Morgan. Geraint Morgan, a Scripture teacher in the local Grammar School and a Calvinistic Methodist elder, had long been disturbed by the doctrinal shift within the denomination. But when the General Assembly declared in 1971 that no church should act in any way contrary to the policy of the Association, he felt he had to resign. This he did, and with five other people began meeting to worship the Lord in his home on Sunday 4 September 1971.[14]

The group agreed on a doctrinal basis adapted from the Westminster Confession, which they translated into Welsh. The church was officially formed on 7 April 1975, but it was five years later, on 3 June 1980, that John Owen and Geraint Morgan were set apart as elders. Eryl Davies and Irvon Parry took the ordination service, and Vernon Higham (Cardiff) preached, taking the third verse of Jude as his text. In 1981 the Fron Community Centre became the venue for services— a Welsh service at 10.30 and an English one at 11.45; and within a month a further service was arranged for 6 o'clock in the evening. The primary concern of the weekly prayer meeting, which continued to move from home to home, was the sorry spiritual condition of Wales, but it also fostered interest in foreign missions and became responsible for the distribution of the prayer letters sent by Mair Davies from Patagonia.

In 1985 Eryl Davies left the pastorate of Ebeneser, Bangor, to become Principal of the Evangelical Theological College of Wales at Bridgend, and Geraint Morgan was called to succeed him. This meant that the burden of preaching fell on the shoulders of John Owen and another elder, Wyn Davies.[15]

Llangefni

The Cil-dwrn Church in Llangefni, Anglesey, is the fruit of conversions during the seventies. The believers felt a desire to meet together, and in 1978 formed a *seiat* with the intention of establishing a church. Weekly house meetings eventually led to the founding of a church in 1979, and a year later they were granted permission to worship in Cil-dwrn chapel, where Christmas Evans once ministered.[16]

During the second week of November 1980, special evangelistic meetings were held on four evenings, and on the Saturday Hywel Davies, from Bala-Bangor College, was inducted as minister of the church. The charge to the new minister was given by Eryl Davies, Bangor, and the preacher in the evening service was Elwyn Davies.[17] On 16 September 1989, Derrick Adams (Bangor) was set apart to assist the minister.[18]

The church takes its duty to evangelise very seriously, and meetings are held in various places on the island. It is also progressive: Sunday services are recorded on cassette; there is video apparatus for the filming of services, and simultaneous translation facilities for the benefit of those who do not speak Welsh. The chapel also has a useful library. To help build bridges with other Christians on Anglesey and in

Bangor, the church organises an annual evening in Coleg Menai for fellowship between evangelical believers. Another outreach tool is the church magazine *Gorwelion* (Horizons), six hundred copies of which are distributed quarterly. At present the minister, Hywel Davies, is assisted by three deacons.[19]

Cardiff

In 1977 E. Wyn James of Troed-y-rhiw, Merthyr Tydfil, became responsible for the Movement's Press at Bryntirion, Bridgend, and a year later Noel Gibbard, pastor of Berea (Independent) in Bynea, Llanelli, was appointed full-time lecturer in the South Wales Bible College, Barry. Both men with their families wished to worship in Welsh, the language of their home. It was suggested that a cause be started in Cowbridge; but Bryntirion, Bridgend, seemed more convenient, and a few meetings were held there led by Elwyn Davies and Noel Gibbard. However, this arrangement was not ideal, and it was increasingly felt that the obvious place to start a new cause was in Cardiff. Although the Heath Evangelical Church held a Welsh service, some felt the need for a Welsh-language evangelical church.[20]

In 1979, a group of Welsh-speaking Christians began to meet in the home of Selwyn and Beryl Williams in Cefn-coed Avenue. Enquiries were made for a suitable venue for Sunday services, and providentially the doors of Tŷ'r Cymry, Gordon Road, were thrown open. The first service was held on 7 October 1979, and the fellowship was constituted as a church on 2 December that year. In 1984 Gwynn Williams with his wife Elisabeth joined the church: he had previously spent ten years in the ministry at Sandfields, Aberafan, and had worked in Bryntirion for a short period before being invited to share the Cardiff ministry with Noel Gibbard. Eight years later, in 1992, he became full-time minister of the church.

The church moved several times: from Tŷ'r Cymry to the Cardiff City Mission Hall, and from there to the Urdd Aelwyd, before being able to purchase a permanent home—Kingsway Hall, the old Forward Movement chapel in Rhymney Street. The move was made in 1997, and at the official opening on 14 March 1998 Dafydd Protheroe Morris of Carmarthen preached on Isaiah chapters 52 and 53.[21] The present congregation numbers some 65 in the morning, and about 55 in the evening.

Carmarthen

Winford Thomas was in a Presbyterian pastorate in Coventry, but the ecumenical developments within the denomination were causing him deep concern, and he began to feel he ought to leave the ministry. When, in addition to this, he was asked to shoulder the burden of caring for more churches, he decided to move to Carmarthen, where he took a secular post as an insurance agent and started gathering together a small group of believers in the town.[22]

The group first met in Winford Thomas's home, moving in 1976 to the Mission Hall in Mill Street. All the members were Welsh-speaking, but a number of non-Welsh-speaking people wished to join them. So English services were started, and this led to the formation of an evangelical English cause. At the beginning of 1980 a week of prayer was held specifically to pray for a new home. In March it was rumoured that the old Presbyterian College was for sale, and taking a step of faith they decided to buy it. The celebration of its opening was on 12-13 June 1981, when the Rev. Omri Jenkins, London (a former student of the Carmarthen College), preached.[23]

From 1980 to 1983, a Welsh service was held at 10 o'clock and an English service at 11, but on 7 December 1983 the church agreed to do everything possible to establish a separate Welsh cause. From 1986 to 1989, Dafydd Protheroe Morris, who led a *seiat* in Llangathen, assisted the work by leading the Welsh service. The Welsh church was instituted on 22 March 1989 under the leadership of Winford Thomas. Three years later, in 1992, Winford Thomas accepted a call to Ebenezer Evangelical Church, Swansea, and he was succeeded by Dafydd Protheroe Morris in the pastorate of both churches.[24]

Talsarnau and Gwyrfai

Both these churches are the fruit of fellowships or *seiadau*. Talsarnau traces its roots to a *seiat* formed in Harlech in 1970 and led by Gwilym Humphreys. In 1977 the group began worshipping in a chapel in Talsarnau. In January 1978, it was agreed to hold a service in Brian Paul's home in Penrhyndeudraeth, under the leadership of Irvon Parry,[25] and that year they were also granted permanent use of the building in Talsarnau.

John Pritchard of Aber-soch had been leading a *seiat* in Gwyrfai, but many of its members felt a strong desire to establish a church. After discussing this with their friends in Talsarnau, the two groups decided to seek a joint pastorate and to call John Glyn from Bala– Bangor College as their pastor.[26] His ordination, by Eryl Davies, took place in Ebeneser, Bangor, on 17 November 1980, when the text of Elwyn Davies's charge was Ephesians 4:12. In 1982 Dewi Tudur, at that time a Baptist minister in Rhosllannerchrugog, joined the group to assist with the work. Four years later the Co-op building in Talsarnau was purchased for the church's use. Between 1986 and 1988 the congregation of the Gwyrfai church increased in number, and in 1991 they purchased the chapel and vestry of Tan-y-coed.

English and Welsh

From 1973, for some years, there was a Welsh evangelical cause in *Bala*, meeting at Bryn-y-groes when John and Buddug West were wardens there. Members eventually moved to other areas, and in later years the English-language church at which the Rev. Ioan Davies now ministers was established in the town.[27]

The *Lampeter* Evangelical Church is an English cause dating back to 1980. It now holds Welsh services regularly on Sunday evenings.[28] Noddfa, *Pontarddulais*, which began in 1971, and from 1989 was pastored by Meirion Thomas, holds a Welsh service on Sunday afternoons and occasional Welsh week-night meetings, at which visiting speakers are invited to deal with central issues of the faith.[29]

Early English causes in North Wales

The church at Plas Bennion, near Wrexham, which was formed in 1970 and became associated with the Movement,[30] comprised a number of individual believers who had come together, rather than disillusioned members or ministers of the traditional denominations. But between 1971 and 1975 five Presbyterian ministers in north-east Wales left their denomination.

Borras Park

First of the five was Glyndwr Jenkins, who, as a student, had helped in the Bala campaign of 1948. After ordination he and his wife spent five years on the Indian mission field in Assam. On returning to Wales, he spent fifteen years ministering in Rossett, Wrexham. He resigned officially on 1 January 1971.[31] Though he asked no one to leave with him, some twenty decided to do so, and they began to meet in the Centre for the Elderly. In 1972 they purchased a piece of land in Borras Park on which to build a chapel. Glyndwr Jenkins retired in 1980, and was succeeded in September of that year by Hywel R. Jones, minister of Grove Chapel, London, and a native of Tai-bach, Port Talbot. He in turn was succeeded by Keith Walker, who left to become Team Leader for UCCF staff working in the Welsh colleges. After three years without a minister, Basil Howlett was ordained as pastor in September 1993.[32]

Caergwrle

Gwilym Roberts, a native of Mold, had been travelling secretary for the IVF before going into full-time ministry, first at Tredegar in the South and then at Holywell in the North. In 1966 he was called to the Wrexham area, to the joint pastorate of Caergwrle, Broughton, Glanrafon and Summerhill. But in 1971, having been a diligent and faithful pastor within his denomination over many years, he felt a compulsion to leave, and after careful consideration he decided to do so.

He, and some from the four churches who decided to leave with him, found a suitable meeting place in the Independent chapel at Caergwrle, which was used on Sunday afternoons only. On Easter Sunday 1972 there were 26 present in the morning service and 36 in the evening. The Lord's provision for Gwilym, his wife and five children was truly wonderful; the generosity of friends enabled him to continue with his ministry and set the church on strong foundations.[33] The church building (Bethel) was purchased in 1981, and in 1984, after a steady increase in numbers, two elders and four deacons were elected. Gwilym Roberts retired after a ministry there lasting twenty-five years.[34]

Holywell

Upon leaving the Theological College at Aberystwyth, Peter Clement assisted with the work in Memorial Hall, Cardiff, before succeeding Gwilym Roberts in Holywell in 1967. In 1972 he decided to leave the denomination, tendering his resignation on 30 June that year. He and those who came out with him worshipped at first in the WRVS centre, and then moved to the Drill Hall. By 1975 the congregation exceeded fifty. Friends showed great kindness to the minister and his family; indeed, one of the members paid the deposit on their home.

It was agreed that the church's doctrinal basis should combine aspects from the Westminster Confession and the Calvinistic Methodist Confession of Faith, and that Independent Confessions should also be consulted.[35] In 1980 two elders were chosen to assist the pastor, and in 1981 an official membership list was created, when 29 members were accepted into the church. That same year Peter Clement left to become pastor of Neath Evangelical Church, and he was succeeded in Holywell by Peter Trumper.[36]

Flint

Born in Cardiff and a student at Aberystwyth, Gilbert Evans was called to the pastorate at Flint in 1963. He was soon to realise that there were difficulties in the church, both locally and in connection with the denomination. Because of ecumenical developments, co-operation with other churches in the town was impossible, and the fact that the denomination fully supported the Ecumenical Movement made his evangelical stance all the more difficult. In 1974 he decided to leave, and soon after his departure he arranged a meeting, not knowing how many would attend. To his surprise, seventy people turned up in a room that had once been a factory canteen. He was further encouraged when people from a nearby estate started coming to the meetings.[37]

In 1975 a large house parallel to the hospital was purchased and adapted as a chapel, its fishpond becoming the baptistry. In 1987 Gilbert Evans left for the pastorate of Upton Baptist Church, Chester, to be succeeded in Flint by John Davies from the Maesteg Evangelical Church. Hugh D. Morgan, Newport, preached at his induction in February 1990. In 1995 the chapel building was extended. Besides regular Sunday and weekday services, the church visits old people's homes, conducts open-air meetings, and arranges a Bible Club for children during school holidays.[38]

Deeside

The last of the five Presbyterians to leave was Peter Milsom. Brought up in Park End Church, Cardiff, he had left his job in insurance to enter Aberystwyth College to train for the ministry. Even before his ordination in Mancot in 1973 he had felt profound unease, as he and four others had been asked to swear an oath of loyalty to the denomination—something never required before. The fact that he felt unable to do so unconditionally gave rise to tension and, despite a measure of blessing in the church, that tension increased until he felt convinced that the right step was to leave the denomination.[39]

He left on 1 January 1975, but remained in the locality because he felt it needed an evangelical ministry. He arranged a meeting in the St John Ambulance Hall, when he and his wife were joined by just one adult and three children. However, his perseverance was rewarded: within a few months the congregation numbered fifteen, and it has steadily increased over the years. The members make every effort to reach the unchurched by arranging home discussion groups and by helping those with special needs, particularly the handicapped. For many years before the calling of Ioan Davies to Bala, the church lovingly cared for the small Bala cause through regular visits by some of its members. Peter Milsom moved south in 1993 to pastor Malpas Road Evangelical Church, Newport, and a year later he was followed in Deeside by Alan Davey.[40]

Early English Churches in South Wales

The sound of departing feet was a notable feature of the early seventies. As in the North, many Presbyterian churches in South Wales completely severed their connection with the denomination. To some, the decision to leave the denomination was a purely personal one: Philip Eveson, for example, of Havelock Street, Newport, left as an individual. Some of them also left their buildings, as did Eryl Davies and over a hundred members of the church in Maesteg,[41] and John Davies and his group in Clydach. Others remained in their buildings: for example, Hugh D. Morgan and his people in Malpas Road, Newport, and Vernon Higham and the Heath Church, Cardiff. More detail can be given concerning Maesteg, Heath and Malpas Road.[42]

Maesteg
Bethlehem Presbyterian Church, Maesteg, experienced much blessing during the period 1965–9. They were also conscious of changes within the denomination and concerned about its links with the World Council of Churches. In 1968 the church passed a motion requesting the

denomination to withdraw from the World Council of Churches and to reinstate the 1823 Confession of Faith. At the same time, the church stated its unwillingness to welcome liberal Presbytery ministers for occasional preaching and decided not to give financial support to liberal missionaries.

In June 1970 the General Assembly voted overwhelmingly against the motion from Bethlehem and gave warning that all local churches should conform to denominational policy. As a result of this decision, on 31 December 1970 the minister, the Rev. Eryl Davies, resigned from the Presbyterian Church of Wales. All the elders and over three-quarters of the congregation joined him to form Peniel Evangelical Church. A local Pentecostal pastor allowed the company to rent his own small church building, arranging for them to buy it after his death. The congregation did so a year later. The work of the new church was consolidated, but there were difficulties with some in the denomination.

Heath, Cardiff

Members of the Heath Church were unhappy with denominational and ecumenical developments. This unease was evident from 1962, when Sir David James offered to donate a sum of money to the Non-conformist denominations in Wales if they agreed to come together. In 1966 the church voted overwhelmingly against a proposed Scheme of Union. A special church meeting was held on 6 December 1967, when it was decided that the only way forward was to form an independent evangelical church.

Another significant development was the release in 1968 of a report by the Commission on the Ministry. Its main recommendation was the formation of a group ministry, but the Heath Church thought this unscriptural. The group ministry was introduced, and the Presbyterian Church also agreed on a levy to support the World Council of Churches. Minister and members of Heath felt strongly on both these matters. A special church meeting was called for 28 November 1969. By this time it was clear that separation was imminent. The final vote for separation was taken on 21 October 1970, to come into effect from 1 January 1971.

In the light of such action, the watch-night service on New Year's Eve 1970 assumed great significance. The meeting was well attended and blessed by a sense of God's presence as Mr Higham preached on the text, 'Who is among you that feareth the Lord, that obeyeth the voice of his servant, that walketh in darkness, and hath no light? Let him trust in the name of the Lord, and stay upon his God' (Isaiah 50:10). The service marked the final gathering of Heath Church as a Presbyterian fellowship.

In 1976 the church bought the building and the manse in Allensbank Road from the Presbyterian denomination. Vernon Higham continues to minister at the Heath Evangelical Church.

Malpas Road, Newport
Hugh D. Morgan began his ministry at the Malpas Road Church in October 1962, and the congregation grew under a biblical ministry and evangelistic vision. But both minister and eldership became increasingly concerned about the ecumenical drift of the Presbyterian Church of Wales and its prevailing theological liberalism. They summarised five areas of concern:

The Scriptures were no longer regarded in practice as inspired or binding on the Presbyterian Church of Wales.

The denomination had departed from its 1823 Confession of Faith and accepted a 'Shorter Declaration of Faith and Practice', which in the view of the Malpas Road congregation was a weaker and inadequate statement.

The 1970 General Assembly had expressed 'complete agreement' with the Ecumenical Movement and had desired all ministers to support its policy towards the World Council of Churches and the British Council of Churches.

The 1975 Wales for Christ campaign, in which the Presbyterian Church of Wales took a leading part, involved co-operation with Roman Catholics and liberals, who had publicly denied the need for new birth and other central doctrines.

At the 1976 General Assembly, as a reaction to evangelicals who had already left the Presbyterian Church of Wales, a 'Declaration of Intent' was passed which stated: 'The time has come to invite those who conscientiously are unable to accept the judgments and decisions of the Connexion, to consider seeking fellowship outside the Connexion.' The minister and elders at Malpas Road understood this to be a declaration that there was no welcome for them in the denomination.

There had been correspondence between the church and the denomination since 1970, and the church had reluctantly withdrawn financial support from activities it deemed unbiblical. After much prayer and discussion, the Annual Church Members Meeting of February 1976 unanimously agreed to secede from the Presbyterian Church of Wales. The denomination asserted its ownership of the premises on the ground of the connexional situation. Though the congregation felt that in natural justice they had a right to the buildings, both confessionally and morally, having been alone responsible for the cost of erection and maintenance, the church committed itself to acting Christianly and not going to law, and so re-purchased the church buildings and manse.

The Malpas Road Evangelical Church continues to adopt the 1823 Confession, with one important amendment: both historic views of baptism are respected in the congregation, thus contributing to gospel unity in a local congregation. In 1988 the church became a founding member of the Associating Evangelical Churches of Wales.

Common ground

The same reasons for leaving were given by all the churches: doctrinal deterioration, which included ignoring the 1823 Confession of Faith; supporting the World Council of Churches, and the denomination's attitude towards those who disagreed with it. Eryl Davies, Vernon Higham and Hubert Clement published a pamphlet explaining in detail their concern about the plight of the denomination.[43] Philip Eveson would add a further cause for concern, namely, the worldliness of the church: in his experience, the church was more prepared to entertain people than to save their souls.[44]

Baptists and Congregationalists

But concern about developments within their denomination was not confined to the Presbyterians. Many Baptists responded angrily to the declaration made by Principal Michael Taylor on the Person of Christ in his address at the 1971 annual meeting of the Baptist Union of Great Britain and Ireland. He stated that God was in Christ as he is in every

95

other person, and that Christ's uniqueness derives from the way he responded to God and the manner in which he operated in the world. In his opinion, Christ could not be both God and man, as was historically believed.[45]

Among those who resigned from the Baptist Union as a result of this address were Philip Hill (Llanwenarth), Sulwyn Jones (Dowlais), Owen Milton (Beaufort) and Graham Tolley (Abertyswg). The same step was taken by some churches—that is, by both minister and congregation—among them Townhill and Penlan (Swansea), Mount Pleasant (Maesycwmmer), Bethel (Cefn Hengoed), Alma Street [now Emmanuel] (Newport), Caersalem (St Mellons) and Alfred Place (Aberystwyth).

Many of these churches declared openly why they were making their stand. Alfred Place, Aberystwyth, underlined the doctrinal shift within the denomination, in particular the denial of Christ's deity by Michael Taylor and the unwillingness of the Baptist Union to remove his name from its list of recognised ministers. The church declared its adherence to the evangelical creed on the Person of Christ and the authority of Scripture and expressed a desire to be in communion with every church of like faith.[46]

In an editorial in the *Evangelical Magazine of Wales* entitled 'Is Jesus God?'[47] Graham Harrison wrote:

> With a boldness that surprised denominational officials . . . Michael Taylor went on record as saying . . . 'It will not quite do to say categorically that Jesus is God' . . . Officially the BU does not countenance creeds and confessions . . . But it does have a Declaration of Principle which is described as the 'basis of the Union', and which forms part of its Constitution . . . this contains a description of our Lord and Saviour Jesus Christ as 'God manifest in the flesh' . . . If there is anything that is central to Christianity, it is the Person of its Founder.
>
> . . . so long as [Mr Taylor] is in error or confusion on our Lord's deity he ought not to hold the position he does or minister to a church, and certainly he ought not to be an officially chosen speaker at the Baptist Union's biggest gathering of the year.
>
> A number of churches . . . at present affiliated to the Baptist Union . . . have a growing uneasiness . . . Perhaps because of the Union's ecumenical participation or its theological comprehensiveness . . .

The witness group based at the *Cylchgrawn Efengylaidd* tent in the National Eisteddfod at Dolgellau, 1949. *Seated from left*: J. Elwyn Davies, Mwynwen Edwards, Emily Roberts, Megan Davies, Geraint Gruffydd. *Standing on extreme right*: Harold Davies

first *Cylchgrawn Efengylaidd* annual conference at Bala, 1952. *Seated from left*: Mari Jones, Emyr Roberts, J. Elwyn Davies, Principal Griffith Rees, T. Arthur Pritchard

Rev. J. Elwyn Davies, General Secretary of the
Evangelical Movement of Wales 1955-90

Rev. T. Arthur Pritchard

Rev. Emyr Roberts

Emily Roberts, Bryn Davies,
Elwyn Davies, John Vevar

Welsh Annual Conference at Denbigh, 1955. *In second row seated:* Bethan Lloyd-Jones, Dr Martyn Lloyd-Jones, I. D. E. Thomas, J. Elwyn Davies, T. Arthur Pritchard, Emyr Roberts, Herbert Evans

Some of the early leaders with their wives: *From left:* Revs. Luther Rees, I. B. Davies, Glyn Owen

Rev. Hugh D. Morgan speaking at an open air meeting on the Aberystwyth sea front during an English Annual Conference

Bryn-y-groes, Bala

Bryntirion, Bridgend

Rev. Derek Swann addressing ministers at a Ministers' Conference (English) in Bryn-y-groes, Bala, 1983

A mountain top experience at a youth camp! *In the front row*: Maldwyn Mundy, Dewi Arwel Hughes, Eryl Davies

Bookshop managers at the Christian Booksellers' Convention, Blackpool, 1987. *Back row from left*: Derrick Adams (Bangor), Stephen Potts (Wrexham), E. Wyn James (Evangelical Press of Wales Director), Mike Hart (Bookshops' Administrator) Matthew Evans (Cardiff). *Seated*: Elaine Harris (Bryntirion), Evelyn Costello (Swansea)

A Senior Camp at Bryn-y-groes, Bala. *Front row, seventh from left and on:* Rev. Neville Rees (chaplain). Mary Lody (women's leader), Alasdair Rose (men's leader). *Seated from right:* Peter and Deanne Hallsworth (Wardens)

Rev. and Mrs Alan Watkins with some helpers who prepared food at the young people's camp at the English Annual Conference

Some campers from a Quinta camp, 1988

side Cardiff Christian
…kshop, Wyndham Arcade
…ng a 'Victorian Week',
… 1988. *From the left*:
…ert Bennett, 'Auntie
…sie' and Matthew Evans
…nager)

…ne of the Office and Press Staff on the occasion of Rev. J. Elwyn Davies' retirement. 1990. *Standing*
…n left: Edmund T. Owen, Jill Richards, Joan Pells Cocks, Elaine Harris, E. Wyn James, Gwynn
…liams. *Seated*: Mair Jones, Mair Eluned Davies, J. Elwyn Davies, Brenda Lewis

Beryl Ebenezer with Tunisian Students at Aberystwyth

Some of the men in the Welsh Ministers' Conference at Bryn-y-groes, Bala, 1993.
Seated: Ifan Mason Davies, Gerallt Wyn Davies, Gareth Davies, Gaius Davies, Eurfyl
Jones, Gordon Macdonald, J. D. Williams, Cecil Jenkins, Sulwyn Jones

Students at the Theological Course (English) in Bryntirion. *From right*: Rev. Andrew Davies, Rev. Graham Harrison (Principal).

Rev. and Mrs Noel Gibbard cutting a 50 years celebration cake in the Movement Tent at the National Eisteddfod in Bridgend, 1998. *Also in the photo*: Ifan Mason Davies (back row, left) and Keith Lewis (back row, right)

they feel in all conscience that they may not be able to continue in membership.

The editorial was afterwards printed by the Baptist Revival Fellowship as a tract.

For English Congregationalists in Wales, the proposed union between the Congregational Union of England and Wales and the Presbyterian Church in England gave cause for grave concern. The first step towards union was to be the establishment of the Congregational Church. In May 1961, Derek Swann spoke against this development in the Congregational Union meetings, because in his view (and that of others of like mind) it was unscriptural. Reporting in *Time and Tide*, Cecil Northcott expressed his admiration for the speaker's toughness, and remarked in passing, 'I liked his lilting speech.'[48] When it was agreed to unite and to form the United Reformed Church, Neville Rees (Morriston), Luther Rees (Llansamlet), Bruce Powell (Tredegar) and Philip Williams (Pontnewydd, Cwmbran) joined the recently formed Evangelical Fellowship of Congregational Churches, while Jeffrey Cox (Gorseinon) left the Congregational Union but did not join EFCC. All these ministers were active supporters of the Movement.

Early in the seventies, a day-conference was arranged to give those who were leaving their churches, or were about to do so, an opportunity to meet, discuss matters together, and pray for God's leading. Forty people came to the first meeting at Bryn-y-groes in January 1971, at which Gordon Macdonald and Gilbert Evans led the discussions. A further conference was held in April, and a similar one arranged in Bryntirion for the people of South Wales.[49]

Associating Evangelical Churches of Wales

By 1988 there had been another important church development. As the number of independent evangelical churches increased, it was felt that a closer relationship between them was desirable. The group of ministers in north-east Wales were convinced of the benefit of this, and a meeting they held to explore the possibility of co-operating and sharing concerns initiated serious consideration of such a relationship in 1985. Interest was aroused among some of the ministers in South Wales (two in particular), with the result that a meeting was arranged in Cardiff on 2 December 1985.[50] After discussing the issue for some time, the group approached the Movement. But there was much unease about such a development, especially within Welsh circles, as was clearly expressed in two meetings of the Welsh Executive Committee held in Bangor and Ammanford.[51]

J. Elwyn Davies and Graham Harrison were appointed to ascertain the general view of ministers within the Movement, and to distribute a short résumé of their responses. This led to further discussion within the Movement, and a meeting was held at Llandrindod to consider the developments. After much deliberation, at a meeting of the Movement's General Committee at Bryntirion on 1 October 1986 it was agreed to support the formation of a fellowship of churches. This led to more specific arrangements, and on 29 October 1987, again in Llandrindod, the Associating Evangelical Churches of Wales (AECW) officially came into being. Of the sixty-six people present, representing thirty-six churches, none voted against the proposal, though six abstained.[52] The AECW held its first meeting on 23 April 1988; by 1989 there were thirty-five associating churches, and by 1998 the number had increased to over fifty.

Even after discussions over many years, the Welsh evangelical churches were none too keen on this development. The Annual Report for 1988–89 suggested reasons for this: among the Welsh there was a more 'independent' spirit; they were also more conservative and concerned to safeguard the relationship between themselves and evangelical ministers within the denominations. By now, however, at least one Welsh-speaking church has joined the AECW.

6
Great Providence of Heaven

Early losses, and the provision of
Eryl Aran, Bryn-y-groes and Bryntirion

In his interesting autobiography, Dr Martyn Lloyd-Jones refers to his belief in providence: 'For me there is nothing in life that is clearer, and I rejoice in the fact.'[1] This belief in God's providence is one of the best means of strengthening the believer's faith, especially in times of difficulty, and that is something the Movement's supporters realised over and over again during the fifty years from 1948 to 1998. Sometimes God saw fit to open a door in an impossible situation: at another time he chose to overrule in bereavement and loss. One or two examples will help us not only to understand better the history of the Movement but also to appreciate this doctrine, which is full of consolation and hope.

Loss and gain
One aspect of God's providence during this period was the number of Christians who died at a young age. Ingeborg Zieseche, whose company the Welsh delegates appreciated so much, was rushed to hospital with TB during the Oslo conference, and from her hospital bed prayed for the Welsh work.[2] She was later sent a map of Wales to help her follow more clearly what was happening in Bala and other areas. Despite the shattering news that she had but a short time to live, and that her brother too was tubercular, her faith remained steadfast, and she graciously submitted to Christ's sovereignty: 'Having accepted him as my personal Saviour, I must acknowledge him as Lord.'[3] Resting on his promise to be with her, and confident of the prayers of friends, she could not see that there was anything to fear.[4] At the age of twenty-three she was taken to be with her Lord.

Celt Hughes hailed from Nefyn, on the Lleyn peninsula. A student at the Bangor Baptist College, he was one of those converted in 1948.

On 11 January of that same year Calfaria Baptist Church, Aberdare, invited him to be their pastor; but the onset of the debilitating illness MS meant that he could not give them a positive answer. He was forced to spend many weeks in hospital, in Caernarfon and then in Liverpool, where the students would visit him in turn and help to feed him. Undaunted, Calfaria arranged the ordination service for 2 September 1948. But he was too weak to move from his bed, so Celt Hughes's chair remained empty that day. Nonetheless he was ordained in his absence, his college Principal's testimony to the radiance of his character and life moving the whole congregation.[5]

J. Elwyn Davies was one of Celt's closest friends, and between 1948 and 1950 they spent much time in each other's company. Elwyn treasures many memories of the period:[6]

> But the one occasion that will always remain with me is the afternoon when I called by, and his Bible class was meeting. I have never seen anything like it, neither before nor after. There was Celt sitting in his chair between two beds, his Bible open in front of him, unable to move hand or foot and having great difficulty in speaking. Slowly I could see his students gather around him, sitting on the two beds, and I joined them there. As we were waiting to start—although, knowing the limitations of the teacher, I had no idea what was going to happen—I could see at the far end of the ward a group of young people who had been playing cards quietly putting them away and going back to bed.

Here was a clear example of God's power being perfected in man's weakness.

Celt Hughes continued to hope to go to Aberdare, and the church there continued to look forward to welcoming him. Elwyn Davies deputised for him twice during this time:[7]

> Twice I preached in the church on his behalf, when he was totally unable to lift hand or foot but still hoped that God would answer our prayers. I shall never forget his telling me, shortly before the second occasion, that he had texts for me to preach on in both the morning and evening service. The first was 'For my thoughts are not your thoughts, neither are your ways my ways, saith the LORD.' He managed to start the second text, 'The LORD reigneth . . .', but could go no further. Seeing that he could not for the life of

him bring out the words, I tried to help him: 'let the people tremble', I said. 'No', said he, laughing heartily at me, his blue eyes sparkling—'let the earth rejoice!'

Celt Hughes's intended ministry at Calfaria never took place, for on 7 January 1950 he was called to a glorious inheritance, where MS would never mar his happiness.

Aled Hughes, another Bangor student and a close friend of Geraint Gruffydd, also died young. Enid Jones, then a child living in the village of Nantlle, was conscious that there was something different about Aled's life, and that the whole community felt a strong desire to see him restored to health. But it was not to be: the bright scholar, ardent Welshman and glowing Christian was called home.[8]

Like Celt, Roland Hughes, from Cwm-y-glo in Caernarvonshire, was preparing for the ministry. He was only twenty-seven when taken ill. His faith shone brightly through the darkness of his final hours and he was able to whisper quietly, 'My feet are on the Rock.'[9]

Grace was a young lady of just twenty when she died on 14 September 1951. Many a time had she stood on the square in Pwllheli witnessing to her Saviour, and she maintained her witness even when confined to a hospital bed in Liverpool.[10] Dyfi Rhys from Gwauncaegurwen was a busy man—busy in his business, but busier on the gospel trail. One August evening in 1956 he was killed near Dolgellau whilst travelling on his motor-cycle to the Movement camp in Glynllifon.[11]

Born in Kidwelly, but later to move with his family to Llanelli, John Thomas, minister of Bethlehem, Sandfields, Aberafan, had always thought he would die at the age of forty. Exceeding his expectation by nearly two years, he was called home in 1969. A close friend of Hugh D. Morgan and, like him, a trophy of the Llanelli campaign of 1945, he studied in Trefecca and Aberystwyth before ordination in 1953. His heart set on fire by the gospel, he laboured with might and main to extend God's kingdom. This is clearly demonstrated in the booklet *Contender for the Faith*, published in 1975 and edited by Graham Harrison with a preface by Hugh D. Morgan. Its concluding section, an article on 'Evangelism' written by John Thomas for the English Magazine, is a fitting memorial to his ardent zeal. The loss of such a valuable worker was sorely felt; many had been enriched by his witness. The short lifespan he envisaged for himself spurred him on to labour more diligently and avail himself of every opportunity to witness to his Saviour.

But God saw fit to raise new workers, as in the case of wardens for the two centres, Eryl Aran and Bryn-y-groes. And when need arose for a gardener to care for the extensive grounds, a praying man was found in the person of Brychan Davies—one who could not only tackle weeds and thorns and briars, but could pray that the wilderness of Wales might once more become a fruitful garden.

God also moved people to areas of his choosing. Elwyn Davies and Herbert Evans went to Blaenau Ffestiniog and were led to the same church. A good number of believers found work in the north-east, and so the Chester *seiat* was formed. Many young people met and found their life-partners in college, camp and conference, and went on to establish Christian families—surely among God's most valuable provisions.

The buildings: a romantic stòry
But we should not forget the story of the buildings. During the Movement's early years J. Elwyn Davies and his family lived at Frondirion in Bala. This house was also the home of the secretary Mair Jones and accommodated the office. As time went by, space became more and more limited, and it became obvious that another property must be found. When Gwilym Humphreys was appointed assistant to the General Secretary, having been ordained to the part-time pastorate of Salim Baptist Church in the town, it was suggested that he and his wife Beth should move into Frondirion and another home be found for the Davies family. On 17 January 1958 the General Committee took the decision to buy a house in Bala, and three days later a phone message was received from Dr Martyn Lloyd-Jones with the news that a woman from Northern Ireland wished to give money to Christian work.[12] She had been to Bala a few years previously and had been warmly welcomed by the people, and her intention, before hearing of the Movement's need, was to revisit the place. Dr Lloyd-Jones was also in close touch with others who were eager to help financially.[13]

Eryl Aran
A house in Bala town was considered, but on 1 February it was learnt that the Fatima Guest House (formerly Eryl Aran) was for sale, and

that the asking price might possibly be lowered from £8,500 to £7,500. This was still a high price, but J. Elwyn Davies, Bryn Davies and the treasurer of the Baptist chapel in Bala were persuaded that they should venture in faith, and Gwilym Humphreys was told of their decision. For some time an order of nuns had shown an interest in the property, and rumour had it that a London syndicate wished to procure it and develop it further as a licensed club. But that very day (1 February), Major Mackenzie the guest-house owner had the staggering news that the growth in his neck was likely to take his life within a couple of months. In view of this he was anxious to sell the property as soon as possible. The nuns made no offer, and on 5 February, just a day before the arrival of the syndicate from London, the Movement bought the place for £7,000, five hundred pounds less than the lower asking price![14]

The Fatima Guest House reverted once more to its original name and became a Protestant evangelical centre. Its name had been changed to commemorate a vision of the Virgin Mary claimed by two children in the Portugese town of Fatima, and also to reflect the name of the shrine to 'Our Lady' in Bala itself. Thousands of pilgrims used to visit, singing their 'Hail Mary, Mother of Jesus' along the town's streets. An altar for celebration of mass had been set up on the lawn, and the stables turned into a drinking club that was open even on Sundays. Gwilym Humphreys expresses the enormity of the change:[15]

> The old house was once again given its old Welsh name. And instead of superstitious pilgrimages it witnessed a deep heart desire to call men back to the Word and to the testimony, to the faith once given to the saints, to the faith of the Protestant Fathers and the old Dissenters, to the faith of Howel Harris, Pantycelyn and Christmas Evans, the faith that set the people of this area and the whole of Wales on fire, and put the language of the Bible on their lips and its truths in their hearts.

The response was astounding. On the Sunday evening before the Movement secured the property, John Roberts had announced from his pulpit in Capel Tegid that he would give anything to see the drinking club closed. A few weeks later he joined with the town's Church Council to express gratitude for the providential way in which this had happened. Indeed, the whole Bala area rejoiced. As to the financial response, the following extract from a written report gives some indication:[16]

> A Welshman from America spending a few days in Britain decided to slip into Wales and, hearing of the purchase of Eryl Aran on the train, gave a hundred pounds there and then. A young teacher, having been left a hundred pounds in an aunt's will, gave it all to Eryl Aran. Indeed more than one person gave a hundred pounds, which meant a great deal of personal sacrifice in those days of scarcity. One's heart is still warmed by the memory of a young Carmarthenshire farmer giving towards Eryl Aran not only the proceeds of the sale of a cow and calf, but rounding the sum to make it a hundred pounds. In a prayer meeting in Eryl Aran the other night, one of our friends, who had given generously before, gave three hundred pounds to the fund.

That is the grace of God at work in a most practical way.

Bryn-y-groes

During 1958 and 1959 Gwilym Humphreys frequently looked over Eryl Aran's boundary hedge at Bryn-y-groes next door. He was not coveting his neighbour's property, but prayerfully hoping for a centre for the Movement that was even better than their present home. After the 1959 camp had been held in Eryl Aran it became abundantly clear that it could not possibly cater for campers as well as two families, Mair Jones, and the Movement office. Bryn-y-groes became a matter of special prayer; but even as early as February 1959 Gwilym Humphreys felt certain that the place would belong to the Movement. After the two families had been praying together one evening, he turned to Elwyn Davies and said, 'Elwyn, God has heard our prayer.'[17] This is an example of what the General Secretary would call a 'given' prayer—that is, God giving the prayer as well as the assurance that it would be answered.

Both Gwilym and Elwyn had to cling fast to the given promise. They knew that the Trawsfynydd Nuclear Authority was interested in the property; but the Liverpool Corporation was also looking for accommodation for its Tryweryn workers, and this posed an even greater threat. It was hearing of the Corporation's intentions that drove the Movement's representatives to approach the owner Mrs Johnston—only to find, much to their surprise, that she was more than prepared to sell Bryn-y-groes to them for the sum offered her by the Liverpool Corporation. She felt strongly that the property should be sold to a Protestant movement that would uphold the traditional religious beliefs of the area, and had been prompted to come to her surprising decision by a verse in *The Times* to this effect, 'Thou shalt not harden thine heart, nor shut thine hand from thy poor brother.'[18]

The prayers offered on behalf of Bryn-y-groes were honoured:[19]

> It is a stepping out in faith, in the certain hope that the great God will lead, and that this venture has a place in the pattern of God's blessing for us. The place is already full for the summer weeks as a Christian holiday camp for young people, but we foresee much wider use of it. A seal was soon set on the venture—a young man sent all he had in the bank, three hundred pounds, before any appeal had been made. A minister and his wife gave us the money they had put by to buy a new washing machine—a sum of seventy-five pounds. Over two thousand pounds have been contributed already.

Activities now centred on Bryn-y-groes, and two years later, with the removal of the Davies family and the Movement office to South Wales, Eryl Aran was sold. Appropriately enough, the couple who first cared for the new centre were Gwilym Humphreys and his wife Beth.

Down the years Bryn-y-groes has been blessed with caring wardens and their wives. Peter and Deanne Hallsworth, who are currently looking after the centre, are no exception; their loving care for the property and its guests makes staying there a pleasure. A complete refurbishment of the house, celebrated on 7 June 1997, was a source of pride both for them and for the friends of the Movement. Prior to moving there, Peter and Deanne had been wardens of Bryntirion, the South Wales centre which, since 1989, has been in the care of Kelvin and Rose Olsen-Vetland.

Bryntirion

The way God's hand steered the buying procedure and provided for the maintenance of the two North Wales centres was thrilling; but it became clear that a similar centre was needed in South Wales. Two possible venues were visited, but both were too expensive. The other possibility was Bryntirion, Bridgend, the home of Ysgol Glyndŵr, the

Welsh school that had been under the care of Mr and Mrs Trefor Morgan. But, again, the asking price was too high. Nonetheless, members of a meeting held in Cardiff insisted that J. Elwyn Davies approach Mrs Morgan. It was with great reluctance that the General Secretary agreed to do so, despite the fact that there was a family relationship between himself and the lady.

When he did so, however, he discovered that the situation had changed considerably. The outcome was that Roy Lee and Keith Lewis, two friends of the work from Cardiff, and members of a subcommittee that had been seeking God's guidance concerning a South Wales centre, purchased (with others) the Undeb Insurance Company, whose assets included Ysgol Glyndŵr. They very kindly offered Bryntirion to the Movement for an annual rent of a thousand pounds, with an opportunity after ten years to purchase it for a further ten thousand. The total sum was only half of its value on the open market.[20] In 1970 this arrangement was entered into, and Bryntirion was later purchased on the generous terms offered.

The building now had to be prepared for use as a camps and conference centre and Movement office. Once again a fitting person was found to care for it in the person of Mrs Eluned Thomas, widow of John Thomas who had been minister at Sandfields. (Indeed, it was he who had particularly advocated the need for such a centre in South Wales.) Much work was needed, and many willing hands were lent for the task. Each Saturday for months, work parties came to Bryntirion from churches within a radius of thirty miles or so (Peter and Deanne Hallsworth of Newport among them). They devoted their planning, plumbing or carpentry skills, painted, decorated and did whatever else was needed to meet the deadline for the first camp in July 1971. And in the ongoing work of the centre, valiant bands of ladies from nearby churches came faithfully each week to help with the cleaning.

The official opening was on 11 September 1971, when some fifteen hundred people gathered in a marquee on the grounds. In the afternoon Dr Martyn Lloyd-Jones preached on 2 Chronicles 20:15, stressing that the battle is the Lord's and we must constantly keep our eyes on him; that is what will give his people hope in sore straits. During the tea interval there was ample time to see the building, and in the evening session J. Elwyn Davies told the story of how it had been acquired, reminding those present of the history of the

Movement from its inception to that day. The large congregation was inspired to look to the future in faith.[21]

The Bryntirion diary filled up rapidly. Besides the numerous Movement activities, churches used it for weekend houseparties and for senior citizens' and young people's groups, and it was booked for missionary society weekends and student conferences. One year the UCCF Welsh Annual Conference managed to squeeze everyone in only by pitching tents in the grounds to accommodate the overflow! Bryntirion had come into the Movement's hands at the very time when it was considering a method of theological training by extension, and in August 1972 its Theological Training Course was launched there.

No one can deny God's leading in the procuring of the two centres, but the faith of the evangelicals was soon to be put to the test. As in the case of a property owned by David Charles in Carmarthen—inspiring the writing of his great hymn 'Rhagluniaeth fawr y nef' (in Edmund Owen's translation in *Christian Hymns,* 'Great providence of heaven')—Bryntirion suffered a fire on 23 March 1978. In Charles's case his rope factory was totally consumed, and there was nothing he could do but pull on the ropes of God's promises. That is precisely what the friends of the Movement did, though providentially the greater part of their building was left unscathed. Arrangements were made immediately to restore the section damaged by fire, and the opportunity was taken to build additional bedrooms, a larger lecture hall, and a more commodious bookshop.

The reopening took place on 5 May 1980 at an open-air service in the grounds led by Neville Rees (Morriston) and Gareth Davies (Ammanford). The service warmed the hearts of the seven hundred people present, and J. Elwyn Davies thanked all who had contributed to the restoration work.[22]

Bryn-y-groes, Bryntirion and camps
In the providence of God, when the Movement purchased the Fatima Guest House in 1958 it acquired much else with it—crockery, cutlery, bedding, kitchen equipment and outbuildings. This naturally raised the question of how these were to be used. A small group of ministers and teachers from South Wales, led by camps enthusiast Brynmor P. Jones and including some with experience of the Inter

Schools Camp at Llanmadoc, Gower, made a day-trip to Eryl Aran to reconnoitre, and they saw real potential for the beginning of an English camps work.

It was decided as a pilot scheme to hold camps at Eryl Aran in the summer of 1959, advertising them in a low-key way through ministers, youth leaders and Christian teachers. The maximum number per camp was to be about thirty, and there were to be separate camps for boys and girls. In the event, about 120 were accommodated in all. Some preparatory work had been done on the outbuildings, but as the proposed extension was not in place, Elwyn and Mair Davies with their young family kindly moved out of their wing in the main house to make their living accommodation available for the camps period. In its review of that summer's activities the Camps Committee recorded 'intense satisfaction that the Lord had graciously blessed both campers and camp officers in a signal and unforgettable way'.

The plan was to extend the camps work at Eryl Aran in 1960 and to hold mixed camps. In early February, bookings were already high, so news of Bryn-y-groes's purchase in March was especially welcome, for the additional buildings proposed for Eryl Aran would not now be necessary. In 1961 the Welsh camps were transferred to Bryn-y-groes from Glynllifon, and in that year the English camps adopted the policy of appointing chaplains as well as leaders.

One of the English camps in 1961 knew remarkable blessing; some of the young people returned home to witness boldly to their faith and organise their own Bible study groups and after-church rallies. A number came from churches in the South Wales valleys, and the ministry they received at camp served to reinforce the work of their evangelical ministers; there were instances of whole families being converted. To encourage campers during the year, Brynmor Jones arranged autumn reunions and young people's rallies (usually in the home church of one group of campers) and launched the magazine *Pathway*.

The work fell into a regular pattern of six English and two Welsh camps each year. But from 1967 on, faced with long waiting lists for some camps, the committee intensified its search for another venue to meet the growing demand. The provision of Bryntirion, therefore, met a real need: five extra camps were organised there in the summer of 1971, and in later years one was also fitted in for the Spring Bank

Holiday week. At one stage, such was the determination of campers to secure a place in the camp of their choice that Richard and Joyce Akrill, who acted as booking secretaries for many years, recall a special mail van delivery on the first booking date! In subsequent years various other centres were used, but since 1987 the camps have happily found a settled third home at Quinta, near Oswestry.

In 1970, prompted by a desire to reach young people in the schools with no church connections, Brynmor Jones pioneered a new project—Adventure (later called Outdoor) Camps. These were tented camps with a more flexible programme and a greater emphasis on outdoor activities. The work was organised by a small committee: those involved needed the energy and practical skills for the many duties required: finding appropriate sites, checking, maintaining and transporting equipment, erecting tents, catering, etc. The task of recruitment in the early years was mainly in the hands of Christian schoolteachers in Glamorgan and Gwent. In 1972, about 140 attended these camps from nine schools, the majority aged between 12 and 15 years, and by 1975 there were 220.

In reviewing the forty years of English camps it is fitting to acknowledge God's goodness and providential care. Mistakes have no doubt been made and lessons learned, but the benefits of the work have been far-reaching. Many Christian parents have been grateful for the clear biblical teaching their children have received, and for its relevant and contemporary application. To youngsters from small churches it has meant a great deal to meet others of their own age and widen their circle of Christian friends. Among long-term benefits are the facts that some who have come to faith at camp have subsequently returned in leadership roles, and that there are many second-generation campers whose parents readily acknowledge their own spiritual debt to the camps work.

Spiritual warfare
The years have certainly brought their ups and downs, times of vision and times of sorrow and distress. But God's people have been enabled to submit to his will, recognising that events are not controlled by fate but are fulfilling his mighty plan, and in so doing their faith has been strengthened to fight the spiritual battle in Wales. Rather than paralysing the workers, such trials have quickened them to challenge

the enemy. When he felt that opposition to the gospel was becoming more fierce, R. Tudur Jones was prompted to ask (and answer) a rhetorical question: 'What is the responsibility of God's soldiers in such straits? The answer is clear and simple—fight.'[23]

But before venturing to the battlefield the soldiers must know exactly what they are fighting for. They must also bear the right arms: spiritual warfare can only be fought with spiritual weapons. What does the Evangelical Movement of Wales stand for? What has it done to safeguard what it stands for? Some answers to these questions have already been suggested, but we must now turn to examine them in more detail.

7

The Faith Once Given

The theological foundations
and the longing for revival

Many attempts have been made to define the characteristics of evangelicalism. According to Dr Martyn Lloyd-Jones, the three essential pillars are the final authority of the Bible, a saving gospel and a holy life.[1] George Marsden agrees with him, but adds, as a fourth, missionary zeal.[2] Dr R. Tudur Jones cites David Bebbington's four emphases—conversion, missionary work, reverence for the Bible, and the sacrificial death of Christ—and adds two more: the social emphasis and the importance given to spiritual revival.[3] All four are agreed on the centrality of the Bible and recognise its unique authority.

The Word of God

The introduction to the Movement's Doctrinal Belief states: 'We accept the holy Scriptures, as originally given, as the infallible Word of God, of divine inspiration. Recognising them as our sole authority in all matters of faith and practice, we believe the doctrines taught therein.' That is the foundation for the acceptance of every other doctrine; and that is why the teaching on the primacy of the Bible needs to be understood.

J. I. Packer's book *Fundamentalism and the Word of God*, published in 1958, is a clear and concise statement of the evangelical teaching on Scripture.[4] Many books on the same theme had been published prior to this,[5] but J. I. Packer's appeared during discussions on fundamentalism and about the same time as the publication of Gabriel Herbert's book, *Fundamentalism and the Church of God* (1957). Packer's book, therefore, was of special significance during the fifties; but it remains a clear statement of the evangelical position. It has been of inestimable value to college students, giving them a strong foundation on which to build, while at the same time stretching their minds.

111

J. I. Packer sets out his argument in contrast to that of the Church of Rome, modernism and ecumenical thought. He emphasises that the Bible alone is the authority of evangelicals, not the Bible plus tradition as the Papists believe; nothing should be placed side by side with Scripture. The modernists, on the other hand, undermine the authority of the Word by stating that only portions of it are God-inspired, the remainder being the product of man's imagination. This theory necessitates finding some method of differentiating between the one and the other, but such is the diversity of opinion amongst modernist scholars that they find it impossible to agree on the canon. Thus, subjectivity has supplanted the objective authority of the Bible. The weakness of ecumenical thought is that it speaks continually of truth, but completely ignores the false. It considers all opinions to be important: one may disagree with another's creed, but one should never refute it. Packer argues that if, as they maintain, truth exists, there must be that which stands in opposition to it, namely, heresy. The only safe path, he maintains, is to be clear on the governing principle in theology, and that is to accept the Bible as the only foundation on which to build. 'The Scriptural approach to Scripture is thus to regard it as God's written testimony to Himself.'[6]

Dr Packer sets great store by the testimony of the Bible to itself. He argues that both Old and New Testaments claim authority, and that the word 'Scripture' unites them. He states, 'The two Testaments are of a piece',[7] a fact underlined by the teaching of our Lord himself. He is utterly convinced that the Word was revealed and safeguarded by the inspiration of God the Holy Spirit. Inspiration expresses itself in words, and because of that the Bible is God's Word to mankind. He is its divine author; but he used human authors, each with his individual personality and style, to record it. God did not dictate his Word; his inspiration fashioned and moulded mind, interest, talent and ability and channelled them to fulfil his purpose. Both God's freedom and man's freedom were safeguarded. The divine and the human came together, as they did in the Person of the Lord Jesus Christ.[8]

This doctrine, like every other Christian doctrine, is to be accepted by faith. The believer believes in order to understand: he does not understand in order to believe.[9] The human mind needs to submit to God's Word, but in submitting it is enlarged—faith quickens the whole man, stretching his mind and freeing his spirit. The believer is enabled to wrestle with the teaching of Scripture, to apply its principles and to present the Christian message to others. These tasks cannot be accomplished without responding with the mind, because 'Obscurantism is always evil and wilful error is always sin.'[10] This does not in any way deride reason, but puts it in its proper place in the process of understanding God's revelation. This is the way to understand the various truths of Scripture, but above all to see who the Lord Jesus Christ really is. The prime purpose of Scripture is to present him. The Christ of Christianity is the Christ of the Scripture.

A clear understanding of the nature of the authority and inspiration of Scripture is an important principle by which to explain the Bible. Knowing that both the Old and the New Testaments were inspired by God gives it unity, and as a result scripture can be compared with scripture. This is one of the basic principles of biblical exegesis. But it ought to be borne in mind that some sections, although inspired, are less important than others. There are no grades of inspiration, but there are grades in the value of different sections. 'Not all parts of Scripture are equally important, or witness to Christ and the kingdom of God in the same way.'[11]

When comparing scripture with scripture one has to consider the nature of different books before attempting a literal explanation—the literal explanation in each case being that intended by the author.[12] A whole book, or section, might be historical, allegorical, apocalyptic or a parable. For example, to understand the Book of Revelation one must try to understand the symbolic meaning of the horse, the sea, the beast, and the numbers seven and ten. Comparing scripture with scripture and trying to understand the nature of the different books certainly demands the response of the whole man, but the believer knows that he has a teacher, the Holy Spirit, to lead him into the truth.[13] The one who inspired the Bible is the same one who can give us better understanding of its contents. When the Christian diligently fulfils his duty to search the Scripture, his teacher never lets him down.

Although evangelicals are in complete agreement about the inspiration and authority of Scripture, it is recognised that there is also room for the individual conscience in the process of reading the Bible. As a result there are different opinions concerning the age of the universe, the nature of holiness, church government and the second coming. This calls for patience, humility, and great care not to foist one's views on another Christian or to tyrannise over his conscience.

No other name

On the sound foundation of the Bible it is possible to develop doctrine. This is of importance to the individual and to the witness of the church. 'It is through doctrine that one grows and matures and gains spiritual power. God has possession of only half of us if he does not rule our mind as well as our heart and will', writes Emyr Roberts. 'And what is more, the Church must be sure of its doctrine to be able to engage in mission.'[14] It is impossible for a doctrinally divided church to teach and evangelise effectively. Uncertainty regarding the Bible and the watering down of the gospel are two of the reasons for the weakness of the Welsh churches. They have lost sight of revealed truth, and sound doctrine counts for little. On the other hand, evangelicals continually need to remember that orthodoxy in itself is not sufficient; orthodoxy must be accompanied by life, the life that issues from the Holy Spirit. It is he who gives life; he is also the spirit of truth who alone can bind us together.

The gospel is the core of revelation, and Jesus Christ is the core of the gospel. The good news is that he came into the world to accomplish man's salvation. The need for salvation can only be appreciated by considering the doctrine of man. For evangelicals, the Fall in Eden is the starting point: when our forefather Adam fell, the whole human race fell, and as a result we are all guilty before God, and sinners under his condemnation. All men are spiritually dead, dying bodily and facing eternal death. Man is described as totally corrupt: that does not mean that he is as bad as he can be, but rather that every part of him is affected by sin. Fallen as he is, man is still God's creation. An unbeliever, because of God's general goodness, can be a good teacher, a successful businessman or a gifted musician. There are many open doors through which he can walk; but the door of heaven is firmly shut against him.

It is the God-man, the second Adam, who saves, and the cross is central to his saving work. Evangelicals believe that the many terms used in Scripture to describe the death on the cross—terms such as 'atonement', 'ransom', 'reconciliation', 'conquering the principalities'— are part and parcel of divine revelation, and not just human theories.

That is why they are loath to let go of the word 'propitiation' in Romans 3:25. One of the features of this doctrine is the penal aspect of Christ's death: when Jesus the sinless one died, he took the place of sinful men. On the cross he was their representative, and so he bore in his body on the tree what they deserved. This meant not only physical suffering, but the wrath of God and death. This plan was of God's making; it was he who gave his Son. In Paul's words, 'God was in Christ, reconciling the world unto himself', and the Son readily submitted to his Father's will. Christ's death on the cross was not the result of the Father losing his temper with his Son, but a demonstration of God's loving, yet just, plan to save sinners. In the words of the Welsh hymnist Ann Griffiths, it was a lawful way for law-breakers to find peace and favour with God.[15]

Christ is a unique person, and in him only is there salvation for men. That is certainly what evangelicals believe, but over the past twenty years there has been a change within the evangelical world. This has happened in at least two areas. Whilst maintaining that Jesus Christ is the only Saviour, and the only way to heaven, John Stott and Philip Hughes believe that it is annihilation and not hell, in the traditional meaning of the word, that awaits unbelievers. And authors such as David Day and Peter Cotterell contend that there are other religions where Christ is hidden, and that the possibility of salvation within these religions must at least be recognised. Neither teaching has been welcomed within the Movement. A session in one of the Welsh conferences was set aside to consider Peter Cotterell's standpoint, and strong opinions were expressed in both magazines. John Benton, for instance, criticised David Day's book *This Jesus* on two counts: the author's loose interpretation of Matthew chapter 25, and what other explicit scriptures say in clear contradiction of his standpoint (Ephesians 2:12; Galatians 5:19; John 6:37).[16]

Spiritualists and occult movements would maintain that they too either lead to God or can connect family members and friends with their departed dear ones. Many people see nothing wrong in dabbling with the occult. Indeed Eryl Davies was sorely criticised for venturing to put forward the biblical standpoint, one critic scornfully calling it mere 'theological claptrap'. Watching films like *The Exorcist* and *The Omen* is thought to be harmless enough, but Eryl Davies produced proof that people suffer emotionally and physically after seeing them.[17]

By his continuing research into the occult Dr Davies has already contributed widely to our understanding of it and has given valuable guidance on how to respond.

A saving gospel

The gospel is the power of God for the salvation of sinners, and it was this power that brought the Evangelical Movement of Wales into existence.[18] During the years 1947 to 1952 an unusual number of people came to know the Lord Jesus Christ, and down the years this emphasis on the experience of conversion has been a characteristic feature.

When R. Geraint Gruffydd entered college in Bangor he was a regular chapel-goer, proud of his denomination and its orthodox tradition, and yet attracted to the liberal emphasis. But gradually the young student was led away from liberalism to 'something very much like the orthodox Christian faith', and there was one person who was a definite influence in the process:

> By the way, the strongest influence in this direction was hearing a lecture by J. E. Daniel during the summer of 1947. I believe that was the most thrilling single lecture I have ever heard, because Daniel showed me once and for all what Christianity was from an intellectual standpoint—not some kind of vague human theory, but a clear and positive revelation given by God.[19]

A few months later Geraint Gruffydd was in a retreat at Plas-y-nant, Betws Garmon, and to his horror J. Elwyn Davies chose to speak on 'the conversion of a sinner'. The truth which he already knew in his mind caught hold of him and shook him to the core. He saw clearly that in dying on the cross Christ had accomplished the work of redemption. All that was needed was to trust in Christ, and by doing just that he received forgiveness and a new life.[20]

Bobi Jones had been an uneasy chapel-goer during his early years in Cardiff. He was religious, in that he attended a place of worship and considered philanthropy of major importance. Indeed, at the age of seven, having listened to a visiting missionary, he decided he would like to go to some foreign country to engage in philanthropic work. When in college in Cardiff he liked to discuss religious subjects and the work of the IVF; but when invited to one of the IVF meetings he refused to go. However, his friend Derek Swann did go, and what he heard led to his conversion. But Bobi Jones was invited to go and hear Dr Martyn Lloyd-Jones during the 1949 National Eisteddfod week at Dolgellau, and this invitation he condescended to accept. He described himself during that period as 'a Hindu and an Independent'.[21]

The 'summons from above' came in Llanidloes. By now Bobi Jones was a teacher, and he attended chapel because it was the social centre of Welsh life. But on a certain communion Sunday everything changed. The minister read from Luke's Gospel, chapter 22, and the arrow that pierced the heart of the listener was verse 21: 'But, behold, the hand of him that betrayeth me is with me on the table.' He realised that his hand was on that table too; and he who had been full of pride and had played with religion, knocked as a sinner on the door of mercy. He went home overcome by strong emotions, fell to his knees in tears before God, and was assured that the door of mercy was still wide open.

In the heat of this moving experience he searched for help to develop spiritually. He followed a Roman Catholic correspondence course and attended Church in Wales services, where he found guidance in the Book of Common Prayer. Eventually he moved to Aberystwyth, and there in Salem chapel (Calvinistic Methodist) he met other evangelicals—some of them children of the 1904–5 Revival, others the fruit of the renewal of 1947 and the years that followed. He also had a cousin who was a minister in the town—Geoffrey Thomas of Alfred Place. He it was who introduced him to the works of Abraham Kuyper, Dooyeweerd, John Murray and others in the Reformed tradition. By now Bobi Jones was totally convinced in his mind that Jesus Christ ought to be Lord of every facet of his life—as a Christian, as a citizen and as a Welshman.[22]

To David Norbury, who was formerly a student in Bangor and is currently Head of School Improvement in the Newport Education Authority, becoming a Christian seemed very dangerous. He would have to give up so much, and his life would be ruined. Anyway, for a sixth-form science student there was very little evidence that there was a God. The idea that Jesus Christ was the Son of God who died and rose from the dead was surely not based on historical facts. As a

Sunday school teacher and fairly regular churchgoer, he began to think it was God who was not there and the Bible was a dead book.[23]

But in his school there were two Christian teachers who were sharing their faith in various ways. On Saturday nights a maths teacher called Fred Williams ran an inter-church youth group called the Young Life Campaign. And an RE teacher called Ralph Gower took RE lessons in the sixth form. He was clear and certain about the truth of the Bible and what it said about God and Jesus Christ. Fred Williams kept on inviting him to the youth group, and both men drew him into the Christian Union in school. 'Despite all my doubts', he says, 'these were exciting days and slowly I was being convinced of the truth. I could never understand why Jesus died. Nevertheless becoming a Christian—that was a step too far!'

But slowly the desire to become a Christian grew. Various Christians tried to help him to make a decision, but however hard he tried it was never real. Then Fred Williams arranged a 'Deeside for Christ Crusade' in Shotton, North Wales. He went along for one reason only—to support a school quiz team, of which a near neighbour was a member. After the quiz there was a closing talk given by Verna Wright.

> For the first time I understood why Jesus had died. I understood that he had given everything for me—he could give no more. For a person like me who had done so much that was wrong! There was no other choice but for me to give everything back to him. The last hymn we sang was 'Out of my bondage, sorrow and night, Jesus, I come to Thee.' That night, with the encouragement of a person who counselled me, I thanked God for giving his Son for me—for giving everything for me—even me! I asked God to accept me as I gave him all that I was and might become.

On the way home he and his friend talked long and hard—not about the quiz but about becoming a Christian—and he believes that later that week she too became a Christian. Fred Williams and Verna Wright became lifelong friends and encouragements in the Lord.

> The path God has laid out for me brought me to a wonderful wife Pat, to three super sons, Tim, Jonathan and Andrew; through four EMW/AECW churches, and eventually to Noddfa church in Pontarddulais.

These experiences have many features in common: conviction of sin and of spiritual need, a turning to God, acceptance of forgiveness, a new life, and a desire to tell others of the experience. But there are differences too. There are varying degrees of the intellectual and the experiential. But all three could name the time and place of their experience—something that is not necessarily true of all who belong to the Evangelical Movement of Wales. Some come to believe in a calm atmosphere, others in an atmosphere that is more exciting. It is equally possible to do so on one's own, with a friend, or in a service.

One of Billy Graham's crusades was the means used to bring one Movement supporter to faith. Geraint Fielder vividly remembers Cliff Barrows marching down Gorseinon's High Street blowing his trombone to announce the evening meeting.[24] Although only ten years old, he went along and heard Billy Graham preach on Belshazzar's feast. When the customary invitation was given at the end of the service, after some hesitation he followed others to the vestry, and was led by the evangelist to accept Christ as his Lord and Saviour. Thankfully, over the years, the Movement's own camps have been used by God to bring many young people to himself, some at a very tender age.

The theological terms used to describe what happened to those mentioned above are regeneration, conversion, and justification by faith. These are the basic elements. Regeneration is solely the work of the Holy Spirit, and it enables the sinner to come to repentance and faith—that is, to turn to God. In accepting him and reconciling him to himself, God forgives his sin and justifies him on the ground of the righteousness of the Lord Jesus Christ.

A holy life

Justification cannot be separated from sanctification: that is, genuine experience must reveal the fruit of the Spirit. In the early years, the Movement had to deal very carefully with this doctrine. The Oxford Group was particularly active in North Wales; and South Wales was especially conscious of the Pentecostal emphasis on the gifts of the Spirit. It was sensed that two colleges, one in Swansea, the other in Birkenhead, posed possible danger. In Swansea it was claimed that perfection is possible in this life and, despite the fact that the Bible clearly states that the precise time of the second coming is a mystery known only to God, it claimed revealed knowledge. During one period people were dissuaded from going to foreign countries and told to remain in Swansea to await the coming of Christ. Geraint Morgan, for one, had an opportunity to enlighten members of the Christian Union in Swansea University and a group of young people in Pontarddulais on these matters.[25]

Some came across influential books, such as *The Law and Faith* by Evan Hopkins, one of the leaders of the Keswick Movement, and J. H. Williams's *Ar ei Ben Bo'r Goron* (On His Head Be the Crown)—in many ways a valuable book, but not free of the Keswick influence. The writings of Oswald Chambers, a man who ploughed his own furrow by maintaining that holiness was both a gift and a process, were read and acclaimed by many. But, thankfully, by far the greatest influence in this area was the works of the Puritans—the emphasis brought out in such a masterly way by J. C. Ryle in his volume *Holiness*. And that is the tradition that prevailed within the Evangelical Movement of Wales.

The gift of the Spirit

The Holy Spirit is constantly at work sanctifying the believer, and the scriptural exhortation is for him to 'be filled with the Spirit'. But the Holy Spirit can also come in an unusual way, as the religious revivals of Wales have frequently proved. It was such a coming, albeit on a smaller scale, that was experienced by the believers in Bangor, Bala and Dolgellau during the Movement's infancy. The same gentle breezes blew over the Cross Hands area between 1949 and 1952. Many a time in the Ministers Annual Conferences the gathered brethren have been aware of the holy presence of God filling the building. When Andrew Davies preached on the cross, all present were overcome by the wonder of God's love; it was as though it were being poured upon them. After preaching from the book of Zechariah in an Aberystwyth Conference, J. I. Packer met with Derek Swann and Eurfyl Jones in the vestry, but so great was the influence of the service that they could do nothing but reverently kneel in worship.

Glynllifon and Cwm-twrch

The campers at the Welsh camp in Glynllifon in 1958 had a similar experience.[26] On the Thursday evening the leaders and some of the speakers met together to pray, and felt an unusual freedom of spirit. They were assured that God had answered their prayer for the following morning's meeting. In that meeting the first hymn was:

> *Fe ddaeth yr Ysbryd Glân,*
> *Mae'n gweithio yn ein plith;*
> *Mae'i ddylanwadau megis tân,*
> *Ac fel y tyner wlith.*

> The Holy Ghost has come,
> He works among us now;
> His power is as a burning fire,
> And as the gentle dew.

The dew fell refreshingly on all present that morning, and a number of young people came to know the Lord Jesus. Many of them have remained staunch Movement supporters.

What happened in Cwm-twrch, Glamorgan, during the late fifties and early sixties remains a source of wonder.[27] The Christians there had been praying for revival, totally unconscious of what was happening in a small village outside Carmarthen. There, a farmer's daughter had a dream, in which she saw herself rushing home with a parcel in her hands. Holding her breath, she hastened to open it, and there before her was a newborn baby. Perplexed, she fasted and prayed that the meaning of her dream might be revealed to her. She was assured that it was a sign of new blessing in a place called Cwm-twrch in nine months' time. Unaware that George Griffiths and members of the Mission Hall had been meeting regularly to pray for revival, she wrote the pastor a letter. On receiving it, George Griffiths charged his flock not to make a public show of the letter but to keep the matter to themselves.

The friends in Cwm-twrch were given grace to continue, as before, to pray each night for revival—no easy task for the same people for some three years! At the end of the nine months of the dream, Peter Scothern visited the Mission Hall, and under his ministry the floodgates of heaven opened. Many people, filled with the Holy Spirit, fell to the ground crying and trembling. George Griffiths, a child of the 1904–5 Revival, had seen similar things happening during that period, and had the spiritual discernment not to refute the phenomena but to realise the dangers of excess. Many turned to Christ, a number of young Sunday school members amongst them.[28]

On a journey in South Wales, Goronwy Prys Owen met two girls who attended the meetings in the Cwm-twrch Mission Hall, and he told J. Elwyn Davies what they had shared with him. On meeting them Elwyn Davies came to the conclusion that the work was of God. He discussed the Cwm-twrch events with T. Arthur Pritchard, and together they went there to a meeting held immediately after the Peter Scothern mission. The nature of that meeting was exactly the same as that of meetings held for many succeeding weeks. The two men repeated their visit, this time taking Gwilym Humphreys with them, and the three were astonished that the meetings still had the same power and influence.

Dr Martyn Lloyd-Jones was told about what was happening in Cwm-twrch, and a letter to T. Arthur Pritchard from a missionary in the Congo describing similar phenomena was also forwarded to him. The minister at Westminster Chapel received the letter a week before he began his series of sermons on Revival. He arranged to meet George Griffiths on his way home from Ireland, where he was to address a meeting held to celebrate the Revival of 1859. The Doctor was met in Liverpool by J. Elwyn Davies and taken to Bryn-y-groes, Bala, where a long and serious discussion on the Holy Spirit's work in revival took place. George Griffiths was also invited by Dr Lloyd-Jones to speak to the ministers at their conference in Cilgwyn.

The close relationship between George Griffiths and the Movement continued. For several years a small group would meet in Cwm-twrch every Friday morning to pray for revival. It benefited both the ministers and the young people of the Mission Hall.[29] Many of the young people would attend the Movement's camps, and in one camp the Cwm-twrch contingent voiced their opinion that every meeting should be like the Mission Hall services. Persuading them otherwise proved difficult, but it was a great consolation that Pastor Griffiths fully understood the situation.

The relationship with Peter Scothern was a different matter. The ministers in the Movement could not see the way clear to working with him. They were not at all happy with the prominent place given to physical healing, nor with his method of pressurising people to accept Christ as Saviour.

The longing for revival

An effective way of nurturing the longing for revival is to recall past revivals, and to find out as much as possible about revivals currently happening in other countries. The 1954 Welsh Conference in Llanelli heard Sidney Evans, brother-in-law to Evan Roberts, recall the events of 1904–5, and in 1959 Dr Martyn Lloyd-Jones addressed a meeting in the Caernarfon National Eisteddfod on the 1859 Revival.

But there were more recent revivals. David Davies (Worldwide Evangelisation Crusade) was able to report on what was happening in the Congo (Zaire), and Nick Willems could tell of the spiritual awakening in Canada.[30] Nearer home, there was a great movement of the Spirit in the Scottish Hebrides during 1948 and 1949. The evangelicals read the reports expectantly and listened to a tape relating its history, and then decided to invite Duncan Campbell to the 1957 Welsh Conference in Rhosllannerchrugog. (This was the only time that the morning addresses were delivered in the English language.) Duncan Campbell also visited places in South Wales, including Llanelli and Merthyr Tydfil.

The nature of revival

Attempts were made not only to chronicle the bare facts of what happened in revivals but also to try and analyse them. Many authors contributed to our understanding of the nature of revival, among them Martyn Lloyd-Jones, Eifion Evans and Brynmor Pierce Jones. Many articles appeared in both English and Welsh magazines, under such titles as 'Can God Possibly?', 'The Need for Revival', 'Is God Able?' and 'Concern for Revival'.[31] Significantly, the first book published by the Movement was *God's Harvest* by I. D. E. Thomas, a collection of articles on revival that first appeared in the English magazine.

All the authors who wrote on the revival theme are agreed that revival is the unusual work of God, his mighty work visiting his people, or God coming down to his people and manifesting his glory. Even when there has been preparation, as on the day of Pentecost, there is a suddenness about it. Eifion Evans describes revival as 'a sovereign, spontaneous, saving work of the Holy Spirit, uplifting Jesus Christ, empowering and quickening the life of the Church, and changing and transforming the world'.[32] The same aspects are emphasised by Emyr Roberts, who explains that there is no qualitative difference between the work of the Holy Spirit in saving an individual and his work in revival. The difference is quantitative, in terms of power, influence and extent. For instance, there will be a general consciousness of the presence of God; the number of converts will be surprisingly high; and when he comes, he accomplishes his saving work among people of all ages and all social classes. The Church tends to have difficulty retaining its hold on certain groups, the young and the working class in particular, but the wind of the Spirit in revival blows into every corner of society.[33] To quote Dr Lloyd-Jones, that is its 'astonishing feature'—'a most astonishing feature, but one which is found with strange regularity in all the stories'.[34]

Another all-important aspect, according to Dr Lloyd-Jones, is the Holy Spirit's primacy in revival.[35] He has sovereign power, and this is manifested in the choice of the instruments used and the places chosen to kindle the flame. Sometimes he chooses to use a prominent man, at other times a mere 'nobody'. A revival can start in a city like Chicago or in a village like Ysbyty Ystwyth. It can be confined to a locality; it can be country-wide; it can spread over a vast area of the world. On the sure foundation of the Word, I. D. E. Thomas argues that revival is supernatural and the prerogative of a sovereign God. He quotes several scriptures, but more especially Amos 9:13, saying, 'This description emphasises a truth that we tend to forget, namely, that the main feature of every true revival is that it is beyond the control of human instruments.'[36]

Phenomena and gifts of the Spirit

The unusual phenomena that accompany revival attract special attention. In his book *Revival* Dr Lloyd-Jones divides them into two classes, the physical and the mental.[37] Among the physical aspects are trembling, falling to the ground and, sometimes, throwing a fit. Among the mental aspects are an unusual clarity when praying and preaching, a quickening of the memory and, in some instances, the ability to prophesy (in its meaning of foretelling). In the same volume he summarises the objections to these phenomena.[38] They are criticised on four counts: that it is a special technique that produces them, that they are but hysteria, that they are psychological, or that they are of the devil. The answer to the first is that the suddenness of revival ensures that it cannot be artificially produced, nor its course determined. To gainsay the hysterical accusation, the Doctor produces concrete medical evidence. If its source is psychological, why cannot thousands of people create a revival at the same time? And it is a weak argument that attributes every phenomenon to the devil, as the scriptures of Luke 11:14-18 and Acts 2:12-15 clearly demonstrate.[39]

It cannot be said that there is the same unanimity regarding the gifts of the Spirit, especially speaking in tongues. A minority are prepared to accept them; many have an open mind; others will argue that the miraculous gifts belonged to the age of the apostles. But there is a general acceptance of the fact that every revival displays the genuine and the counterfeit.[40] Since renewal does not remove the weaknesses of human nature, care must be taken; emotion can get out of control and lead people to act foolishly. Believers can so easily allow pride to slip in and nurture a critical spirit. Everything must be tested by the infallible Word of God and evaluated by the amount of glory given to the Lord Jesus Christ.

Biblical examples and promises

Not only does Scripture provide us with the principles of revival, but it also gives us notable examples. One of the best in the Old Testament is what happened under the leadership of Nehemiah; but the New Testament gives us the best example of all in its report of the day of Pentecost. Because of similarities to what happened in the book of Acts—the power of the Spirit, the presence of God, conviction of sin and great numbers being saved—the word 'pentecost' has been used historically to describe revival. Although it is true to say that the New Testament Pentecost was a once-for-all event which signified the coming of the Holy Spirit to abide in the Church, it was none the less a sign of the beginning of a new era, the era of the Holy Spirit. One can expect powerful or less powerful demonstrations of his activity from time to time in the history of the Church.

The source of our confidence for praying for revival is the promises of God in his Word, but there are also other reasons for doing so. The desperate condition of society is one of them. Such is the indifference, immorality and materialism, and such the inability of the Church to reach the people, that nothing but supernatural power will shake the country. To explain this, Dr Lloyd-Jones uses the failure of the disciples to cast out the spirit, as recorded in Mark 9:28-29. Although there are many things to be considered, 'The first of these considerations is the appalling need.'[41] As a result, the church should feel helpless, humble itself before God, and confess that it is in a crisis.

It was the writer's hope that small groups would meet together in homes and churches to pray specifically for revival. He refers to chapters 62 and 63 of Isaiah with their strong emphasis on prayer.[42] The prophet, on the one hand, is troubled by the sorry plight of Zion, but on the other hand sees her as she should be. This drives him to pray, and to persevere in prayer: 'For Zion's sake will I not hold my peace, and for Jerusalem's sake I will not rest.' The Doctor urges his readers to do the same, and longs for the time when the 'Oh' of Isaiah 64:1 might again be heard in the prayers of God's people.

The Movement considers it vitally important to pray for and to expect revival. It believes that the secret for reviving the churches lies in the doctrine of the work of the Holy Spirit. Rather than striving to protect themselves as organisations, the churches need to seek new spiritual life. To quote Emyr Roberts, an organisation has everything—order, worship and the sacraments; in the catholic tradition 'the shop is always open', even when nobody calls. Welsh chapels can be such organisations—social or cultural organisations[43] that find the Holy Spirit a bit of an embarrassment. But it is the Holy Spirit who protects the Church as a company of true believers depending completely on the sustaining power of God.

The churches of present-day Wales are in a pretty feeble state, and there are no visible signs of revival. But we ought not to grow weary. What ought we to do? Here is part of Eifion Evans's prescription: God's Word must be faithfully proclaimed through evangelising and preaching; in all humility we must contend with God and claim his promises; and we must study past revivals so that we may thirst once more for the refreshing visitations of the Holy Spirit.[44]

8
Faith for our Time

Nationhood and social issues

It was a thoroughly Welsh group that came together in 1948, and until 1955 all activities were conducted in the Welsh language. The only exception was the occasional English article in *Y Cylchgrawn Efengylaidd*. The early leaders were very conscious of Welsh culture—indeed they were part of it, many of them contributing to its literature; several were pacifists; and the majority attended chapel faithfully.

Welshness

The blessing of 1948 and 1949 gave the evangelicals a clearer vision than before of the relationship between the gospel and culture. They realised the danger of putting the cart before the horse, that is, giving priority to culture; but as Bobi Jones says, 'Because you are a Christian you will agree that culture is a part of religion, and not religion a part of culture.'[1] The battle to protect the language and its culture continues, even after the coming of the Welsh Assembly; but the battle to protect the Christian faith in Wales is a matter of life and death. Bobi Jones points out another danger: that of separating culture from the gospel—separating the emphasis on the individual's experience from his place in society. He refers to the argument between Mari Lewis and her son Bob in Daniel Owen's novel *Rhys Lewis*. Bob's secular philanthropy made many evangelicals nervous, with the result that they hid comfortably behind Mari Lewis. 'But Mari Lewis and her ilk, being Christians, must be held totally responsible for what happened to the Christian witness in Wales in the succeeding generation.'[2]

In the Pentecostal tradition, native Welsh-speakers have a tendency to speak English and to read their Bible in that language. There are some within the Evangelical Movement of Wales who do the same, and one finds fluent Welsh-speakers worshipping through the medium of English even when there is opportunity for them to do so in their own tongue. The early leaders recognised the danger of outside influences and agreed that they should go back further than the 1904–5 Revival, and 'not allow movements with their headquarters in England to take hold of the reins, as happened to such an extent after the Revival of '04, but to nurture our own leaders'.[3]

What the Movement seeks to do is to proclaim the good news in Wales, and that cannot be done without considering both the plight of the language and the plight of society. On the one hand, evangelicals must see their unity in Christ: on the other hand, they must see the diversity that exists among believers after their conversion. Conversion does not remove personal characteristics nor national status. Dr Martyn Lloyd-Jones explains this truth in the light of Galatians 3:28:[4]

> Everyone—every nation—will have the same opportunity to be saved, but that does not mean that the Jew and the Greek will then be one. The Jew remains a Jew and the Greek a Greek. The Jew does not become a Greek. A man of little ability does not receive super intelligence and so forth. These basic things are left as they were.

In Christ the 'middle wall of partition' is removed; but in Christ the differences between man and man and nation and nation are also sanctified by grace.

Keeping the old and the new within the Labour party is no easy task, nor is it easy to keep the balance between right and left. It is just as difficult at times to reach a mutual understanding between the Welsh-speaking and the non-Welsh-speaking and the English. Bobi Jones is saddened by the fact that the attitude of some Welsh people towards our nation is much the same as that of many English authors. After acknowledging the value of O. R. Johnston's booklet, *Nationhood, Towards a Christian Perspective*, he adds, 'This is quite a positive little book. And yet, I am afraid that English people in general, sterling Christians such as Fred Catherwood and O. R. Johnston himself amongst them, have but a comparatively shallow comprehension of the nation's significance.'[5]

One thing is certainly true about the standpoint of the English people mentioned: there is no room for 'nationalism', but only for 'patriotism'. Within the Movement we have both nationalists and patriots, but we also have some who have nothing to say to either emphasis, and who condemn any mention of the language. On one occasion when the language was given some prominence in the English Magazine, a correspondent described it as 'bizarre'.[6] And when Dr Lloyd-Jones' attitude to nationhood became known to a Chester doctor he protested vehemently against such an emphasis.[7] Yet there is unity, and the fact that so many are now learning the language is encouraging. Because these learners not only value the Welsh language but have also experienced the frustration of being unable to speak it, they have a key role to play in keeping the various factions together. They will be able to pull down barriers rather than put them up. Wales desperately needs the gospel in both languages, and we have to be on the watch constantly lest we destroy the unity in Christ.

At times the General Committee and Welsh Executive Committee have had to set aside time to deal specifically with the Welsh language. Occasionally a complaint would be voiced that too little use was made of Welsh in the operations of the Movement.[8] Principles had to be considered, and on one occasion Dr Geraint Gruffydd was asked to prepare two papers, one assessing the situation in Wales, the other dealing with the scriptural principles that should govern the believer's relationship with the nation and the state. He presented the fruit of his labour to the Welsh Executive Committee and, under the leadership of the Rev. Gareth Davies, heated discussion followed. It was agreed to ask the Welsh Literature Committee to prepare articles on relevant themes, and also to arrange an annual Welsh meeting in North and South Wales.[9]

National Eisteddfod

The National Eisteddfod has offered evangelicals an opportunity to explain the evangelical faith to their fellow countrymen. Until recently, under the auspices of the Evangelical Library, an annual lecture was arranged dealing with a person who had played a key role in our religious past. Among them were Islwyn, Christmas Evans, J. E. Daniel and Sarah Charles. In the 1967 lecture at the Bala Eisteddfod, when the four-hundredth anniversary of the translation of the New Testament into Welsh was being celebrated, Gwenallt presided, and the speakers were Geraint Gruffydd and R. Tudur Jones.

Many evangelicals have had some success in the National Eisteddfod, and a choice few have carried away the major prizes: Emyr Roberts and Dafydd Ifans were awarded the Prose Medal, and Siôn Aled and Einir Jones are crowned bards.[10] Their prize-winning work was published by the Eisteddfod itself, but several of the lectures also saw the light of day in the Evangelical Library of Wales series edited by E. Wyn James.

Publications

The evangelical witness was also strengthened by other works published by the Evangelical Press of Wales (now Bryntirion Press). The Welsh were reminded of several aspects of their country's history—by Gwyn Davies in his book *Griffith Jones, Llanddowror* (1984); by John Aaron in *Torf Ardderchog* (A Wonderful Throng, 1992); by Noel Gibbard in *Elusen i'r Enaid* (Alms for the Soul, 1979), an introduction to the works of the Welsh Puritans; by Eifion Evans in his books on revival; and by E. Wyn James in his volumes on hymns and carols.[11] The Christian parents of Wales were greatly encouraged by the publication of a children's Bible, *Beibl i Blant* (1991), and of *Taith y Pererin i'r Teulu* (Pilgrim's Progress for the Family, 1997) based on Bunyan's classic which, with the Bible, has had such an influence on our country's past. When *Christian Hymns* was published in 1977, the outside world was given the opportunity not only to appreciate some Welsh hymns in translation, but also to see the hymnody of the Welsh in the development of the broader tradition of the hymn.

Through the medium of the two magazines the great names of our evangelical heritage were introduced to the present generation by regular contributors such as David Boorman, Eifion Evans, Geraint Gruffydd, Gwilym Humphreys and Noel Gibbard.[12] Readers had opportunity to see the original versions of well-known hymns by Edward Jones (Maes-y-plwm), Pedr Fardd and Thomas Charles,[13] and new hymns appeared in both languages.[14] The Welsh Magazine had the privilege of publishing contributions by prominent living writers—two articles by Keri Evans on the hindrances to a spiritual life;[15] two poems by Gwenallt Jones[16] and another by Nantlais Williams;[17] three translations by J. Vernon Lewis,[18] and one of Elvet Lewis's hymns.[19] Gwyn Walters (then of Cardiff) translated one of the few hymns of John Calvin, linking the new movement with the Protestant Reformation.[20]

Bobi Jones has been a regular and valuable contributor to the Welsh magazine over many years. His two series, 'Dogfennau Mawr y Ffydd' (The Great Documents of the Faith) and 'Y Dreftadaeth Deg' (The Fair Inheritance), were written to remind readers of our glorious evangelical past. The first included, among other works, Vicar Prichard's metrical versions of Psalms 121, 126 and 19,[21] and a letter from William Williams Pantycelyn to Thomas Charles; the second, observations on the literary contribution of a variety of authors, such as Ellis Wynne; Robert Jones, Llanllyfni[22]; Owen Evans ('the J. C. Ryle of Wales'); Owen Thomas ('the greatest biographer in the Welsh language'); Ann Griffiths; Daniel Owen, the renowned late-nineteenth-century novelist, and more recent authors such as R. Tudur Jones and Emyr Roberts.[23] Another series of articles, 'Cewri'r Diwygiad' (The Giants of the Revival) was contributed by Robert Ellis—a series that was published in translation under the title *Living Echoes of the Welsh Revival 1904–5* (London, no date).

Welsh Bible

Much attention has been paid over the years to the traditional Welsh version of the Bible, known as the William Morgan translation. When it was decided to produce a revised version of the New Testament, the task was entrusted to Cecil Jenkins, Emyr Roberts, Gordon Macdonald and Edmund Owen, the last-named devoting much of his time with the Press to this venture. The revised version of the 1620 New Testament was published in 1991.

Since then, many laborious hours have gone into studying the original Hebrew and Greek texts, so that changes to the current version of *Y Beibl Newydd Cymraeg* (the New Welsh Bible published by the Bible Society) can be suggested to the editorial panel before a revised edition appears. The men involved in this work are Gordon Macdonald (Aberystwyth), Iwan Rhys Jones (Bridgend), Cecil Jenkins (Llwyn-hendy) and Arfon Jones (Cardiff). Using the same revised text, it is hoped to publish a Study Bible, and the task of editing the explanatory notes has been given to Gwyn Davies (Aberystwyth), author of many commentaries in the *Bara'r Bywyd* (Bread of Life) series, which, ever since the appearance of the first volume in 1980, have been edited by Edmund Owen.

Foundations

It is vital that Welshness should be firmly based on biblical principles; otherwise what is in itself good will become an idol. This is what has happened in a number of African countries, where nationalism has been based on principles that are anti-God. Fortunately the Christian influence still prevails to some extent in Wales, though a number of nationalists are prone to go to extremes. In his book *Crist a Chenedlaetholdeb* (Christ and Nationalism) Bobi Jones writes, 'In this little book I have tried to argue that one of the theological areas where classical Christianity in Wales could make an original contribution to current thought would be in the interpretation of nationalism.'[24] And since the Movement claims to promote 'classical Christianity', it would be as well to try to understand what some of its people have said about this matter.

In the first chapter of his book on Christ and the nation, 'Gwaith Duw a'r Genedl' (God's Work and the Nation), Bobi Jones states categorically that the nation is a 'creation of God'. Like another scholarly Christian, J. E. Daniel, he appeals to Acts 17:26—'And he has made from one blood every nation of men to dwell on all the face of the earth, and has determined their preappointed times and the boundaries of their habitation' (NKJV).[25] Consequently the Christian should think of his responsibility to his nation as one aspect of his responsibility to God. He refers to the cultural commandment, which is bound up with creation and the general grace of God: 'Be fruitful and multiply; fill the earth and subdue it . . .' (Genesis 1:28).

But when were nations formed? Both Bobi Jones and R. Tudur Jones are agreed that a quotation from the work of the pioneer educationalist Griffith Jones, Llanddowror, serves to answer the question:[26]

> Therefore, God's mercy is apparent in his work of mixing the languages and scattering the people, giving them different languages. And if this general rule proclaims the goodness and love of God, could it be denied that it is true of any particular example of it? And if we try to wipe out a certain language—and especially one which is as old as any existing in the present world—should we not be truly terrified lest we fight against the laws of heaven and undermine the verdicts of divine providence?

God saw fit to overrule the intentions of men. 'Where man was building uniformity, God insisted on creating variety':[27] when he was seeking to be free to fulfil his own wishes, God was putting the bit in his mouth and reining him in. 'Language and nationhood act as a restraining force on man's pomp and pride, they are a stumbling block and a hindrance to overruling ambition and presumptuous greed.'[28] To quote Martin Luther, serving one's nation is 'life's school', because doing so enables one to see the need for serving humanity.[29]

This emphasis on the Tower of Babel does not forget the Fall in Eden nor the element of judgement associated with the event. There is, nonetheless, a difference of opinion among evangelicals with respect to the significance of that judgement. Some would say that scattering the languages was the judgement and, consequently, that we should not speak of national differences; others would refer to the second chapter of Acts and argue that God through the gospel restores the right relationship between nation and nation, rather than obliterating the differences between them.[30]

One of the features of the doctrine presented by both Bobi Jones and R. Tudur Jones is the emphasis on 'sphere theology'. This is how it is expressed by Bobi Jones:[31]

> The simple plan is this: that there are on earth comparatively independent spheres of activity ('federal' is the best word), so that each one has its purpose, its conditions, and its own attributes— spheres such as the family, the state, mathematics, the local church, language, art, and so forth.

Each sphere has its own sovereignty, but in that order it is possible for one sphere to serve another sphere. That is the way to protect against the authoritarianism which can slip into any one of the spheres or circles.[32]

In a radio talk, subsequently published in *Y Cylchgrawn Efengylaidd*, Geraint Gruffydd suggests that there are three important things that we should bear in mind when considering the Welsh language and our culture.[33] In the first place, if we have the language we should speak it, teach it to our children and encourage others to learn it. In the second place, we should be concerned about righteousness in the life of our nation. 'Righteouness exalts a nation', and we should be watchful that other countries deal righteously with it.

And in the third place, we should not separate this righteousness from personal righteousness before God. What Wales needs is new people, people who are counted righteous before God, and have received new life from him.

The believer must consider his responsibility within the Church as a Welshman and as a citizen. He has the privilege of being not only a heavenly citizen, but also an earthly citizen, and he must of necessity safeguard the right relationship between them. He ought not to forget the earth when he thinks of heaven, nor ought he to forget heaven when he thinks of earth. As a citizen of two worlds the believer can contribute not only to the Church but to society also.

Salt and light

Emyr Roberts is absolutely clear in his mind as to what the chief work of the Movement should be. 'The Evangelical Movement need not apologise even if it were true that it had no other favour to offer the nation but to proclaim that Christianity means personal repentance and a living faith in the Lord Jesus Christ and a life that seeks to glorify God.'[34] Because of this central emphasis the Movement is frequently accused of ignoring social problems, especially political issues, and even of shutting its eyes to them. In accordance with his basic statement Emyr Roberts reminds the critics that they are passing judgement on an Evangelical Movement: what binds its supporters together is the gospel and not political dogma.[35] Within the movement there are nationalists, socialists, Tories and the occasional non-political animal, as is true of the Ecumenical Movement and of our country's churches as a whole.

Nonetheless, the evangelical person is no less a person than anyone else, nor is he less of a citizen. Indeed, he has a new way of looking at everything: at himself, at man, at the Church, at the world around him, and at creation. He acknowledges that he lives in God's world, and that as a consequence all things belong to him who is both Creator and Saviour. On the other hand, he realises that he lives in a fallen world, and that the fingerprints of sin have tainted every corner of it. He must never forget that. We have in Emyr Roberts's words a timely warning:[36]

> If history teaches us anything it teaches us this: that the seeds of corruption are present in every social revolution, whatever ideals

its leaders might cherish, and that in the end it is bound to become evil and corrupt (and the same law applies to the Church as an organisation), unless the fear of God and the motives of grace are a power in the life of the people.

This is God's world, but its enemies are trying to possess it, and the believer must make it clear that he is on God's side.

Every Christian should feel that it is his bounden duty to be a responsible member of the family and of society. When problems arise in these circles it is the custom of the Movement to encourage both individual supporters and committee members to bring the issues to the notice of the churches. Occasionally a day-conference is arranged to discuss a particular matter.

Broadcasting Bill

Sometimes an official statement is made on the Movement's behalf, as happened in the case of the Broadcasting Bill in 1990.[37] There were fears on two counts: namely, that freedom of opinion would be restricted, and that Christianity as one of the beneficial influences on society in general would be ignored. In this area, as in other areas, there is danger that the wealthiest organisations will have the greatest influence. Although society is largely secular, the bill proposed to give broadcasting time to religious minorities and argued that the time allotted to different church bodies should be according to their membership numbers.

The Lord's Day

The attitude of the people of Wales to the Lord's Day has changed drastically over the last quarter of a century. In the first of a series of articles written for the Welsh magazine Gwyn Williams of Cardiff states that there are three things to be considered.[38] First is what we read in Genesis 2:1-3 of God resting on the seventh day, thus ordaining the Sabbath. 'This ordination of the Sabbath is referred to by theologians as one of "the ordinances of creation", that is, a feature of a world and a life that is to exist as long as creation lasts.' Secondly, it is a day of remembrance: that is what it was in Old Testament times according to Deuteronomy 5:15, and that is most certainly what the first day of the week in the New Testament is—a celebration of the resurrection, or the exodus, of our Lord from the grave. Thirdly, it is an opportunity to look forward, since there remains a rest for God's people (Hebrews 4:9), that is, an eternal rest in heaven.[39]

Evangelicals are agreed that Christians should keep Sunday as a special day, but opinions differ on at least two matters: how exactly it should be kept, and whether unbelievers should be expected to acknowledge this day. Most evangelicals will attend two services and Sunday school. Some will be very particular about their arrangements for the rest of the day, and will only do what is absolutely necessary; while others will be happy to watch television or attend concerts. The Movement is strongly of the opinion that Sunday is of benefit to man as man, even if he does not appreciate the significance of the resurrection.[40]

The issue of Sunday observance was given more prominence when opening shops for trading became legal. The Movement strongly opposed the new law, and the General Secretary made a statement on its behalf, answering the arguments put forward in its favour.[41] Some Christians contended that Sunday differed from the Old Testament Sabbath, but others counter-argued by emphasising the ordinances of creation. There were Christians of the opinion that it is wrong to foist one's ideas on others, but they were reminded that many people—individuals, shopkeepers and members of trade unions—were opposed to Sunday opening, albeit not on Christian grounds. The argument that championed the freedom of the individual to do as he wished on Sunday was a non-starter, because each person should think not only of himself but of his fellow man. The large companies would be reaping the profits of the extra day's trade, and the small companies would be bound to suffer. The majority in Parliament favoured the change, but it was not too late to write to local constituency members, and that is what the Movement's statement urged its supporters to do.[42]

Homosexuality

Because of a stand made by the Aberystwyth Evangelical Church opposing homosexuality, the Movement attracted some unexpected publicity. The local church felt unable to send a representative to appear on the current affairs programme 'Byd ar Bedwar' (The World on Four), and Gwynn Williams was asked to voice the Movement's opinion. Later, the Aberystwyth church made a statement explaining its stance on the basis of Genesis 2:24-25, emphasising that it was condemning the homosexual act, in accordance with Leviticus 18. Whilst admitting that it was only one of many sins, they were certain that it was none the less a sin: 'We believe that we have to stand on the testimony of the Word of God, and we state our opposition to anything that gainsays that Word, especially when an attempt is made to justify that which God condemns.'[43] It is surprising how little support there was for the Aberystwyth church, though there was eloquent support for the opposition.

The 'gay' opposition to the Movement continued. On the final day of the 1992 National Eisteddfod in Aberystwyth, a group that was anxious to promote homosexuality attacked the Movement's bookstall, upsetting the tables and scattering the books. The Eisteddfod Director asked the group to promise not to repeat their act of vandalism the following year, but they argued that they were acting as individuals and not as a cell, and could therefore promise nothing.[44]

The family

Other issues deserving attention were birth and death and the family. Many Movement supporters, among them Keith and Rhiain Lewis, contributed extensively in these areas, and are members of the anti-abortion movement 'Bywyd' (Life). In the first chapter of his book *Y Teulu Cristnogol* (The Christian Family), Keith Lewis deals with the scriptures that are the foundation of family life, Genesis 1:28, 2:18; the husband and wife relationship, Ephesians 5:24-25; teaching children, Psalm 127:3, Ephesians 6:4; and the responsibility of children, Exodus 20:12, Proverbs 6:20, Ephesians 6:2. And there is constant application of Scripture in the chapters on 'Sexual care', 'Discipline' and 'Three attitudes'. The aim is to create and nurture a loving relationship between parents and their children, a relationship where they can be completely open with each other, children honouring their parents and parents loving their children, not forgetting that they are sinners. The unmarried are also included in the family: they are instructed how to accept their situation, and offered helpful advice taken from the work of Dr A. N. Martin.[45]

In a similar book written in English—*Christian Family Matters* (1985)[46]—the family unit is based on the same Christian principles. The contributions are varied, and include 'The Marriage Covenant' by J. Elwyn Davies; 'Divorce' by Neil Richards; 'Abortion and Family

Planning' by Brian Harris, and 'Fostering and Adoption' by Stuart Olyott. An attempt was made to deal with matters in the light of the ordinances of creation, the effect of the Fall, and the relationship between the two Testaments, Old and New.

Education

It was the demands made by the world of education that brought together a number of teachers to form the Association of Christian Teachers of Wales. In 1981 the Christian Council for the Schools of Wales was formed by representatives of the Association of Christian Teachers, the Scripture Union, the Evangelical Movement of Wales and the University and Colleges Christian Fellowship. In 1983 David Underhill was appointed full-time worker, to be followed by Allan Rees (1990–95).[47] Because teachers were acutely conscious of the moral deterioration and anti-Christian philosophy so frequently apparent in educational policies, lectures dealing with problems in the teaching world were regularly held and the material published. The following titles give an idea of the issues that concerned teachers and parents: *The Place of Authority in Education* by Alan F. Francis; *Christian Schools* by D. Eryl Davies; *Declining Moral Standards in Schools: Cause, Effect and Response* by Glyn Baker; *The Battle for Ascendancy in Education* by J. Hefin Elias; *Stress and Commitment for the Christian Teacher* by D. Alun Watkins, and *Whose Child?* by Fred Hughes.

Let us look more closely at two of the published works. According to Fred Hughes (*Whose Child?*), humanism with its emphasis on reason had greatly influenced education in Britain, with the inevitable result that man had not only been placed at the centre of things but was considered self-sufficient. In keeping with this belief in the centrality of man, the structure of traditional authority had been challenged, with more time allotted to other religions to the detriment of Christianity. The author followed this analysis with the biblical argument in favour of authority in the family, in school and in government.

Christian Schools forcefully presented the case for the separate schooling of children from Christian homes. Because of the general moral deterioration and the constant changes being made to the curriculum, it argued that education should be the responsibility of the home and the church rather than that of the state. Needless to say, there was fierce opposition to what was seen as segregation.[48] The counter-argument was largely based on the nature and extent of parental responsibility. Parents are certainly to teach their children Christian precepts and to bring them up in the fear of the Lord; they are to see to their general welfare; but they should also accept the state's responsibility to organise education. God did not intend parents to be responsible for schools, and many a parent would not have the ability for such a task. Furthermore, segregated Christian schooling poses its own dangers: an obvious one is that it affords fewer opportunities to serve the wider society; but another, and more serious one, is that there is no guarantee that it will of necessity protect a belief and a way of life that is in accordance with Scripture. The enemy is as well-equipped to work within the Christian circle as without it—to quote the words of one correspondent, 'Better the enemy we know than the one we don't know.'[49]

War and peace

An issue that creates dissension is that of war and peace. It would seem that there are more pacifists among Welsh-speaking supporters of the Movement, and Arfon Jones is certainly one of the most ardent. He explained his stance very cogently in his book *Rhyfel yr Oen* (The War of the Lamb),[50] which also brings us into contact with some of America's evangelicals, authors such as Jim Wallis and Ronald Sider.

But it was an Englishman ministering in Wales, Richard Ross, who sounded the alarm against the use of nuclear arms. He was responding to an article by Welsh-speaking Welshman Gwyn Davies, who condemned the unjust attack of one country on another, and yet argued that it was right to threaten and, if need be, use nuclear arms to defend a country. The Englishman contended that the use of nuclear arms was immoral, whatever the circumstances. It would cause untold havoc—and that in a world created by God, with man as the pinnacle of his creation. And how does one decide whether an attack is just or unjust? On the international level, what is frequently of importance is defending the power and interests of the stronger countries. The Christian, of all people, should condemn this. The issue remains a topic of discussion, but it is unlikely that there will ever be unanimity on this, any more than on many other issues discussed within the Movement.[51]

Social issues

In 1987, although some within the Movement believed that this was unnecessary and would divert attention from more important considerations, the Movement established a Social Issues Committee. One English evangelical church in particular expressed strong opposition, and even some of the leaders within the Movement recognised that there were dangers, especially should it follow the trend of the radical evangelicalism of America. Yet it prospered for a number of years. The first lecture on 'Is there a need for a Christian political party?' was delivered in 1987 by Donald Macleod of Edinburgh. The following year Fred Catherwood spoke on the subject of 'Human Rights'.[52] J. I. Packer was the invited speaker on one occasion, and his visit was of particular significance because he had adopted an inter-church policy very different from that of the Movement. He was also given opportunity to address a ministers' meeting in Bryntirion.

Unemployment

At a time when there was a substantial increase in unemployment in Wales, a group of people came together to consider the matter in order to help individuals and churches. As part of the process, Gerallt Wyn Davies issued a discussion document, which was later published as a booklet, *The Christian, the Church and Daily Work*.[53] The year was 1984, when 'More than one in three unemployed men in Wales have been without work for over a year', and in the EEC a quarter of all young people under 25 years old (28% in the UK) were unemployed. Asking if society can be built on leisure, he sets out the biblical teaching on work, tracing that through the Protestant work ethic to 'what might be called "the death of work" in our generation'.

The Christian should be clear in his own mind about the nature of work, and prepared to oppose any threat against it, of whatever kind it might be. On the one hand it is possible to make work an idol: on the other, it is possible to degrade it. God created man to be a steward of his estate; he was created to worship, yes, but he was also created to work. It is a basic Christian principle that work is essential to the wholeness of man's well-being, and that is why individuals and churches should assist those who are out of work and give particular attention to the sick and the needy. Church leaders should meet and suggest to their members various ways of helping; the unemployed should be offered counselling; financial help should be available; and the out-of-work encouraged to do voluntary jobs. A group of churches could even consider a work creation scheme.

Special needs
There is always the possibility of the unemployment rate falling substantially, but there is little likelihood of a sudden change in the number and condition of the disabled. The Movement has tried to wrestle with some aspects of their need. Although it was financially impossible to open centres, it was possible to collaborate with other organisations and encourage individuals and churches to do what they could.

With Dr Joy Pryce of Colwyn Bay making the necessary arrangements, a number of camps were held for those with special needs—in Aberdesach, Bod Difyr, and Llanbedr, Harlech.[54] Having spent ten years in medicine before specialising in child psychiatry, Dr Joy Pryce was the ideal camp leader. She was ably assisted by Brynmor P. Jones, who took responsibility for the morning addresses and the epilogue, and looked after the equipment borrowed from the Movement centres. These camps were totally different from the usual Movement camps. There was no compulsion to attend even the epilogue—indeed, some campers chose to go fishing rather than attend a meeting! Dr Joy Pryce also contributed valuable articles to the Welsh magazine—articles such as 'Ysbytai'r Meddwl a Chyfrifoldeb y Cristion'[55] (Mental Hospitals and the Christian's Responsibility), which enlightened readers on psychiatric illnesses and disorders.

The Movement has always been more than ready to help Tear Fund and Cause for Concern.[56] An increasing number of churches support Tear Fund, and for some years the two movements have shared a tent on the National Eisteddfod field. When David Potter felt the need to establish A Cause for Concern, his article appeared in the *Evangelical Magazine of Wales*,[57] and there was an immediate response from Alfred Place Baptist Church, Aberystwyth. It was decided to open a home in the town, and a meeting was held in Cardiff so that South Wales Christians might learn what was happening in Aberystwyth. Plas Lluest was purchased in 1977, the home established in 1979, and officially opened in 1981.[58] Many of those who attend the two annual conferences in Aberystwyth pay a visit to the home, which is situated above the village of Llanbadarn. Present at the opening were Mr and Mrs Murphy, who were moved to sell their home for a reasonable price in order to establish a centre in their home town of Deganwy. No one church is responsible for this venture, but many individuals and churches support it as they feel able.

In dealing with social matters the purpose of the Movement was twofold: to teach people to think biblically about various issues, and to enable them to act responsibly. Adapting the principles to specific situations was generally left to the churches. But the Movement itself would have liked to open a home for older people on land which it owned in Bryntirion, and it was a matter of bitter disappointment when the local council refused to grant building permission.

The Movement sets great value on the faith given once for all to the saints. It is prepared to present that faith to the present generation, and also ready, as in the past, to face the battles of the faith. We shall look more closely at that aspect in the next chapter.

9
Battles of the Faith

'Can two walk together, except they be agreed?'
(Amos 3:3)

Some time during 1958 a friend asked the Rev. L. D. Richards, Cwmafan, about the religious situation in Wales. 'He maintained that there were in Wales within *Yr Hen Gorff* [the Calvinistic Methodist denomination] three movements, namely the "Evangelical" movement, the "Healing" movement, and the "Ecumenical" movement, and that every minister of note within the connexion belonged to one of them.'[1] It is of no consequence who the 'ministers of note' were, but the classification is interesting. L. D. Richards, whose sympathies were obviously with the Ecumenical Movement, goes on to say that in his opinion the Evangelical Movement is far too prone to give priority to the words of the Bible rather than the Word. They should, he says, take into account the new knowledge concerning the Bible, and reconsider the nature of inspiration and authority.[2]

'Fundamentalism'

The Rev. L. Haydn Lewis, Ton Pentre, thought that clinging to the old concept of the Bible as the inspired Word of God was none other than rank 'fundamentalism'. Those who belonged to the Apostolic Church of Pen-y-groes, Carmarthenshire, were in his opinion 'the most zealous supporters' of Welsh fundamentalism, but it grieved him that the belief was 'already lifting its head in our National Colleges and our Theological Colleges'.[3]

The supporters of the Movement were, and still are, regarded as 'fundamentalists'. The columnist Theophilus, writing in *Y Goleuad*, stated: 'We know that one fundamentalist movement has captured one section of the young people. As a result these are found to be more conservative than their grandparents, and also more unwilling to welcome new light.'[4] He adds that the development could not be confined to one generation. The editor of *Seren Cymru* had this to say: 'The emphasis of these people [the conservatives] on the divinity of Scripture reminds us of the widespread belief that the divine nature of Jesus Christ had swallowed up his human nature so that he was God assuming the semblance of man.'[5] Within a year the 'conservatives' had become 'fundamentalists', which meant that they were people who 'accepted the perfect inerrancy of the Bible'. That was the basic difference between them and the liberals: 'The primary bone of contention between those who are theologically conservative and those who are liberal is the doctrine of the inspiration of the Bible.'[6] A correspondent to *Y Faner* asked the Movement to state its opinion of the Bible, because he would like to know more about the belief that every event in the Bible was 'historically true to the letter'.[7]

In the above quotations the word 'fundamentalism' is used rather emotively, but the editor of *Seren Cymru* saw fit to trace the source of the term, reminding his readers that it was a word used to describe a group in America trying to defend the essentials of the faith against the attacks of theological liberals; the inspiration of Scripture was only one among many issues. What the editor said was of course true, but it should be remembered that the group responsible for *The Fundamentals*, which first appeared in 1909, consisted of British, Canadian and South African as well as American authors.[8] The editor continues, 'To a large extent the Evangelical Movement has inherited the standpoint of the early fundamentalists, and that is why this name is given them by those who oppose them, a name which tends to be misleading.'[9] He was right to call the term 'misleading', but it is very doubtful whether supporters of the Movement would consider themselves 'heirs' of the *Fundamentals* group. It is true that they would be in total agreement with the authors of *Fundamentals* on the inspiration of Scripture, but as 'heirs' of the old Welsh Protestant tradition their source of inspiration is the Welsh tradition of John Penry, Vavasor Powell, George Lewis, Cynddylan Jones, Wyre Lewis and R. Tudur Jones. It should also be remembered that the Fundamentalist Movement, in the United States especially, developed into small fundamentalist factions, and that the Evangelical Movement of Wales is less than happy with many of those developments.

But L. Haydn Lewis, in his articles, chose to forget the wider tradition. He contends that there are three important things that need to be remembered: 'that it is the dowry of the last century and the continuation of a by-product of the Revival upheaval at the beginning of this century'; that it is 'a reaction against two World Wars', and that there is 'a hint of it even on the pages of the New Testament itself, especially in the Johannine literature'.[10] Defending the New Testament against such an accusation is a needless task, but it is significant that L. Haydn Lewis makes no reference to the evangelical literature available at that time—literature explaining the source and meaning of the term 'fundamentalism' and the evangelical teaching on the authority of the Bible.[11] By the way, the term 'fundamentalist' was not used until 1920.[12] Although the Evangelical Movement of Wales stands resolutely for the essentials of the faith, it is loath to use that adjective to describe its belief.

Evangelicals and the Bible

For the Movement, as for the Church down the centuries, there is a special meaning to the word 'inspiration', one that is based on the teaching of the Bible itself. We have already, in chapter seven, referred to the teaching of the Lord Jesus Christ and to scriptures such as 2 Timothy 3:16 and 1 Peter 1:21,22. Nevertheless, the Movement is accused of all kinds of errors concerning the Bible. It is said that evangelicals—the 'fundamentalists' of the critics—do not accept the mistakes made down the centuries by those copying the manuscripts. According to L. Haydn Lewis, verbal inspiration does not acknowledge the faults of print-setters, printers or publishers.[13] In any case, it is argued, the Bible is only a human attempt to express eternal truth. We ought to bear in mind, says Rhys Nicholas, 'that the writers and the copiers and the translators were human beings, and that it is possible to make mistakes when transcribing documents'.[14]

Responding to the articles written by L. Haydn Lewis in *Y Drysorfa*, Emyr Roberts (Rhyl) expressed surprise at both their content and their spirit, adding that their greatest fault lay in the adoption of the experimental method in dealing with the Bible. Consequently they lost sight of the uniqueness of the Christian revelation—that God has addressed us once and for all in Scripture. The duty of believers is to seek a better understanding of what God has said, and to do so under the guidance of the Holy Spirit, who himself inspired Scripture. Nor did Emyr Roberts think that even his fellow liberals would agree with

L. Haydn Lewis, especially with the statement that the Bible was a human attempt to understand eternal truth.[15]

This is what one of the evangelicals said on the subject of errors: 'It is fair to accept that errors can be made in translating and copying—what human work is without errors? . . . But we cannot accept that there are errors in the original revelation, which was breathed out by God himself.'[16] There is a fundamental difference between the work of the Holy Spirit inspiring the original writers and the Spirit leading the copiers and the translators. 'Inspiration', when applied to the Bible, has a specific meaning: the original text was the one inspired. Because that is not available, a mass of manuscripts that have been safeguarded down the ages have to be studied to try and find the most reliable. Not all evangelicals are agreed on the best text, but they are wrestling with the problem.

Variety

The other danger, according to the Movement's critics, is to ignore the variety within the Scriptures. This is how the editor of *Seren Cymru* put it: 'What is more, the conservative standpoint does not do justice to the glorious variety of literature found in the Bible.'[17] One way of proving the inaccuracy of this statement would be to turn to the *New Bible Dictionary* published by the IVF (1962). Among its many entries there are articles on 'The Language of the New Testament', 'Judaism', 'Eschatology' and 'Bible Criticism'. Another way would be to listen to the view of one conservative, doubtless speaking for all his fellow conservatives:

> That is what makes the Bible so interesting—there is something in it to suit all tastes. We should be on our guard not to impose a uniform pattern on something which is essentially varied in its literary expression. Because of this variety, it is important to consider each verse in its context, and it is to this aspect that we shall turn in the following points.[18]

The 'following points' include an emphasis on the importance of explaining the words of Scripture in their usual meaning; of interpreting them according to the circumstances of the particular book, and of bearing in mind the unity of the Bible.

The words and the Word

Sometimes there is venom in the criticism that supporters of the Movement set more importance on the words than on the Word.[19] There are two ways of responding to this criticism. In the first place the Movement's detractors should realise that its supporters are wrestling with the relationship between the words and the Word in the belief that understanding the words illuminate the Word. Is not personal knowledge of the Lord Jesus Christ, the Word made flesh, the cornerstone of the Movement? Not a single supporter would attempt to come into a living relationship with 'words', 'facts', or 'statements'.[20] In the second place, the words of Scripture are not fallible words, and evangelical conservatives cannot accept the idea that God speaks his infallible Word through fallible words.

Christ and the Old Testament

Another aspect of liberal criticism is to maintain that the authority of Jesus Christ overrules the authority of the Old Testament. Matthew chapter 5 is cited, and the verses that begin 'You have heard that it was said' are contrasted with those that begin 'But I say unto you'. It is claimed that these words of our Lord are the first to criticise the Old Testament, and that the fifth chapter of Matthew's Gospel is 'as critical and as presumptuous as Biblical Criticism might appear to some today'.[21] Here is a précis of Dr Lloyd-Jones' response:[22]

> He gives us his own positive exposition of the Law, and he also contrasts it with the false teaching of the Scribes and Pharisees. Indeed, there is a sense in which it can be said that the whole of the remainder of this Sermon, from verse 21 right through to the end of chapter 5, and chapter 6 and chapter 7, is nothing but an elaboration of that fundamental proposition, that our righteousness must exceed that of the Scribes and the Pharisees if we are indeed to be citizens of the kingdom of heaven.

As the Son of God, the Lord Jesus Christ could rightly interpret Scripture and, in so doing, demonstrate his own authority. The words referred to as being critical of the Old Testament must be interpreted in the light of verses 17 and 18, where the Lord firmly puts his stamp on its authority.

Use of the mind

But what the Movement's supporters lack most, according to its critics, is the ability to think. They are people who simply accept everything on the basis of external authority, without bothering to think for themselves. According to one critic, 'There is more truth in the little finger of one who honestly doubts, than in the whole body of one who mindlessly accepts everything.'[23] But the most sweeping statement is possibly this: 'But once Biblical Criticism had seriously started its work, no one could thereafter accept the infallibility and literalism of the Bible without being either dishonest or ignorant.'[24] Such words could suggest a touch of pride and arrogance, for they completely ignore what the evangelicals say, and the literature they have produced. Here is what one person who had believed for many years had to tell a young believer:[25]

> What gladdens my heart in your letter is the fact that you are obviously *thinking seriously* about matters relating to our faith. We are to love the Lord our God with all our *mind* as well as with all our heart and soul (Matt. 23:37). We can never *think* too much about our faith.

By now there has been a tremendous increase in the amount of evangelical literature that deals with the inspiration, authority and interpretation of the Bible.

Pinnacles of the faith

There prevails an impression that the only matter of dissension between evangelicals and their critics is that concerning the Bible. In his constant criticism of fundamentalists W. J. Edwards maintains that all the denominations are evangelical, and when the Evangelical Theological College of Wales was established at Bryntirion he posed the question, 'Is not every theological college in Wales an evangelical college?'[26] It would be well to pose a few pertinent questions before responding more fully. Is conversion given the same primacy in the denominations as it is in the Evangelical Movement? How much room is there for God's judgement in today's sermons? Is the doctrine of the atonement acceptable? How often is the second coming mentioned?

Emyr Roberts, apologist

Emyr Roberts of Trefor (and subsequently of Rhyl) was not only a lifelong preacher of the gospel but also an apologist for the evangelical faith. Immediately after his conversion he began corresponding with Gwilym O. Roberts, the most daring representative of the radical modernists. Emyr Roberts had, in the first place, responded to an article by L. D. Richards in *Y Drysorfa* (1949), and his reply had moved Gwilym O. Roberts to write, from Hanley, the first of his letters, dated 21 June 1949 and signed 'The little man buried here'.[27]

In this first letter he expressed admiration of Emyr Roberts's honesty and independent mind, but felt sad that an intellect that Christ could ill afford to lose could churn out such other-worldly stuff.[28] He obviously saw no dishonesty or ignorance in the evangelical conservative! But he preferred the 'psychological-scientific' emphasis; the 'floppin Barthian or the Niebuhrian'[29] was 'anathema' to him. If God has become flesh, then it must be the things of earth that count, and one must wrestle with the best way of enthroning love instead of selfishness. The difference between himself and Emyr Roberts was the difference between 'other-worldliness' and 'naturalism'. Without mincing his words, Emyr Roberts replied that the God of 'naturalism' had no salvation for anyone who was getting on in years or dying of consumption.[30]

The Hanley exile read one of Emyr Roberts's letters before breakfast. He was, he writes, astounded by the minister's creative ability—'This paragraph [on Fromus] is a gem'[31]—and realised that the writer wished to see everything in the light of the gospel. That, he believed, meant that they were getting nearer to one another. The apologist was in no way convinced, and had great doubts when he read the psychologist's prophecy for 1970: 'Within the 1970 religious framework—when the minister of the Gospel will also be a clinician—the ministry will suit me.'[32] By now both felt that they were destined to fight on opposing sides, but that the contest should be a friendly one. The psychologist published his ideas in books, and in articles sent to the Welsh papers, especially *Y Goleuad* and *Y Cymro*. These ideas were obviously very extreme, and many outside the Movement opposed them. And yet, when the writer spoke in the Bala Association, one of the denomination's periodicals referred to his 'memorable address'.[33] And when the wife of one Calvinistic Methodist minister wrote a letter of criticism to *Y Goleuad*, the editor sided with the psychologist.[34]

Y Goleuad

The next scene of discussion and debate was staged by the *Goleuad*, in 1963 and 1964 in particular. Gwilym O. Roberts expressed his ideas just as eloquently, and Emyr Roberts continued to oppose him, but another character now came to the fore, namely Theophilus.[35] Though rather more conservative than the 'exile', he could not swallow many of the old doctrines, among them the miraculous birth and the atonement. In a long series of articles Theophilus dealt with every aspect of the birth of Jesus, and during the series many joined the fray in defence or criticism. The titles of contributions by the original contestants are significant: Emyr Roberts's was 'Cristnogaeth Efengylaidd a Moderniaeth' (Evangelical Christianity and Modernism); Gwilym O. Roberts responded with 'Protestaniaeth Radicalaidd a Christnogaeth Radicalaidd' (Radical Protestantism and Radical Christianity).[36]

Gwilym O. Roberts welcomed Theophilus' radical ideas, and also took the opportunity to chastise some of his fellow modernists for concealing what they believed from the people. They were, he said, too afraid 'to come out of their holes' and lacked 'the guts' to do so, especially some of the college professors.[37] He appreciated the honesty of Theophilus, a man who loved God and the truth. But Emyr Roberts strongly disagreed: he thought the ideas of both men were crude, and proclaiming the faith once given to the saints was an urgent necessity.[38] The *Cymro* columnist could not take such an old-fashioned Christo-logical response seriously, calling on J. R. Jones, Dafydd Ellis Thomas and Froude to back him.[39] But, according to Emyr Roberts, these men were just as guilty, in talking about Christianity whilst rejecting the testimony of those whom Jesus had chosen to be his witnesses.[40]

The Cylchgrawn

Both Gwilym O. Roberts and Theophilus came under the scourge of 'Meirchion' in *Y Cylchgrawn Efengylaidd*:[41]

> It is difficult to tell which is the more old-fashioned. There is Theophilus, nailing his flag to the mast of Dean Inge's ship, which ceased plying the contemporary theological seas some years ago.

And in the field which includes the 'clinical psychiatry' that Mr Roberts is so fond of amusing us with, it is difficult to get a doctor who uses clinical psychiatry in his day-to-day work to accept, without a pinch of salt, the Freudian system which he practically accepts as religion.

'Meirchion' also expresses surprise that the two contributors are given so much space in the Welsh papers, reminding readers that in the debate as to whether or not to believe, scholarship is neutral.

Honest to God

During that same period Bishop John Robinson's *Honest to God* appeared. R. Tudur Jones responded to its publication in an article bearing the equivalent title in Welsh, *Wir Dduw* (a term likewise used colloquially to avow the veracity of a statement). He summarises Robinson's standpoint under two headings: his desire to make Christianity more acceptable to 'the secular men of our generation', and to proclaim that Christianity is for everybody, not just those who are religious and who feel guilty because of sin. 'In a word, the Bishop favours a Christianity plucked clean of its supernatural elements, a religionless Christianity.'[42] Accepting Robinson's claim meant putting aside the Bible and getting each one for himself to respond to the One who is the root of our existence. *Honest to God* was also guilty of misinterpreting grace and salvation, and of seeing prayer as 'openness to the ground of our being' and not as a child talking to its father.[43]

Church Unity

'This year [1962] we are in the strange position of being bombarded by much talk about uniting the churches and, at the same time, celebrating the memory of those who tore the Church apart three centuries ago.'[44] So wrote the author of the 'Sylwadau' (Comments) column in the Welsh magazine. Naturally it was the evangelicals who most frequently mentioned the celebration, the ecumenists being much troubled because of the unhappy dissensions. But that same year they were greatly encouraged by the generous promise of Sir David James to give a sum of money, on condition that the denominations move towards unity and collect a specific sum themselves.

The author of the 'Sylwadau' column expressed his fears about the proposal, and 'Meirchion' shared those worries.[45] Both saw the ecumenical activity as clearing the path for the establishment of one Protestant church. But they acknowledged the force of some of the arguments: that denominationalism was losing its meaning, that the Baptists and the Independents were more ready to accept a measure of centralisation; and, of course, the promise made by Sir David James. However, the basic question was, On what conditions could the Church expect God to be on its side? The ecumenical activity, with its emphasis on unity which might only be outward, could be a 'red herring' on the path of genuine Church renewal.[46]

'Meirchion' welcomed the writer Kate Roberts into the fray: he praised her article in *Y Drysorfa*, in which she argued for a return to the simplicity of the New Testament, meeting in homes, and giving generously to the needy of the world.[47] The 'Sylwadau' column welcomed E. Tegla Davies's daring statement in *Y Cymro*: 'In every period of renewal there is a shattering of unity similar to the shattering of a shell in spring so that the kernel might find earth to grow into a tree.'[48] Dr Martyn Lloyd-Jones also longed to see something new come into being, as he made abundantly clear in his television interview with Aneirin Talfan Davies.[49] The differences between interviewer and interviewee were obvious: the first stressed the importance of continuation, catholicity and the middle road; the second saw the urgent need for a new evangelical unity based on sound Biblical doctrine.

Tuag at Uno (Towards Unity) was published in 1963. The introduction explained that there should be theological agreement and agreement on church order. The doctrinal foundation for unity lay in the truths that had always been believed by the Church, and the church order should enable all its members to live together and promote the missionary witness. The central argument for unity was that it was God's will, and that divisions not only hindered the mission of the Church but denied its very nature. The publication enlarged upon the theological and organisational aspects, giving four and a half pages to the first and twelve to the second.

Both the *Cylchgrawn Efengylaidd* and the *Evangelical Magazine of Wales* were of the same opinion—that the respective space allotted to the two issues was very significant. Church organisation was given careful scrutiny, while the short doctrinal section was extremely ambiguous. The ambiguity could be likened to a solicitor reading out a will and telling the family not to worry about the meaning of the terms—they could interpret them in their own way.[50] Being too dogmatic about doctrine, it was said, posed the danger of restricting the Holy Spirit.[51] 'Did the 1823 Confession of Faith restrict the Holy Spirit?' asked the *Evangelical Magazine of Wales*. Were not the Methodist fathers abundantly blessed, and did they not enjoy the mighty power of the Holy Spirit in their churches?

The Christian Church

After many pamphlets had appeared in the name of the Movement, *The Christian Church* was published in 1966.[52] It was Dewi Eirug Davies who gave most attention to the booklet.[53] It must be said that some of his accusations were true: the booklet, and some individuals within the Movement, were too prone to condemn organisation and to doubt the intentions of ecumenists. Nevertheless, the two articles he wrote illustrate the chasm that can exist between the Evangelical Movement of Wales and its opponents.

The nature of the Bible

It is no surprise that one of his three central points was the nature of the inspiration and authority of the Bible. In the writer's opinion, the booklet failed to differentiate between the Bible, and the Word of God *in* the Bible. The evangelicals, he maintained, were guilty of stressing the letter rather than the saving works of God, as is true of the Protestant tradition: 'The Protestant emphasis is on the *works* of God , whilst the literalist emphasises the words recorded on the pages of the Bible.'[54] This is a misrepresentation of the truth. Neither Calvin nor even Luther would separate the words from the works as Dewi Eirug Davies maintains. Nor would anyone within the Evangelical Movement of Wales consider that there is such a separation.

The Movement claims a marriage, not a separation. It claims the sufficiency of the Scriptures not only as a basis for creed and conduct, but above all that we might discover the mind of Christ. The booklet states that very clearly. The Scriptures, it says, 'are sufficient, and the mind of Christ will never be found in the violation of them or of the principles which they enjoin'.[55] Who is to decide which portions of the

Bible are the Word of God? Is it the Pope, the Church, experience or reason? Dewi Eirug Davies is silent on the issue.

The nature of the Church

The other bone of contention is the nature of the Church. Who belongs to it? According to the Movement, those who have been born again. But according to Dewi Eirug Davies that emphasis is unscriptural, and he offered two reasons in support of his argument: that not everyone in the churches had experienced a vivid conversion, and that there are always wheat and tares in the church.[56] But the issue is not whether a person has experienced a 'vivid conversion', but whether he has experienced conversion. The nature and details of conversion are variables: the experience itself is not. Doubtless, for some of the Movement's supporters, conversion has been a 'Damascus road' experience, but all can testify to a personal knowledge of the Lord Jesus Christ. And were the New Testament authors not addressing believers—those who had been 'quickened', 'had passed from death to life', 'had received the implanted word' and been 'born from above'?

The argument about the wheat and the tares is a very precarious one. If Dewi Eirug Davies is referring to the biblical parable, then it is perfectly clear that the field is the world and not the Church. How strange that an Independent should argue like Augustine of old, whose emphasis promoted the idea of the Church as an establishment and not a fellowship of believers! His own denomination until recently held that the Church was a body of those who had believed in Jesus Christ. It is true that one can never be perfectly sure that every church member is born again. Church leaders are fallible, and they can make mistakes when receiving members, but each applicant should be accepted on the basis of faith in the resurrected Lord. The desire of the Movement is to see churches as pure as possible, while acknowledging at the same time that there is no such thing as a perfect church.

But despite every effort made by the Movement to explain its teaching, some critics insist on ignoring what it says about the Church. According to Gwyndaf Jones, it is trying to create perfect churches, though this has been firmly denied. He maintains that the New Testament way was to accept members 'on the basis of faith in Christ as a Saviour'. In *The Christian Church* it is stated that membership should be restricted to those who profess 'faith in Jesus Christ, the eternal Son of God, as Saviour, Lord and God, whose death in their place constitutes the only ground of their salvation'. The critic maintains that 'faith' and not 'experience' is the basis of church membership. The Movement argues that they cannot be separated. Faith in Christ is essential, but if it is not conjoined with experience there is a danger of believing with the mind only. Faith in Christ brings about a change in the believer's life, and one should 'examine with charity all candidates for membership, so as to ensure as far as humanly possible' that such a change has occurred. But it is faith in Christ that is the main consideration.[57]

A monopoly of truth

The third issue that troubles Dewi Eirug Davies is that the Movement is too ready to claim that it has a monopoly of the truth: it is always right and everyone else wrong.[58] It is possible to respond in two ways. The Movement believes that the truth has been revealed once and for all time, and it proclaims that positively; but it does not claim a monopoly in the understanding of it. For instance, Jesus Christ is the true Son of God; in him dwells 'all the fulness of the Godhead bodily'. This was not decided by the Movement; it is the irrefutable testimony of Scripture. Should the Movement be more broadminded and accept those that deny the divinity of Christ? If it were to do that, not only would it be disobedient to Scripture, but it would be denying his existence. The other thing that ought to be mentioned is that the Movement does acknowledge individuals, movements and evangelical churches that disagree with it on some matters of faith and church order.

The Movement ought not to avoid criticism, but such criticism should be fair, and based on the statements and literature of the Movement itself. Dewi Eirug Davies is inclined to pick out a certain point from the booklet and then generalise, oftentimes creating a fantasy of its contents. The booklet says that financial matters are 'secondary', but the critic says 'unimportant'. The booklet was introduced to facilitate country-wide evangelical unity, but Dewi Eirug Davies maintains that the interest of the Movement lies in 'spiritual' unity. He claims that in condemning good works the booklet is unscriptural, whereas in doing so it is in fact completely scriptural, because the clause mentioned is in the context of justification by faith alone, and 'alone' is the key word.[59] Sarcastically the writer says that there is some passing reference to showing mercy. So there is, but that is in the clause which refers to the work of the church; and the critic also fails to notice the reference to holiness in one of the clauses (4c). One could quote numerous other examples.

The author of the two articles does not like the dogmatic spirit of the evangelicals; he prefers to be broadminded. It is such a shame, he says, that the Movement presents a particular interpretation as the final truth. One would therefore expect Dewi Eirug Davies not to be dogmatic, and not to present a particular interpretation authoritatively. But when dealing with the Bishop of Woolwich and the ascension, this is what he says: 'Luke never thought of heaven as a place, and neither did he think of a body literally ascending to a place above the heavens.'[60] This sounds very much like a dogmatic statement. And he goes on to say that what we have is 'Luke's attempt to present a truth which is beyond the ability of words to express.'[61] If truth is beyond expression in words, then no one can know what the truth is.

In order to put the Movement in its place, Dewi Eirug Davies resorts to sarcasm. He refers to the statement that no difference should be made between clergy and laity—a statement made in the context of church leadership, and in the light of the priesthood of all saints. The booklet, he maintains, contradicts itself when it says that members do not have to understand the doctrines in their entirety, that only the leaders have to be able to do that. This has nothing whatsoever to do with the difference between a clergyman and a lay person; it merely accepts what is obvious to all, that leaders have a better understanding of doctrine than those seeking membership. The critic unsheathes his sword and takes a swipe: 'I dare say many a lay person thanks his lucky stars that infallible men sometimes slumber.'[62]

Neither the Evangelical Movement of Wales nor the booklet claims infallibility. Here is a statement from the booklet:

> If in any way at all we have strayed from the teaching of the Bible, then we invite our readers to inform us—and we trust we shall have the grace to be corrected. It is the desire to honour God by obeying Him that moves us.

Church developments

The committees of the Evangelical Movement of Wales urged individuals to be awake to church developments. From amongst the Baptists, Sulwyn Jones[63] and Gwilym Humphreys stated their opinions very clearly, as did Noel Gibbard from amongst the Independents. In the correspondence, there was no way of avoiding such vital issues as the authority of Scripture, the essentials of the faith, and church order. According to J. S. Williams, Tumble, those who could accept the authority of the Scripture were 'cranks'.[64] This statement clearly angered Gwilym Humphreys, and he responded that it was such attacks that brought people to a crossroads where they had to make a choice. J. S. Williams, he writes, ought not 'to find fault with us for bidding you farewell, and for saying why, and for promising to do our level best to prevent the people from following you.'[65]

Among the Independents, Huw Ethall and Emrys Jones were staunch ecumenists. The former was responsible for 'Colofn Undeb Eglwysig' (The Church Unity Column) in *Y Tyst*. He presented the usual ecumenical arguments, that unity was in accordance with the will of God, and that it was essential to promote the mission of the Church. 'Denominationalism' no longer counted, but rather 'catholicity'—a readiness to accept Christian unity everywhere without exception, of all denominations and of all countries.[66] In his respose Noel Gibbard dealt with the meaning of the words 'church' and 'churches', and argued in the light of this that the title 'The United Church of Wales' was misleading. The debate also encompassed doctrinal matters, Huw Ethall maintaining that there was already basic agreement, Noel Gibbard denying this, noting in particular the doctrine concerning the Person of Christ.[67]

The parameters of the discussion were widened after the Joint Committee of the denominations met following the Conference in Carmarthen in 1963, and *Yr Alwad i Gyfamodi* (The Call to Covenant) and *Cyfamodi* (Covenanting) were published, in 1966 and 1968 respectively. Initially, representatives of the Church in Wales, the Methodist Church, the Presbyterian Church of Wales and the Union of Welsh Independents met together; then representatives from the Welsh Province of the Congregational Church of England and Wales and the South Wales Area of the Baptist Union of Great Britain and Ireland were appointed, but representatives of the latter were unable to be present. Representatives of the Roman Catholic Church joined as observers in 1967.

In his column 'Sylwadau' in the *Cylchgrawn*, 'E. R.' drew attention to church developments. In his opinion, what was proposed in *Cyfamodi yng Nghymru* (Covenanting in Wales) was not the way to put first things first. 'Is that what comes first in the Ecumenical Movement: planning a better, stronger and more inclusive organisation?'[68] He could find no reference to grace, repentance and saving faith 'within its covers'. Aled Williams could not understand this objection to the desire to covenant. The formation of one Church was a World Council of Churches ideal, but it must begin locally. He maintained that the characteristics of the Church were clear in the booklet and that there was a way forward towards unity. 'E. R.' drew attention to the fact that only about a dozen paragraphs dealt directly with doctrine, whereas forty-one were given to the subject of the ministry. He also pointed out how the work of the Protestant Reformers divided the Church. If divisions call for repentance, then the Reformers were the most guilty in the history of the Church.[69]

Wales for Christ

During the same period the churches expressed a desire to work together in order to evangelise. In the 1968 annual meetings of the Union of Welsh Independents, Glyn Thomas (Wrexham) called the denominations to unite in a campaign to call Wales back to Christ. At the request of Trebor Lloyd Evans, the Administrative Committee of the same Union called a meeting in Aberystwyth in March 1969.[70] That meeting agreed to ask the Welsh Council of Churches to arrange a conference. It was held on 21 July, with a further meeting on 8 September, and the following were represented: the Society of Friends, the Presbyterian Church of Wales, the Methodist Church, the Roman Catholic Church, the Congregational Church of England and Wales, the Union of Welsh Independents and the Baptist Union of Great Britain and Ireland.

As part of the campaign it was agreed to distribute the Gospel of Mark, and the Movement was invited to join in the venture. The matter was discussed in the English Executive Committee under the leadership of Hugh D. Morgan on 20 November 1973. It was decided not to accept the invitation because of the difficulties of co-operating with those who were not only non-evangelical, but in some cases anti-evangelical; and there was the added difficulty of the presence of Roman Catholics. J. Elwyn Davies arranged to meet Morgan Mainwaring and Ieuan S. Jones in order to explain the Movement's standpoint. He was kindly received, and both men fully understood the feelings of the evangelicals.[71]

But many people in Wales were angered by the Movement's stance. *Y Cymro* seized on the story and gave it much publicity, mentioning remarks by Emyr Roberts and Gareth Davies, who was chairman of the General Committee at the time.[72] What worried Emyr Roberts was the danger of over-organisation, and he reminded the readers about 'Ymgyrch y Deffro' (The Awakening Campaign)—'a campaign that caused no one even to turn in his sleep'.[73] Gareth Davies was more concerned that it was putting the cart before the horse, but he was attacked by the editor of *Y Tyst*, suggesting that the presence of the Roman Catholic Church was the big bogey for the Evangelical Movement of Wales, and rejecting the 'fundamentalist shibboleths' of the evangelicals. Responding, Gareth Davies set before the readers a possible scenario—two people of opposite convictions evangelising with Wales for Christ, and someone asking them to explain the Gospel of Mark and enquiring about the way of salvation. Would that person not get two totally different—indeed two contradictory—answers?[74]

R. Tudur Jones in 'Tremion' (Glimpses/Views—his column in *Y Cymro*), did not totally condemn the campaign but was very critical of it. He mentioned that some campaign supporters were very dissatified with the 'prickly' way in which the editor of *Y Tyst* had handled the matter.[75] He also acknowledged the 'prudent' contribution of Gwynn Williams in *Y Cylchgrawn Efengylaidd*. But he was scathingly critical of 'Arweiniad Poblogaidd' (A Popular Leading): in his opinion it read like a 'short story'; it was offensive and a perfect example of middle-class snobbery. Many of the students of Bala-Bangor had ripped this page out of the booklet, 'and I heartily approved their action'.[76]

Criticism of the Movement's response to the Wales for Christ campaign also came from W. Eifion Powell. He considered its attitude immature, and thought its unwillingness to co-operate with other Christians a clear demonstration of pride. He was also concerned that the Movement was making missionary work a matter of public bickering.[77] The gist of the reply given by D. G. Davies of Cardiff was that there was a difference between distributing the Gospel of Mark and offering the gospel. Distributing posed no problem, but evangelising did, because the latter required credal agreement, not disagreement as, for instance, between Protestant and Papist.[78] Whilst disagreeing with Papists on some matters, W. Eifion Powell did not believe they taught heresy.[79] Noel Gibbard sent him a copy of the *Cylchgrawn* that explained the position of the Movement, but he remained critical, and attacked Cecil Jenkins for daring to say that in his opinion the Gospel of Mark was not the ideal choice because of the disagreement about the lengthy closing paragraph (though he himself accepted it). In response, W. Eifion Powell drew attention to the fact that the portion was italicised.[80] Gradually the storm subsided.

The Roman Catholic Church

The reign of peace was short-lived. During the Wales for Christ debate, frequent reference was made to the role of the Roman Catholic Church in the campaign, and one of the complaints against the Movement was its unwillingness to co-operate with Papists.[81] When plans were afoot to invite the Pope to Wales, and the Movement stated that as Protestant evangelicals they could not join in the welcoming ceremony, the peace was shattered.

When a joint statement was issued by a member of the Catholic Church, an ecumenical Presbyterian and an evangelical, the Movement decided to issue a statement to the Press.[82] It was published in a number of papers on Saturday 29 May 1982, but Celtic Press Limited refused to publish it in any of its papers in Glamorgan and Gwent.[83] J. Elwyn Davies expressed the Movement's disappointment at the refusal, and the editor-in-chief promised to include the statement as an advertisement; but when it came to settling terms, even that was refused. The explanation offered was: 'While we do not think that the copy would contravene our legal requirements, the content is such that we would exercise our right to refuse to accept the copy.'[84] The Celtic Press was littered with articles about the Pope's coming, but there was no space to express opposition.

In its statement, and in both its magazines, the Movement explained its position. This was not only a pastoral visit but also a diplomatic one. Immediately before the Pope was to leave Rome, it was announced from the Vatican—not from the Foreign Office—that the diplomatic relationship between Britain and the Holy See was to be raised to ambassadorial level. The Queen, the titular head of the Church of England, was to invite the Pope to Buckingham Palace. Never had any national leader received such a welcome in Britain. It was concern about this kind of development that Graham Harrison expressed in his article in the English magazine;[85] it was also what troubled the British Evangelical Council. The Council's statement, printed in the English, and also translated in the Welsh, magazine, expressed concern that 'a professed branch of the Christian Church dared to act as an earthly state', adding that 'historically the Roman Church has persistently sought to pursue its religious ambitions under secular as well as ecclesiastical auspices'.[86]

The all-important question was 'Has Rome changed?' Both Graham Harrison and Eryl Davies (writing in the *Cylchgrawn*) gave the same emphatic answer: 'Basically, no.'[87] They accepted that there had been some changes (for instance, the people had the Bible in the vernacular and were being urged to read it), but the Church of Rome could not change radically without denying its principal claim, '*Semper eadem*' (always the same). The two evangelical ministers were agreed that the face of Rome had changed. Since the Second Vatican Council (1962–1965), Protestants were no longer thought of as heretics but as 'separated brethren'; and as a result of the Charismatic Movement members of the Roman Church had come into a closer relationship with Protestants. The tragedy was that the Protestant Church had changed drastically, so much so, indeed, that one of the leaders of the Church of Scotland could suggest that past differences be forgotten.

J. Elwyn Davies enlarged upon some of the principal doctrines of the Church of Rome.[88] For one thing. it believes that regeneration happens at baptism—the child is cleansed from the stain of original sin and becomes a Christian. And this was certainly the teaching of the Second Vatican Council. What happened at baptism is then confirmed in the ceremony of confirmation. This is completely at odds with biblical teaching. The Word teaches that regeneration is the work of the Holy Spirit. One becomes a Christian by faith and repentance; one comes to God on the basis of the finished work of Christ and not through the mass; it is the good news about Christ, as preached by the apostles, which reconciles a sinner to God, not the sacraments. As a consequence of its teaching, the Church of Rome is an organisation which sees fit to lean on the power of the human arm to achieve its purposes. How, in all honesty, could the Church of Rome be considered a proper Church? This is the Church that accepts unrepentant sinners into its bosom, pronounces anathema on the doctrine of assurance, and insists that good works, penance, the mass and purgatory are essential to salvation. Cardinal Hume said that the Pope had a message for those outside the Papal fold; J. Elwyn Davies suggested that the evangelical faith also had something to tell the Roman Catholics.[89]

The Gospel and the Church

By the end of the eighties it was possible to look back upon ecclesiastical developments from the time of the meetings of the World Council of Churches in Montreal, Canada, in 1963, and the Second Vatican Council, 1962–1965. These developments were encompassed by Hywel R. Jones in his book *Gospel and Church* (Evangelical Press of Wales, 1989). He expresses the opinion that it was significant that the Catholics were present in Montreal as observers. During those meetings an attempt was made to understand the relationship between 'Tradition', 'tradition' and 'traditions'. The gospel is the 'Tradition'; the process of development which can elaborate on the 'Tradition' is the 'tradition'; the variety in the expression of the 'Tradition' and specific creeds within the different churches are the 'traditions'.[90]

This is the way, according to the ecumenical argument, not only to bring the Protestant churches closer together, but also to include the Church of Rome. That Church claims on the basis of 'tradition' that its doctrines concerning Mary the mother of Jesus should be accepted. That is made manifestly clear in the reports of the Second Vatican Council. The discussions between Anglicans and Catholics— 'The Anglican–Roman Catholic International Commission' (ARCIC)— were, according to Hywel Jones, similarly inclined. According to *Final Report* (ARCIC), the authority of God's Word is found through the written word, and one must therefore listen for that Word. It is the effect of Scripture, not its nature, that is given priority: it is the function of the Bible, and not its inspiration, that is all-important. Consequently, the central position is given to understanding the 'tradition' rather than the ultimate authority of the Word of God.[91]

This, according to the author of *Gospel and Church*, is a dangerous development. It is a denial of the historical Protestant teaching, and it means that any theological discussion must be an ecumenical discussion. The governing principle now is what promotes church unity; all other things are minor considerations. Whilst the Roman Church is putting more stress on the Bible without denying its own central teaching, the Protestants are putting more stress on the Church; but it is doubtful whether they can do so without losing sight of the central doctrines of Protestantism. The theological discussions have developed into ecclesiastical discussions, which means that the authority of the Bible has become a side issue.[92]

Hywel R. Jones also deals with other doctrines. He refers to the Eucharist, noting the use of the term 're-present' when referring to the death of Christ during the Mass—another attempt to bring Anglicans and Catholics closer together. The word protects the Roman doctrine, and gives Anglicans a means of explaining the term in the light of the Thirty-nine Articles. Not all within the Church of England accepted this. In the opinion of J. I. Packer, 'This may not be *exactly* a return to the Mass but it is *certainly* a reversal of the Reformation.'[93] The attitude of the ecumenical mind to the doctrine of justification by faith is precisely the same. In the volume *Salvation and the Church* (1987), the report maintains that the Council of Trent was criticised not by the reformers of Britain but by the reformers on the continent; but this analysis was refuted by many, including Alister McGrath, David Wright and Roger Beckwith.[94]

The key term is 'justification'. What does the word mean? Although *Salvation and the Church* accepts that it means 'proclaiming just', it does not refute the meaning 'making just'—yet another ecumenical attempt to bring Papists and Protestants together. It suggests that if faith is central, it can be explained in the Papist way or the Protestant way. That means that justification by faith is no longer one of the tests of the true church. The teaching of both Martin Luther and the Pope must be accepted. According to the report, 'Justification and sanctification are two aspects of the same divine act.'[95]

In the light of these developments, small wonder a change occurred in the attitude towards the mission of the Church. Hywel Jones traced this back to the replacing of the centrality of reconciliation between man and God by the relationship between man and his fellow man. It is man's welfare that is paramount, and social work is an essential part of mission. The author of *Gospel and Church* argues that this is unscriptural, but he also reminds his readers that the World Council of Churches refused to listen to critics within its own ranks, especially so Visser 't Hooft.[96] The Frankfurt Declaration (1970), formulated by Peter Beyerhaus of Tubingen and supported by others,[97] also expresses concern, and advocates a return to calling people to God through Christ, the only means of salvation. This was a complete antithesis of the emphasis that had prevailed since the days of the New Delhi meetings in 1962, when it was declared that there was a possibility of salvation for those who had never heard the gospel, because of the presence of Christ—'the anonymous Christ', so-called—behind all other religions.[98]

On the basis of this change in mission it is possible to focus on bringing people together, people of every tongue and religion. This is how Hywel Jones puts it: 'A cosmic Christ unites Jesus of Nazareth and other religious prophets and leaders, and a world spirit replaces the Holy Spirit of God and Christ.'[99] Another way of presenting the same message is to speak of the gospel of the kingdom, and explain this in socio-political terms. If social justice is not proclaimed, it is said, then the gospel is not being proclaimed. But the Movement argues that man must first receive that righteousness which is found in Christ, and then that righteousness must bear fruit in every part of his life. There is a difference between justification and sanctification, but they cannot be separated.

Fifty years

We have referred in this chapter to some of the most important events in the religious world during the half-century 1948–1998. The Evangelical Movement of Wales could not ignore them; they played a vital role in its task of putting its house in order.

At the same time it compelled it to look more carefully inside the house. Doubtless different people would see within the Movement different strengths and weaknesses. A few individuals were too harsh-spirited in its defence, and sometimes a conscientious Christian was unfairly condemned. During some periods the Movement was over-dependent on individuals, and sometimes mistakes were made in the appointment of workers. Nor did the Movement at all times succeed in keeping Welsh-speaking and non-Welsh-speaking members together, and some would be of the opinion that it neglected the Welsh witness. Whatever the faults, the Evangelical Movement of Wales is more than ready to accept that it will not prosper in its task unless it is ready to walk the path of submission and repentance.

Appendix 1
Doctrinal Basis

We accept the Holy Scriptures, as originally given, as the infallible Word of God, of divine inspiration. Recognising them as our sole authority in all matters of faith and practice, we believe the doctrines taught therein. We believe in particular the following:

1. in the only true and living God, the Holy Trinity of Divine Persons in perfect unity, Father, Son and Holy Spirit, each of whom is co-equal and co-eternal, and sovereign in creation, providence and redemption.

2   in the God and Father of our Lord Jesus Christ, who is holy, righteous, full of grace, mercy, compassion and love. In his infinite love he sent forth the Son, that the world through him might be saved.

3. in the Lord Jesus Christ, the incarnate Son of God, whose true humanity and full deity were mysteriously and really joined in the unity of his divine Person. We believe in his virgin birth, in his perfect life and teaching, in his substitutionary, atoning death on the cross, where he triumphed over Satan, sin and death, in his bodily resurrection and his ascension into heaven, where he now sits in glory at the right hand of God.

4. in the Holy Spirit, the third Person of the Godhead, whose work is indispensable to regenerate a sinner, to lead him to repentance, to give him faith in Christ, to sanctify the believer in this life and fit him to enjoy fellowship with God. For spiritual power and effectiveness his ministry is essential to the individual Christian and to the Church.

5. that as a result of the Fall all men are sinful by nature. Sin pollutes and controls them, infects every part of their being, renders them

guilty in the sight of a holy God, and subject to the penalty which, in his wrath and condemnation, he has decreed against it.

6. that through faith (and only faith) in the Lord Jesus Christ, whose death was a perfect oblation and satisfaction for our sins, the sinner is freely justified by God, who, instead of reckoning to us our sins, reckons Christ's righteousness to our account. Salvation is therefore by grace and not by human merit.

7. that the Lord Jesus Christ will return personally, visibly and gloriously to this earth, to receive his saints to himself, and to be seen of all men. As the righteous Judge, he will divide mankind into two, and only two, categories—the saved and the lost. Those whose faith is in Christ will be saved eternally, and will enter into the joy of their Lord, sharing with him his inheritance in heaven. The unbelieving will be condemned by him to hell, where eternally they will be punished for their sins under the righteous judgement of God.

Appendix 2
The Evangelical Press of Wales

The Evangelical Press of Wales (Gwasg Efengylaidd Cymru), now known as Bryntirion Press (Gwasg Bryntirion), produces books that present the Christian faith and tries to build up Christians. Since the early seventies, the number of titles in both Welsh and English has increased substantially, the English books by now selling in more than twenty countries worldwide. Already some 75 Welsh titles have appeared—excluding the 36-volume series *Bara'r Bywyd* (The Bread of Life)—and some 80 in English.

Selecting from the Welsh section, four groups of books may be mentioned. Firstly, the popular narrative essays of Mari Jones, *Trwy Lygad y Bugail* (1970, third edition 1989), *Yng Nghysgod y Gorlan* (1979, reprinted 1983), and *Daw'r Wennol Yn Ôl* (1992), translated into English under the titles *In the Shadow of Aran* (1972, six reprints), *In the Shelter of the Fold* (1979, second edition, 1992) and *When Swallows Return* (1992). Then there are two volumes dealing with theological matters, namely *Ysgrifau Diwinyddol I* (1979) and *II* (1988)—collections of theological essays written by men of evangelical and reformed persuasion, and edited by Noel Gibbard. One of the two most important single publications, possibly, was *Y Beibl i Blant mewn 365 o Storïau*, an adaptation by Julie Rhys Jones and Elisabeth James of *The Children's Bible* (Mary Batchelor). So far, 12,000 copies have been sold. The second is *Y Testament Diwygiedig Newydd* (1991), a revised version of the New Testament of 1620; 40,000 copies of this have already been distributed in our schools by the Gideons.

A great deal has been produced in English, the nine books by Peter Jeffery topping the sales chart. *All Things New* is especially valuable for those enquiring about the faith and those beginning the Christian life, and it has already been reprinted nine times. His *Christian Handbook* provides a simple and clear introduction to the Bible, church history, and Christian teaching. By 1992, J. Douglas

169

Macmillan's inspiring study of Psalm 23, *The Lord Our Shepherd* (1983), had seen six reprints. Eifion Evans' historical accounts of revivals, reminding us of God's mighty work in Wales in times past, are in regular demand. *Revival Comes to Wales* (1959), which deals with the 1859 revival, and *The Welsh Revival of 1904* (1969) have seen nine and seven reprints respectively. *Fire in the Thatch* (1996) is a volume of articles on the history and nature of revival, and *Pursued by God* (1996) comprises a metrical translation of *Theomemphus* by Williams Pantycelyn, together with an introduction to his life and work. Another valuable volume on the 1904 Revival is *Voices from the Welsh Revival* (1995) by Brynmor P. Jones.

But the most substantial publication, without doubt, is *Christian Hymns*, a collection of 901 hymns first published in 1977 under the editorship of Graham Harrison and Paul E. G. Cook. Besides being widely used in the four home countries it has been sold throughout the English-speaking world. Its continuing appeal rests largely on the fact that it caters for a wide variety of legitimate tastes and contains a good proportion of hymns with a healthy biblical, experiential content. Allied to this is the number of hymns written at times of spiritual awakening. Together with many tunes that are part of the rich heritage of Welsh hymnody, it contains several translations of Welsh hymns that otherwise would be unknown to English-speaking congregations, some of which were commissioned specially for the book. Despite the fact that a number of other hymnbooks have been published in recent years, *Christian Hymns* continues to be in demand both at home and abroad.

Many individuals have worked in the Press since its inception, several of them deserving special mention. E. Wyn James, with his administrative gift and editorial diligence, was largely responsible for its development during the years 1977–1993; Edmund T. Owen assisted in both the Movement Office and the Press from 1974 to 1996, and continues to do some voluntary work. From 1964 until her retirement in 1997, Brenda Lewis, on top of administrative work in the Office, was responsible for editing many of the English books (and continues to lend a ready hand), and for a number of those years she also undertook copy-editing for the *Evangelical Magazine of Wales*. Mair Jones, from 1956 until 1997, managed the Office and took on the onerous task of being chief compositor for Press books and magazines, and she too continues to help after retiring. Between 1996 and 1999 David Kingdon was manager of the Bryntirion Press.

Linked with the Press and the Movement, the Christian Bookshops have been of service to individuals and churches down the years. At present the Movement has nine shops: at Bangor, Wrexham, Bala, Ammanford, Swansea, Neath, Bryntirion (Bridgend), Llandrindod and Cardiff. Manning a stall in the annual Christian Booksellers Convention was for some years a boost to the work.

Since 1949 the Movement has had a tent on every National Eisteddfod field. Its sales there were at first confined to *Y Cylchgrawn Efengylaidd* and a few books, but by now they extend to a wide range of titles—it has indeed been another shop window for Press publications as they have increased from year to year. Advantage has also been taken of the Urdd Eisteddfod, more especially to exhibit and sell children's books.

Notes

Chapter 1

1. 'The greatest thrill was the nationalisation of the coal industry, the high water mark of fifty years' struggle', John Davies, *A History of Wales* (Penguin, 1990), 593.
2. Simon B. Jones and E. Lewis Evans, editors, *Sylfeini Heddwch* (Cymdeithas Heddwch yr Annibynwyr, 1945).
3. e.g. *Y Faner*, 2 February 1947.
4. J. E. Daniel: a theologian of note and a staunch nationalist; a professor in Bala–Bangor College. He left in 1946 to work in the Welsh Department of the Ministry of Education. The subject of a recent study by Dafydd Densil Morgan, *Torri'r Seiliau Sicr* (Llandysul, 1993).
5. Dewi Eirug Davies, *Diwinyddiaeth yng Nghymru, 1927–1977* (Gwasg Gomer, 1984), 242-3. A remark in *Y Dysgedydd*, 'The Fall and original sin are not mentioned in the volume [*Sylfeini Heddwch*], April 1945.
6. 'Yr Anifail Bras', Eples (Gomer, Llandysul, 1951): a volume of poems written by Gwenallt between 1943 and 1951.
7. Dewi Eirug Davies, *Diwinyddiaeth*, 238.
8. He published his pamphlet in 1947; dealt with it in an article, 'In Favour of Demolishing 75% of the Buildings', *Y Faner*, 5 October 1949.
9. It began among the Independent ministers, and developed into an inter-denominational movement, R. Tudur Jones, *Yr Undeb* (Abertawe, 1975), 357-8; W. B. Griffiths refers to this, 'Efengylu Heddiw', *Y Dysgedydd*, February 1947; the movement introduced, 'Nodion y Mis', *Y Dysgedydd*, September 1946.
10. Geraint D. Fielder, *Excuse Me, Mr Davies—Hallelujah!* (Evangelical Press of Wales, Bridgend, 1983), 82-5; there are also more details about the work in the colleges in the volume.
11. ibid., 115; Eluned Thomas, 'I Was There', *The Evangelical Magazine of Wales*, August–September 1998.
12. Personal interview with J. D. Williams, December 1997.
13. Personal interview with Herbert Evans during the Welsh Evangelical Conference in Aberystwyth, 1998; Kevin Adams notes, Bryntirion, Bridgend.
14. Personal interview with Harold Jones, 27 July 1998; he remembered Bessie Roberts, David T. Davies, Maldwyn Edwards [Lewis?], Mair Williams and Celia Davies.
15. Personal interview with John and Mari Jones, Bryn and Sylwen Davies, 28 July 1998.
16. J. Elwyn Davies, *O! Ryfedd Ras* (Gwasg Bryntirion, 1998), 13-16; personal interview with Elwyn and Mair Davies, 21 May 1998.
17. 'Parseli'r Bala Wedi Cyrraedd', *Y Faner*, 23 April 1947.
18. ibid., 'Y Newyn yn Ewrop', 15 October 1947.
19. *O! Ryfedd Ras*, 19.
20. ibid.
21. Personal interview with Elwyn and Mair Davies, 21 May 1998.
22. *O! Ryfedd Ras*, 19-20.
23. Personal interview with Elwyn and Mair Davies, 21 May 1998.

24. 'Cynhadledd Cristnogion Ieuanc y Byd', *Y Faner*, 20 August 1947.
25. *Y Faner*, 17 September 1947.
26. That man was Dan Jones, Goginan; his articles, 'Yr Ysgrifau o'r Almaen', 1 October 1947, 'Rwsia a'r Almaen', 29 October 1947.
27. Personal interview with Elwyn and Mair Davies, 21 May 1998.
28. ibid.
29. ibid.
30. A reference to this in 'Golwg ar Gymru', *Y Cylchgrawn Efengylaidd*, 21:5, 1984; the home was that of Mrs Eirwen Humphreys.
31. 'Dros Ysgwydd y Blynyddoedd', the autobiography of Emily Roberts in the care of John Emyr, Cardiff.
32. ibid.
33. ibid.
34. Personal interview with Mrs Eirwen Pritchard, 9 July 1998.
35. ibid. Daniel Powell Williams (1882–1947): see Eifion Evans, *The Welsh Revival of 1904* (Bryntirion Press, 2000), 193ff.
36. 'Dechreuadau', *Y Cylchgrawn Efengylaidd*, XI:1, 1969.
37. Personal interview with Elwyn and Mair Davies, 21 May 1998, and with Herbert Evans during the Welsh Evangelical Conference in Aberystwyth, 1998.
38. ibid.
39. Personal interview with Elwyn and Mair Davies, 21 May 1998.
40. According to Sylwen Davies, this was the verse, and not the one mentioned in *Excuse Me, Mr Davies—Hallelujah!*, 134. Personal interview with Bryn and Sylwen Davies, Elwyn and Mair Davies. For some reason Arthur Pritchard speaks of the vision on the Saturday, but many of those who were there testify that it occurred on Monday morning.
41. ibid.
42. ibid.
43. ibid.
44. Personal interview with Geraint Gruffydd, 2 September 1998.
45. Personal interview with Elwyn and Mair Davies, 21 May 1998; Kevin Adams notes, Bryntirion, Bridgend.
46. Personal interview with Gwilym Humphreys, 14 May 1998. Gwilym Humphreys became a Baptist minister in Llanllechid and Bethesda in North Wales; the warden of Bryn-y-groes, while caring for the Baptist cause in the town; a schoolteacher; and he now takes a leading role in the Evangelical Church at Talsarnau, near Harlech.
47. Personal interview with Harold Jones, 27 July 1998.
48. 'Ymgyrch dros Grist yn y Bala', *Y Seren*, 28 March 1947, 4.
49. *O! Ryfedd Ras*, 31.
50. ibid.
51. Personal interview with Elwyn and Mair Davies, 21 May 1998.
52. ibid.
53. Personal interview with Rina Macdonald, 10 July 1998, and a letter from Emily Roberts to Rina Macdonald, dated 22 April 1948, *Y Cylchgrawn Efengylaidd*, Winter 1995–6. The testimony of Meirionwen Davies can be found in Geraint D. Fielder's *Excuse Me, Mr Davies—Hallelujah!*, 143.
54. 'Yr Ymgyrch', *Y Seren*, April 1948, 5.
55. Personal interview with Elwyn and Mair Davies, 21 May 1998.

56. Personal interview with John and Mari Jones, Bala, 26 July 1998.
57. Personal interview with Arthur Wynn Williams, 27 July 1998.
58. A letter from I. D. E. Thomas, 30 December 1998.

Chapter 2

1. I. D. E. Thomas, 'Y Saith Mlynedd Hyn', *Y Cylchgrawn Efengylaidd*, III:5, 1955; he writes of three people going to Mr Evans, but there were four: J. Elwyn Davies, Arthur Pritchard, I. D. E. Thomas and Herbert Evans.
2. A personal interview with Elwyn and Mair Davies, 7 September 1998.
3. It appeared in November–December, 1948, and not in 1949 as reported in Iain Murray's *David Martyn Lloyd-Jones*, vol. 2, 247.
4. The names of the *Cylchgrawn* committee were first published in the March–April issue, 1:3—the three editors and Elwyn Davies; the Rev. W. H. Davies, Llanybydder (Chairman); Mr Arthur Pritchard, Blaenau Ffestiniog; Mr Geraint Griffiths, Aberystwyth; the Rev. Glyn Williams, Bethel; and Miss Emily Roberts, Derwen.
5. Gwyn Walters: for more information: 'Holi Dr Gwyn Walters', *Y Cylchgrawn Efengylaidd*, 24:1, 1987; 'Cofio Gwyn Walters', ibid., Winter 1993–4.
6. A letter from I. D. E. Thomas, 30 December 1998.
7. A personal interview with Geraint Morgan, 10 May 1998.
8. Information received from Elwyn Davies.
9. A personal interview with Eirwen Pritchard, 9 July 1998.
10. An undated letter from Emyr Roberts to Glenys Jones (mother of the Rev. John Glyn, Waun-fawr), in the care of John Emyr.
11. 'Atgofion', Mrs Grace Roberts, by kind permission of John Emyr.
12. Many tributes were paid to Emyr Roberts in various publications. Two of them: R. Geraint Gruffydd, 'Emyr Roberts', *Y Faner*, 13 May 1988; J. Elwyn Davies, 'Yr Anwylaf o'r Anwyliaid', *Y Cylchgrawn Efengylaidd*, 25:3, 1988. Examples of the works of Emyr Roberts: *Y Ffydd a Roddwyd* (Y Bala, 1957, 2nd edition Pen-y-bont ar Ogwr, 1980), *Mae Heddiw Wedi Bod* (Llys Eisteddfod Genedlaethol Cymru, 1973), *Dyddiau Gras* (Pen-y-bont ar Ogwr, 1993).
13. 'Dan Groen y Gweinidog', *Y Cylchgrawn Efengylaidd*, 22:3, 1985.
14. A personal interview with Rina Macdonald, 30 July 1998.
15. ibid.
16. A letter from Mari Davies (later Jones) to 'Dear friends' (the family of Emyr Roberts, Trefor), 11 May.
17. Personal interview with Mari Jones, Bala, 28 July 1998. Also, Iain Murray, *David Martyn Lloyd-Jones*, vol.2, 210-11.
18. Personal interview with Geraint Morgan, 10 May 1998. A report of the Eisteddfod may be seen in *Y Faner*, 10 August 1949.
19. 'Arwyddion yr Amseroedd', *Y Cylchgrawn Efengylaidd*, 1:7, 1949.
20. ibid.
21. 'Eisteddfod Dolgellau', 1:6, 1949. Elwyn Evans, the son of Wil Ifan, arranged this: Iain Murray, *David Martyn Lloyd-Jones*, 211.
22. Diary (1), Emily Roberts.
23. ibid.
24. Mair Eluned Davies and Rina Macdonald, 'Emily Roberts', *Y Cylchgrawn Efengylaidd*, October 1995.
25. Diary (1), Emily Roberts.
26. 'Y Dyddiau Cynnar', *Y Cylchgrawn Efengylaidd*, X1:1, 1969.

27. Diary (2), Emily Roberts.
28. A personal interview with Geraint Gruffydd, 2 September 1998.
29. The Rev. H. H. Williams: a native of Tal-y-sarn, Caernarvonshire; he ministered in the Rhondda, in Whitland and Cross Hands in Carmarthenshire, in Hirwaun in Glamorgan, and Cemaes in Montgomeryshire; on his retirement, moved to Tŷ-croes, Ammanford.
    This period was of great benefit to me personally; I used to join the group in Cross Hands regularly, and had the privilege of being present in the Foelgastell campaign.
30. 'Pabell y Cylchgrawn', *Y Cylchgrawn Efengylaidd*, 3:2, October 1954.
31. Information from Elwyn Davies; an announcement inside the back cover of *Y Cylchgrawn Efengylaidd*, 2:12, 1953-4.
32. A report in *Y Cylchgrawn Efengylaidd*, 2:7, 1952. It is difficult to understand this remark by Iain Murray: 'Humanly speaking, this came more by accident than design', *David Martyn Lloyd-Jones*, vol. 2, 247.
33. A personal interview with Derek and Ceinwen Swann, 15 September 1999.
34. 'Cynhadledd y Cylchgrawn Efengylaidd', *Y Faner*.
35. *Y Faner*, op.cit.
36. Diary (2), Emily Roberts.
37. 'Cynhadledd y Cylchgrawn', *Y Cylchgrawn Efengylaidd*, 111:VI, 1955-6; personal memories.
38. A personal interview with Geraint Morgan, 10 May 1998.
39. 'Y Cylchgrawn Mewn Gwledydd Tramor', *Y Cylchgrawn Efengylaidd*, 111:1V, 1955-6.
40. ibid., 'Hwnt ac Yma', 2:10, 1953.
41. ibid.
42. A personal interview with Elwyn and Mair Davies, 24 September 1998.
43. A personal interview with Rhiain Lewis, 2 September 1998.
44. ibid.
45. ibid.

Chapter 3

1. A summary of events in the history of the Evangelical Movement in a leaflet found among committee minutes in Bryntirion.
2. Diary (4), Emily Roberts, 4 June 1954.
3. Dr Martyn Lloyd-Jones favoured 'evangelical movement' because the churches in general were moving further away from the historical Protestant faith, but his ideal was to see the establishing of 'evangelical churches'. There is an account of the Denbigh Conference in *Y Cylchgrawn Efengylaidd*, III.VI, 1955-6.
4. A typewritten sheet in the records: 'Evangelical Movement Sub-Committees'.
5. Diary (6), Emily Roberts.
6. e.g. *Dechrau Canu: Rhai Emynau Mawr a'u Cefndir* (Gwasg Efengylaidd Cymru, 1987); *Carolau a'u Cefndir* (Gwasg Efengylaidd Cymru, 1989); ed. *Rhyfeddaf Fyth* (Gwasg Gregynog, 1998).
7. 'and he gave some . . .' (tributes to J. Elwyn Davies), *The Evangelical Magazine of Wales*, June–July 1990; 'Sgwrs â J. Elwyn Davies' (ed.); Hywel Davies, 'Ar Yr Aelwyd', *Y Cylchgrawn Efengylaidd*, Summer 1990.
8. 'Meeting Point: an Interview with G. Wyn Davies', *The Evangelical Magazine of Wales*, October–November 1993; 'Sgwrs â Gerallt Wyn Davies', *Y Cylchgrawn Efengylaidd*, Autumn 1993.

9. *The Evangelical Magazine of Wales*, first issue, March 1955. The first committee: the two editors, the Revs J. Elwyn Davies, Blaenau Ffestiniog, and J. Glyn Owen, Wrexham; the Revs I. D. E. Thomas, Caernarfon; J. D. Williams, Ammanford; T. Arthur Pritchard, Llanelli; Emyr Roberts, Trefor; J. Haines-Davies, Aberystwyth; Mr Geraint Gruffydd, Aberystwyth; Mr Herbert Evans, Blaenau Ffestiniog; and Miss Emily Roberts, Llanymawddwy.

10. The Conference was welcomed to Sandfields by John Thomas in an article in *The Evangelical Magazine of Wales*, 1:7, 1957.

11. A letter from Eluned Harrison, 26 October 1998.

12. A personal interview with Elwyn and Mair Davies, 7 September 1998.

13. A personal interview with Derek and Ceinwen Swann, 15 July 1999.

14. A personal interview with Elwyn and Mair Davies, 7 September 1998.

15. Iain Murray, *David Martyn Lloyd-Jones, Letters 1919–1981* (Banner of Truth, 1994), 136. 'It seems to me that you [Elwyn Davies] and Elizabeth Braund and Packer should meet fairly soon in order to plan the first issue. It is very important that it should be done properly.'

16. *The Evangelical Magazine of Wales*, 1:16, 1960.

17. ibid., a series during 1960–61. Eryl Davies, 'An Address' (unpublished), 'The Bala Ministers' Conference'. Minutes of General Committee, 26 December 1956; 'Y Daflen Newyddion', 11 November 1959; 'News Sheet', 1, 1960.

18. ibid., 1:10, 1959; also, 'On the Study of God', first of series, 1:23, 1961.

19. ibid., 1:16, 1960.

20. ibid., 1:13, 1960. The arrangement between the two committees (England and Wales) continued until 1962, Minutes of the General Committee, 10 April 1962.

21. Minutes of the Fellowship of Presbyterian Ministers.

22. ibid., 27 January 1956. Malcolm Evans and Derek Swann (Cong.), and Vernon Higham (CM) were present.

23. Cilgwyn, June 1957. The matter was broached for the first time by Russell Jones, Minutes of Executive Committee, 5 November 1956.

24. Eryl Davies, 'The History of the Bala Ministers Conference'.

25. *The Evangelical Magazine of Wales*, special issue, April 1981; another example in Iain Murray, *D. Martyn Lloyd-Jones*, vol. 2, 700-1.

26. Eryl Davies, 'The History of the Bala Ministers Conference'.

27. Minutes of the Ministers Committee for the different years.

28. *Theological Training Course*: Graham Harrison, Hywel Rhys Jones and Andrew Davies, assisted at the time of writing by Philip Eveson, Derek Swann, Roger Welch, Peter Clement and Stephen Clark.
    Welsh Theological Course: this began as meetings in Bala under the leadership of Elwyn Davies, Gwynn Williams, Geraint Morgan and Noel Gibbard; then meetings were arranged in South Wales, in Tŷ Brasil and Bryntirion, Gwyn Davies and Iwan Rhys Jones joining as tutors.
    Christian Study Course: Eryl Davies, Gwilym Roberts and Noel Gibbard.

29. Graham Harrison, *The First Eight Years, 1972–1980*; information from Graham Harrison.

30. An English committee was formed: Derek Swann (chairman), Gerald Smith, John Thomas, Brynmor Jones (secretary), Dilys John, Mary Lewis, Pam Williams, Ceinwen Matthews, Brenda Lewis, Brian Holding, J. Elwyn Davies. There was already a Welsh committee.

31. Minutes of the General Committee, 18-20 April 1961. J. Elwyn Davies and

Gwilym Humphreys were asked to formulate the appeal.

32. A personal interview with Elwyn and Mair Davies, 24 September 1998.

33. The Movement representatives were Elwyn Davies, John Thomas and Emyr Roberts, Minutes of the General Committee, 27-28 September 1961.

34. Minutes of the General Committee, 23, 24 February, 10 April 1962 The following were asked specifically to keep an eye on developments within the denominations: B. J. Alsopp and Gwilym Humphreys (B), Noel Gibbard and Derek Swann (I), Eifion Evans and John Thomas (CM), and Gordon Macdonald (W), Minutes of the General Committee, 26 June 1962.

35. Observations on the Report of the Joint Committee of the Four Denominations; another was written by Gwilym Humphreys, *Ai Uno Yw'r Ateb?* (Is Union the Answer?).

36. Iain Murray, *Letters*, op. cit., 163-4, 169-70.

37. Minutes of Ministers Committee, 24 June 1964; Executive Committee, 8 November, 14 December 1965; General Committee, 14, 15 January 1966.

38. Minutes of Ministers Committee, 14 June 1966.

39. Iain Murray, *D. Martyn Lloyd-Jones*, vol. 2, 314-20.

40. ibid., 544-50, and the discussion, chapter 17.

41. Minutes of General Committee, 1 May 1967.

42. J. Elwyn Davies, *Striving Together* (1984), 52(ii).

43. ibid., 'Appendix B' for full details.

44. J. Elwyn Davies, 'British Evangelical Council', *The Evangelical Magazine of Wales*, 6:6, 1967/68. The British Evangelical Council was formed in Edinburgh in 1952. Evangelical churches in membership could not only discuss relevant matters together but also act together upon decisions taken. Membership terms are not as broad as those of the Evangelical Alliance.

Chapter 4

1. 'Yma a Thraw', *Y Cylchgrawn Efengylaidd*, 1:2,1:3, 1:4, 1:5.

2. ibid., 1:4.

3. ibid.

4. Diary (1), Emily Roberts, 26 April 1950; the speakers were Idris Davies, Ammanford; David Shepherd, Gorseinon; Glan Rees, Llandudno; Gwyn Walters and others.

5. Personal interview with Elwyn and Mair Davies, 9 July 1998.

6. *Y Cylchgrawn Efengylaidd*, 2:12, Winter 1953–4.

7. 'Hwnt ac Yma', *Y Cylchgrawn Efengylaidd*, 3:3, Winter 1954–5.

8. Diary (4), Emily Roberts, 22-24 September 1954.

9. 'Y Daflen Newyddion', 1, 1959.

10. 'From the Secretary's Desk', *The Evangelical Magazine of Wales*, 2:12, 1964.

11. ibid., 'News and Comment', 7:6, 1969.

12. e.g. 5:2, 5:3, 1966.

13. Information from the late Brynmor P. Jones.

14 'An Opportunity', *The Evangelical Magazine of Wales*, 2:11, 1964.

15. Minutes of the General Committee, 15, 16 September 1967.

16. ibid., 17, 18 November 1969.

17. Minutes of the Welsh Executive Committee, 26 March 1971, 19 February, 13 October 1980.

18. ibid., 1 October 1973.

19. Minutes of the General Committee, 12 October 1973.
20. An Open Letter, *Y Cylchgrawn Efengylaidd*, XIII:5, 1974.
21. 'Efengylu yng Nghymru', *Y Cylchgrawn Efengylaidd*, XV:3, 1975 (not XV:2 as stated on cover).
22. A personal interview with Ifan Mason Davies, 2 September 1998. See also 'Y Fan Lyfrau', *Y Cylchgrawn Efengylaidd*, XV:2, 1975.
23. 'O ddrws i Ddrws', *Y Cylchgrawn Efengylaidd*, Winter 1993-4.
24. First edition, 1970, ed. D. Bryn Jones; second edition 1973, eds. Dilys C. Evans, Ceinwen Elias and Brenda Lewis.
25. Minutes of the General Committee, 28,29 March 1979.
26. 'Y Disgwyl Am . . .', *Y Cylchgrawn Efengylaidd*, Winter 1991-2.
27. 'I Batagonia Bell', *Y Cylchgrawn Efengylaidd*, Summer 1996. Eluned Morgan (1870–1938): author and religious leader in Patagonia; born on board ship in the Bay of Biscay, she was the daughter of Lewis Jones, one of the pioneers of the Colony in Patagonia, and was deeply influenced by the Revival of 1904–05, *Dictionary of Welsh Biography*.
28. Gerallt Wyn Davies, 'Tyrd â'r Llyfrau', *Y Cylchgrawn Efengylaidd*, Summer 1996; Ian Shaw, 'Bring the Books', *The Evangelical Magazine of Wales*, 28:2, 1989.
29. A letter from T. Arthur Pritchard to Emyr Roberts, 4 May 1959.
30. A letter from Emyr Roberts to 'My dear friends' (Pantyneuadd), 22 January 1951.
31. ibid.
32. ibid., 'Sunday morning', no date, to 'Miss Glenys Jones'; later the mother of the Rev. John Glyn, Waunfawr.
33. A letter from Joan Hughes, Caernarfon, 4 March 1998.
34. Personal interview with Harold Jones, 27 July 1998.
35. Information from Geraint Morgan, Rina Macdonald, and Mr and Mrs Arthur Wynn Williams.
36. Diary (2), Emily Roberts, 29 August 1951.
37. A letter from Mari Davies (later Jones) to Emyr Roberts, 29 November 1950.
38. Diary (1), Emily Roberts, 9 June 1950.
39. ibid., (3), 21 February 1953.
40. ibid., (2), 19 May 1951.
41. ibid., (5), 9 September 1959.
42. ibid., (3), 14 July 1953.
43. A letter from Emyr Roberts to Mari Davies (Jones), 22 January 1951.
44. Information from Geraint Morgan and Meirion Thomas.
45. Information from Leslie James and Eryl Davies.
46. Information from Dilys John and Bryant Seymour.

Chapter 5

1. 'Pay the Cow-shed Ten Shillings', *The Evangelical Magazine of Wales*, 9:6, 1970.
2. ibid.
3. ibid., 11:1,3,4, 1972.
4. Personal interview with Gordon Macdonald, 9 September 1998.
5. ibid.
6. ibid.
7. ibid. [Agreed] 'to invite Mr Macdonald to become Assistant Secretary for North Wales, and as such to have pastoral and evangelistic oversight of the work in North Wales, and also to assume for the time being, administrative responsibility for

Bryn-y-groes.' Minutes of the General Committee, 1 May 1967.

8. *Y Cylchgrawn Efengylaidd*, 34:4, 1997.
9. ibid.
10. *Y Cylchgrawn Efengylaidd*, XI1:1, 1971, and information from the Rev. Dafydd Job.
11. ibid.
12. ibid.
13. ibid.
14. *Y Cylchgrawn Efengylaidd*, 21:5, 1984.
15. Information from John Owen and Alun Williams, Colwyn Bay.
16. *Y Cylchgrawn Efengylaidd*, 21:5, 1984.
17. ibid., 19:3, 1980–81.
18. ibid., 26:5, 1989.
19. The magazines mentioned above, and information from the Rev. Hywel Davies.
20. 'Cartref Newydd yn y Brifddinas', *Y Cylchgrawn Efengylaidd*, Spring 1998; personal information.
21. ibid.
22. Information from Winford Thomas, Swansea, and Robert Rhys, Carmarthen.
23. 'Adfer yng Nghaerfyrddin', *Y Cylchgrawn Efengylaidd*, 19:6, 1981.
24. *A Church is Born* (1999), 'The story of the formation, establishment and development of Carmarthen Evangelical Church'. Information from Winford Thomas, Swansea, and Robert Rhys, Carmarthen; in 1999 Dafydd Protheroe Morris resigned from the ministry of the Welsh church in order to focus his attention on the English cause, and in the same year Geraint Lloyd accepted the invitation of the Welsh church to be their minister.
25. *Y Cylchgrawn Efengylaidd*, 19:2, 1980.
26. ibid.
27. Information from Ioan Davies, Bala.
28. Information from Gareth Jones, Lampeter.
29. Information from Meirion Thomas, Pontarddulais.
30. *The Evangelical Magazine of Wales*, 9:3, 1970.
31. ibid., 'Focus on Wales', 10:1, 1971; 'Five New Churches in Clwyd', *Evangelical Times*, March 1975.
32. ibid., information from Arthur Wynn Williams and Basil Howlett, Borras Park.
33. *Evangelical Times*, March 1975.
34. Information from the Rev. Gwilym Roberts. In 1999 Wyn Hughes began his ministry in Caergwrle. A member of the Cardiff Welsh Evangelical Church, he studied in the London Theological Seminary.
35. *Evangelical Times*, March 1975.
36. ibid., 'Holywell Evangelical Church', *The Evangelical Magazine of Wales*, 21:3, 1982.
37. *Evangelical Times*, March 1975; *The Evangelical Magazine of Wales*, 14:4, 1975, 15:3, 1976.
38. An anniversary leaflet from John Davies, Flint, 'Flint Evangelical Church, The First 25 Years, 1974–1999'. John Davies ministered in Clydach, Swansea Valley, before succeeding his brother Eryl Davies in Maesteg.
39. *Evangelical Times*, March 1975.
40. *Church Handbook* (Deeside Evangelical Christian Church), 1984, 1994; *Evangelical Times*, March 1975.

41. *The Evangelical Magazine of Wales*, 10:2, 1971. The churches of Mount Pleasant and Bethel, Ely, left in 1968 without contacting the Evangelical Movement. *Whether It Be Right?* was published to explain their standpoint.
42. ibid., 10:2, 4, 1971. Maesteg: information from Dr Eryl Davies; Heath: Leighton Hargest, compiler, *Holding Forth the Word of Life* (Heath Christian Trust, 2000); Malpas Road: information from Meirion Thomas.
43. Eryl Davies, Vernon Higham, Hubert Clement, *If We Neglect*, April 1970. Hubert Clement did not leave the denomination.
44. *The Evangelical Magazine of Wales*, 10:3, 1971.
45. Robert Horn, 'Crying Peace When There is None', *The Evangelical Magazine of Wales*, 11:3, 1972.
46. ibid., 11:1, 1972.
47. ibid., 10:3, 1971.
48. Cecil Northcott, 'With the Congs', *Time and Tide*, 25 May 1961.
49. 'Emerging Churches Confer', *The Evangelical Magazine of Wales*, 10:2, 1971.
50. Information from the Rev. Gwilym Roberts, Caergwrle; Minutes of the General Committee, 1, 2 October 1986.
51. Minutes of the Welsh Executive Committee, 23 January, 11 March 1987.
52. Minutes of the General Committee, 17, 18 November 1987, stating that 66 were present in Llandrindod, 'Brief Report' says 65: 'A brief report of the meeting of delegates from Evangelical Churches in Wales to inaugurate an Associating Churches Council'; an English letter to ministers and church leaders, signed by Elwyn Davies and Graham Harrison and dated December 1987. It explains the relationship between the Associating Churches and the Movement: 'Through taking its place as an integral but autonomous part of the EMW, and being represented on its General Committee by eight representatives which it shall appoint, the ACC will be linked with the provision for ministry, fellowship and witness already established through the work of EMW.'

Chapter 6

1. *Y Llwybrau Gynt*, vol. 2, 25.
2. J. Elwyn Davies, 'I Gofio Ingeborg', *Y Cylchgrawn Efengylaidd*, 1:2, 1949.
3. ibid.
4. ibid.
5. *Canmlwyddiant Capel Calfaria Aberdâr, 1852–1952*, 32-6.
6. J. Elwyn Davies 'Cofio Celt', *Gorwelion*, Llangefni Church Magazine, Winter 1998.
7. ibid.
8. Personal interview with Enid Jones, Dowlais, 14 July 1999; 'I Gofio Aled', *Y Cylchgrawn Efengylaidd*, 1:11, 1951.
9. 'I Gofio Rol', *Y Cylchgrawn Efengylaidd*, 2:3, 1952.
10. ibid., 'I gofio Grace'.
11. 'Dyfi Rhys', *Y Cylchgrawn Efengylaidd*, 111:V111, 1956.
12. J. Elwyn Davies, 'Adroddiad', typescript in Bryntirion.
13. Iain Murray, ed., *Letters*, 134-5.
14. J. Elwyn Davies, 'Adroddiad'.
15. 'Eryl Aran', *Y Cylchgrawn Efengylaidd*, III:12, 1958.
16. ibid., IV:2, 1958; 'Gwaith Duw ym Mryn-y-groes', Summer 1997.
17. ibid.

18. ibid.
19. ibid., editorial, IV:8, 1960.
20. Personal interview with Elwyn and Mair Davies.
21. 'A Day To Remember', *The Evangelical Magazine of Wales*, 10:5, 1971; 10:2 of the same year.
22. ibid., 'Focus on Wales', 19:3, 1980.
23. 'Cenedlatholdeb y Cristion', *Y Cylchgrawn Efengylaidd*, IX:4.

Chapter 7
1. *Y Cylchgrawn Efengylaidd*, I:1, 1948.
2. *Evangelicalism in Modern America* (Eerdmans, 1984), ix; ibidem, *Evangelicalism in Modern Britain* (1993, second edition), 2-3.
3. R. Tudur Jones, *Grym y Gair a Fflam y Ffydd* (Bangor,1998), chapter 14.
4. Reviews of the book appeared in Welsh: T. J. Russell Jones, *Y Cylchgrawn Efengylaidd*, IV:1, 1958; Noel Gibbard, *Y Tyst*, 24 July 1958.
5. e.g. N. B. Stonehouse and Paul Woolley, *The Infallible Word* (Tyndale, 1964); B. B. Warfield, *The Inspiration and Authority of the Bible* (London, ed. 1951); Douglas Johnson, *The Christian and his Bible* (IVF, 1953), and E. J. Young, *Thy Word is Truth* (Eerdmans, 1957).
6. J. I. Packer, *Fundamentalism and the Word of God*, 89.
7. ibid., 76.
8. ibid., 79, and Appendix 1.
9. ibid., chapters V and VI.
10. ibid., 127.
11. ibid., 85.
12. ibid., 102-4.
13. J. Stafford Wright, *Interpreting the Bible* (IVF, 1955); A. M. Stibbs, *Understanding God's Word* (IVF, 1950).
14. Emyr Roberts, *Cyrraedd Trwy'r Glustog* (Gwasg Gee, 1971), 85, 86.
15. e.g. Eryl Davies, *The Ultimate Rescue* (Evangelical Press, 1995), chapters 21 and 26. A book which continues to be influential is James Denney's *The Death of Christ*, first published in 1902; the 1952 edition was edited by R. V. G. Tasker (London, Tyndale Press).
16. 'Can People Be Saved Without the Gospel?', *The Evangelical Magazine of Wales*, 19:6, 1980-1; Hywel R. Jones, *Only One Way* (Bromley, 1996).
17. Eryl Davies, 'The Dark World of the Occult', *The Western Mail*, 11 August 1992; ibidem, the same title in *The Evangelical Magazine of Wales*, 31:4, 1992. Regarding deviations from the faith: Eryl Davies, *Truth Under Attack* (Darlington, Evangelical Press, 1990, 1995).
18. See also chapter 1.
19. Personal interview with Geraint Gruffydd, 2 September 1998, and his article, 'Atgof am J. E. Daniel', *Y Cylchgrawn Efengylaidd*, XV111:4, 1979.
20. Personal interview with Geraint Gruffydd, 2 September 1998.
21. Personal interview with Bobi Jones, 3 September 1998.
22. ibid. John Emyr's *Writers of Wales: Bobi Jones* (Cardiff, 1991) is an excellent introduction to the work of Bobi Jones.
23. Information from David Norbury.
24. 'Billy the Kid in Wales', *Evangelicals Now*, November 1966.
25. Personal interview with Geraint Morgan, 10 May 1998.

26. Personal memories; interview with Elwyn and Mair Davies.
27. Personal interview with Elwyn and Mair Davies.
28. ibid., George Griffiths, *What God Hath Wrought* (Port Talbot, 1962), 10-11.
29. ibid. When Emily Roberts and Elwyn Davies were on a journey in South Wales, they visited the signal box 'where Cecil Griffiths works, his prayers for revival rising like incense heavenwards', Diary (5), Emily Roberts, 2 September 1959.
30. 'Focus on Wales', *The Evangelical Magazine of Wales*, 12:5, 1973.
31. *Y Cylchgrawn Efengylaidd*, IV:6, 1959, XV:1, 1972; *The Evangelical Magazine of Wales*, 1:20, 1961, 4:3, 1965.
32. Eifion Evans, *Fire in the Thatch* (Evangelical Press of Wales, 1996), 13-14.
33. Emyr Roberts, R. Geraint Gruffydd, *Revival and its Fruit* (Evangelical Library of Wales, 1981), 4.
34. D. Martyn Lloyd-Jones, *Revival* (Marshall Pickering, 1986), 105.
35. ibid., 108-10.
36. I. D. E. Thomas, *God's Harvest*, 16.
37. *Revival*, 134-5.
38. ibid., 136-42.
39. ibid.
40. *Revival and its Fruit*, 10-11; *Fire in the Thatch*, 18.
41. *Revival*, 7.
42. ibid., chapters 20 to 24.
43. *Revival and its Fruit*, 4-5.
44. *Fire in the Thatch*, 18.

Chapter 8

1. 'Y Diwylliant Cymraeg a'r Beibl', *Y Cylchgrawn Efengylaidd*, VI:5, 1965.
2. *Crist a Chenedlaetholdeb*, 40. The novel *Rhys Lewis* is available in an English translation.
3. 'Sgwrs â J. Elwyn Davies', *Y Cylchgrawn Efengylaidd*, Summer 1990.
4. ibid., 'Os Wyt Gymro', 24:2, 1987. Also J. Elwyn Davies, 'Nationhood and Language', *The Evangelical Magazine of Wales*, 28:4, 1989.
5. *Crist a Chenedlaetholdeb*, 127.
6. 'Daniel',' 'Comment', *The Evangelical Magazine of Wales*, 27:4, 1988; Editorial, *Y Cylchgrawn Efengylaidd*, 26:1, 1989.
7. *Crist a Chenedlaetholdeb*, 8.
8. J. Gwyndaf Jones, *Y Cylchgrawn Efengylaidd*, X:3, 1969; minutes of the General Committee, 9, 10 October 1964.
9. Minutes of the Welsh Executive Committee, 15 October, 12, 13 November 1971, 28 January, 17 April 1972.
10. Emyr Roberts in 1973, *Mae Heddiw Wedi Bod*; Dafydd Ifans in 1974, *Eira Gwyn yn Salmon*.
11. e.g. Eifion Evans, *When He is Come* (1959) and (under another title) *Revival Comes to Wales* (1979), *The Welsh Revival of 1904* (1969), *Fire in the Thatch* (1996); E. Wyn James, *Trysorau Gras, Detholiad o rai o emynau gorau'r Gymraeg* (1979), *Dechrau Canu* (1987), *Carolau a'u Cefndir* (1989).
12. e.g. David Boorman in *The Evangelical Magazine of Wales*, 'Vavasor Powell' 21:3, 1982, 'Howell Harris', 22:1, 1983. In *Y Cylchgrawn Efengylaidd*: Eifion Evans, 'Walter Brute', 10:1, 1971, 'Daniel Rowland', V:7, 1963; Gwilym Humphreys, 'Ar Drywydd Vavasor', XVIII: 1,2,3, 1979, 'Cynfal Fawr a Rhai o'i Bobl', Spring

1998, 'Hugh Owen, Bronclydwr', Summer 1998; Noel Gibbard, 'Stephen Hughes', 'Vavasor Powell', V:4, 5, 1962.

13. *Y Cylchgrawn Efengylaidd*, 20:1; 21:5.
14. e.g. Siôn Aled, John Mainwaring, Dafydd Job and Noel Gibbard, and Geraint Gruffydd praised the poems of Bethan Jenkins and Mair Eluned Davies. Examples in English: Edmund T. Owen, 'I cast my burden', *The Evangelical Magazine of Wales*, 30:2, 1991, and Lynne Davies, 'Imagine me, a sinner' , ibid., 35:2, 1996 (translations); Noel Gibbard, 'A Hymn', ibid., 25:2, 1986; Alan Clifford, 'Revival', ibid., 27:5, 1988. Vernon Higham published two bilingual volumes: *Giving Thanks* (1968), and *Joy Unspeakable* (undated). The Movement also published a volume of poems edited by John Emyr, *O Gylch y Gair* (1987).
15. 'Rhwystrau'r Bywyd Ysbrydol', *Y Cylchgrawn Efengylaidd*, VII:2, 1965, VII:3, 1965-6.
16. ibid., X:2, 1968-9, IX:3, 1967-8.
17. ibid., 1:7, 1949.
18. ibid., 1:2, 4, 6, 1949.
19. ibid., 2:12, 1953-4.
20. ibid., 2:9, 1953.
21. ibid., X:1, 5, 1969; XI:2, 1969-70.
22. ibid., Summer 1990.
23. The others in order: Winter, 1990-91, Winter 1992-3, Spring 1991, Winter 1991-2, Autumn, 1993, Winter 1997, October-December 1997, Spring 1992 and Spring 1994.
24. *Crist a Chenedlaetholdeb*, 91, and J. Elwyn Davies, 'Nationhood and Language', *The Evangelical Magazine of Wales*, 28:4, 1989.
25. *Crist a Chenedlaetholdeb*, 17.
26. R. Tudur Jones, 'Cenedlaetholdeb y Cristion', *Y Cylchgrawn Efengylaidd*, 1X:4, 1968, and also *Crist a Chenedlaetholdeb*, 124, 125.
27. R. Tudur Jones, 'Cenedlaetholdeb y Cristion'.
28. Emyr Roberts, *Cyrraedd Trwy'r Glustog*, 56.
29. ibid.
30. J. Elwyn Davies, 'Nationhood and Language'.
31. R. M. Jones, *Llên Cymru a Chrefydd* (Abertawe, 1977), 41.
32. One of the influences on the authors is Abraham Kuyper; see article by R. Tudur Jones, 'Abraham Kuyper', *Ysgrifau Diwinyddol II* (1988), ed. Noel Gibbard.
33. *Y Cylchgrawn Efengylaidd*, XIII:2, 1979.
34. Emyr Roberts, *Cyrraedd Trwy'r Glustog*, 55.
35. ibid.
36. ibid., 36.
37. 'Y Mesur Darlledu Newydd', *Y Cylchgrawn Efengylaidd*, Winter 1990.
38. 'Y Sabath', *Y Cylchgrawn Efengylaidd*, 23:2, 1986.
39. ibid., the second article, 23:3, 1986.
40. ibid., 23:4; 'The Lord's Day', *The Evangelical Magazine of Wales*, 25:1, 1986.
41. ibid., 'Give an Hour to Save a Day', 24:4, 1985.
42. ibid.
43. 'Tu Allan i Ffiniau Priodas', *Y Cylchgrawn Efengylaidd*, Spring 1992.
44. ibid., 'Pen Tŵr', Autumn 1992; Minutes of the Welsh Executive Committee, 15 October 1992.
45. Keith Lewis, *Y Teulu Cristnogol* (Gwasg Efengylaidd Cymru, 1984).

46. *Christian Family Matters*, foreword by Sir Frederick Catherwood (Evangelical Press of Wales, 1985).
47. 'Focus on Wales', *The Evangelical Magazine of Wales*, 22:3, 1983. Chris Wales is currently doing the work. Among the dedicated workers were Chris Hess, Anne Lewis, Glyn Baker and Ian Garrero.
48. ibid., 8:1, 1969. Geoffrey Thomas, 'Christianity and the Schools—*Quo Vadis?*'
49. ibid., 8:22, 1969, Hywel R. Jones, one of three responses: 'Christianity and the Schools—Three Comments': also, 'From Our Mailbag'.
50. Cyhoeddiadau Bywyd Newydd, 1984.
51. *The Evangelical Magazine of Wales*, 25:6, 26:4, 1986-7; *Y Cylchgrawn Efengylaidd*, 23:4, 1986.
52. *The Evangelical Magazine of Wales*, 27:5, 1988.
53. Evangelical Press of Wales, 1984.
54. 'The 1976 Bod Difyr Camp', *The Evangelical Magazine of Wales*, 16:3, 1977; 'Brenig Fellowship Camp', ibid., 23:1, 1984.
55. 'Ysbyty'r Meddwl a Chyfrifoldeb y Cristion', *Y Cylchgrawn Efengylaidd*, XII:1, 1971; ibid., Geraint Morgan, 'Cofio Joy Pryce', Spring 1994.
56. Frequent references to 'A Cause for Concern' in *The Evangelical Magazine of Wales*: 14:3, 1975; 15:3,4, 1976; 24:4, 1985; 25:2, 1986.
57. 'Focus on Wales', *The Evangelical Magazine of Wales*, 15:4, 1976; 21:6, 1982-3; 24:4, 1985.
58. 'Llewyrch Lluest', *Y Cylchgrawn Efengylaidd*, 19:6, 1981; *The Evangelical Magazine of Wales*, 20:1, 1981.

Chapter 9

1. 'Mudiadau', *Y Drysorfa*, October 1958.
2. ibid.
3. ibid., 'Y Ffwndamentaliaid Yma', September 1956, the second article in a series of three.
4. 'Hawl ac Ateb', *Y Goleuad*, 6 May 1964, 5; the attitude is the same throughout the series.
5. 'O gadair y golygydd', *Seren Cymru*, 9 November 1984, 4.
6. ibid., 15 March 1985, 4.
7. 'Taro'r Post', *Y Faner*, 6 December 1985, 2.
8. e.g. Campbell Morgan, Robert Anderson and H. G. C. Moule.
9. *Seren Cymru*, op. cit.
10. *Y Drysorfa*, August 1956.
11. See chapter 7.
12. 'The Word Fundamentalism', *The Evangelical Magazine of Wales*, 1:VII, 1958; also: John R. Stott, *Fundamentalism and Evangelism* (Crusade, 1956).
13. His second article in *Y Drysorfa*.
14. 'Maen Prawf ein Cristnogaeth', An Address to the Union of Independents, 1982.
15. *Y Drysorfa*, February 1959.
16. Gwyn Davies, *Y Grym a'r Gwirionedd* (Gwasg Efengylaidd Cymru, 1978), 24-5.
17. *Seren Cymru*, 9 November 1984.
18. *Y Grym a'r Gwirionedd*, 35.
19. D. R. Thomas, *Y Cymro*, 25 May 1988.
20. Dewi Eirug Davies, *Diwinyddiaeth yng Nghymru*, 111.
21. ibid., 123.

22. *Studies in the Sermon on the Mount* (Inter-Varsity Press), 214.
23. L. Haydn Lewis, article 3, *Y Drysorfa*, 1956.
24. Dewi Eirug Davies, *Diwinyddiaeth yng Nghymru*, 127.
25. 'My Dear Jonathan', *The Evangelical Magazine of Wales*, 1:4, 1955-6.
26. 'Y Defaid a'r Geifr', *Y Faner*, 15 June 1984, 9, ibid., 'Y Ni a Nhw', 5 December 1986, 8.
27. A letter dated 15 June 1949; this letter, and the other letters, in the care of John Emyr, Cardiff.
28. Letter dated 21 June 1949.
29. Letter dated 26 June 1949.
30. According to a letter sent by Gwilym O. Roberts to Emyr Roberts, 1 July 1949.
31. Letter dated 1 July 1949.
32. Letter dated 13 July 1949.
33. 'Gwyddoniaeth a Chrefydd', *Y Ffordd*, January 1956.
34. A letter written by Arthur Pritchard to Emyr Roberts, 13 May 1964.
35. 'Hawl ac Ateb', *Y Goleuad*, 6 November 1963, 5.
36. 15 July 1964, 4.
37. 'Tros y Tresi', 29 April 1964, 2.
38. *Y Goleuad*, 13 May.
39. 26 August 1964.
40. 15 July 1964.
41. *Y Cylchgrawn Efengylaidd*, 6:1, 1964.
42. ibid.. Summer 1963.
43. ibid.
44. *Y Cylchgrawn Efengylaidd*, V:3, 1962.
45. ibid.
46. ibid., V:3, 1962.
47. ibid.
48. ibid., V:5, 1962.
49. *Barn*, March, April, May; Letters, 143-63. Also D. Martyn Lloyd-Jones, *Llais y Doctor* (Gwasg Bryntirion, 1999), 90, 93.
50. 'Comment', *The Evangelical Magazine of Wales,* 2:7, 1963.
51. ibid.
52. The statement in *Y Cylchgrawn Efengylaidd*, VII:6, 1966.
53. 'Y Mudiad Efengylaidd a'r Eglwys Gristnogol', two articles in *Y Dysgedydd*, 1966.
54. Article 2.
55. *The Christian Church* (1966), 5.
56. Many references in Article 1.
57. 'Ystyriaethau ar Natur Eglwys', *Y Tyst*, 29 January 1987. *The Christian Church*, 8, 9. Standard works on this matter: Geoffrey F. Nuttall, *Visible Saints* (Oxford, 1957); Edward Morgan, *Visible Saints* (New York, 1963).
58. Article 1.
59. Clause 3 (g), 'Through faith (and only faith) in the Lord Jesus Christ, the sinner is freely justified by God.' There is no gospel apart from this. Philip Eveson, *The Great Exchange: Justification by Faith* (Bromley, 1996).
60. Article 2.
61. ibid.
62. ibid.
63. 'Y Bedyddwyr a'r Cynllun Uno', *Seren Cymru*, 15 October 1965.

64. ibid., 22 October 1965.
65. ibid., 26 November 1965. Also: J. S. Williams, 'Ateb Byr i'r Parch. G. L. Humphreys', 31 December 1965; Noel Gibbard, 'At y Golygydd', 11 February 1966.
66. 20, 27 January, 3 March 1966.
67. 'Y Cynllun Uno', 10 February, 10 March, 17 February 1966.
68. *Y Cylchgrawn Efengylaidd*, X:3, 1969.
69. ibid., 'At y Golygydd', 4, 1969.
70. 'I'r Holl Fyd', *Y Tyst*, 25 December 1969.
71. Minutes of the General Committee, 7,8 February 1974.
72. 'Cymru i Grist', *Y Cymro*, 28 January 1975, 1, 10; ibid., 'Ysgwyd y gambo ecwmenaidd', 11 March 1975.
73. Editorial, 13 February 1975.
74. ibid., 6 March 1975, 5.
75. 'Cymru i Grist', *Y Cymro*, 25 March 1975, 5.
76. ibid.
77. 'Llythyr Agored at Aelodau'r Mudiad Efengylaidd', 27 March 1975.
78. 1 May 1975.
79. 'Ynglŷn ag Ymgyrch "Cymru i Grist"', *Y Tyst*, 15 May 1975, 2.
80. June 1975.
81. Protests prior to this: Bangor Evangelical Church, 'Protest at Bangor', *The Evangelical Magazine of Wales*, 10:1, 1971; D. Martyn Lloyd-Jones, *Ar Gyfeiliorn* (undated).
82. Minutes of the General Committee, 23, 24 November 1981, 17 March, 14 September 1982.
83. 'The Pope's Visit to Wales', *The Evangelical Magazine of Wales*, 21:3, 1982; and the same statement in *Y Cylchgrawn Efengylaidd*, 20:3, 1982.
84. ibid.
85. 'A Pope for Pontcanna', *The Evangelical Magazine of Wales*, 21:2, 1982.
86. *The Evangelical Magazine of Wales,* 21:1, 1982; *Y Cylchgrawn Efengylaidd*, 20:2, 1982.
87. *The Evangelical Magazine of Wales*, 21:2, 1982; *Y Cylchgrawn Efengylaidd*, 20:2, 1982.
88. 'An Earnest Appeal', *The Evangelical Magazine of Wales*, 21:2, 1982.
89. ibid.
90. *Gospel and Church*, 36-8.
91. ibid., 50, 52.
92. ibid., 52.
93. ibid., 81.
94. ibid., 89-90, 91.
95. ibid., 98.
96. ibid., 136.
97. ibid., 136-8.
98. ibid., 137, 147-50.
99. ibid., 140.

Index